What people are

The Christian M... y

A departure at right-angles to thinking in the modern Western world. An important, original work that should get the widest possible hearing.
Iain McGilchrist, author of *The Master and his Emissary* and fellow of All Souls Oxford, on the author's previous book *Middle Way Philosophy 1*

The author describes the aim of this book as being to present "the case against Christian belief but for Christian faith". In my view his aim is amply fulfilled in its ten chapters, which begin with a discussion of "faith without belief" and end with a discussion of Christian ethics and politics. Reflecting the author's sojourn in Buddhism, there is much talk of "The Middle Way". Jesus, enlightened like the Buddha, is no absolutist; rather, in his life and teaching he provides an example of a wholesome balance between the left and right hemispheres of the brain. As the Christ, he is "the balancer, the mediator, the transformer, the bridge-builder that we find within ourselves. This is a densely argued book, needing, and deserving, time to digest; and to work out, with the author's help, the implications of approaching religion in general and Christianity in particular, in terms of the Middle Way.
Edward Walker. author of *Treasure Beneath the Hearth*

The recognition of the different functions of the brain's two hemispheres provides a whole new approach to thinking about the meaning and values of human life, that can be applied in the context of every philosophy and religion. Robert M Ellis here uses it to distinguish between abstract left hemisphere belief

and live embodied faith in the Christian tradition: an important consideration for anyone influenced by Christianity.
Roderick Tweedy, editor of Karnac Books, author of *The God of the Left Hemisphere: Blake, Bolte Taylor and the Myth of Creation*, and editor of *The Polticial Self: Understanding the Social Context of Mental Illness*

The Christian Middle Way

The case *against* Christian belief but *for* Christian faith

The Christian Middle Way

The case *against* Christian belief but *for* Christian faith

Robert M. Ellis

CHRISTIAN ALTERNATIVE

Winchester, UK
Washington, USA

First published by Christian Alternative Books, 2018
Christian Alternative Books is an imprint of John Hunt Publishing Ltd.,
No. 3 East Street, Alresford, Hampshire SO24 9EE, UK
office1@jhpbooks.net
www.johnhuntpublishing.com
www.christian-alternative.com

For distributor details and how to order please visit the 'Ordering' section on our website.

ISBN: 978 1 78535 756 5
978 1 78535 757 2 (ebook)
Library of Congress Control Number: 2017942268

A CIP catalogue record for this book is available from the British Library.

Design: Stuart Davies

Printed and bound by CPI Group (UK) Ltd, Croydon, CR0 4YY, UK

Contents

By the same author

A Theory of Moral Objectivity
A New Buddhist Ethics
The Trouble with Buddhism
Theme and Variations (fiction)
North Cape (poetry)
Truth on the Edge: A Brief Western Philosophy of the Middle Way
Middle Way Philosophy 1: The Path of Objectivity
Middle Way Philosophy 2: The Integration of Desire
Middle Way Philosophy 3: The Integration of Meaning
Middle Way Philosophy 4: The Integration of Belief
Middle Way Philosophy Omnibus Edition (combining the 4 previous volumes)
Migglism: A Beginner's Guide to Middle Way Philosophy
Parables of the Middle Way
The Jungian Middle Way: How Jung's *Red Book* parallels the Buddha's method of human integration (forthcoming)

Dedicated to the memory of my late father,
Rev Geoffrey Ellis, 1927-2015: liberal Baptist minister and
Congo missionary

We all must do just what Christ did. We must make our experiment. We must make mistakes. We must live out our own vision of life. And there will be error. If you avoid error, you do not live.

Carl Jung

Acknowledgements

I would like to thank the following people, who all provided initial reading and helpful comments before publication: Barry Daniel, Susan Averbach, Richard Flanagan, Barbara Mills, David Lambourn and Edward Walker. More broadly I would also like to thank both the Middle Way Society and the Sea of Faith Birmingham Group for their supportive response to the project.

1

Introduction

Despite a Christian family background, I have never managed to be a Christian in the way defined by most churches. I am not a 'believer', and could recite no creed without a sense of hypocrisy and conflict. But after many years of engagement with other traditions – Buddhist, philosophical and psychological – it has become increasingly clear to me that 'belief' is not what Christianity is most importantly about. It is quite possible to drink deeply of what Christianity has to offer, indeed to be 'Christian' in all the ways that matter – morally, spiritually and intellectually – without 'believing' such absolute propositions as that God exists, or that Jesus is the Son of God, or that Jesus saves believers from sin. Indeed, I will go further. Such beliefs have no positive practical effects on the lives of Christians, beyond being shortcuts to group conformity which may also have many negative effects. That is the conclusion of an argument that will be unpacked as this book progresses.

But this book is not merely about the disavowal of Christian 'belief'. It is also about something much more positive: the value of the meaning and faith that people find in their experience of the Christian tradition. Later I will go into the question of exactly what I mean by terms like 'meaning' and 'faith', but for the moment let us just mark them out as the bearers of all that is good in Christianity. It is God, or Christ, who inspires Christians to campaigns of justice and acts of love: not because they have committed themselves to abstract propositions about God, but because they experience the inspiration of God, who fills them with positivity and confidence. Belief is in no way necessary to inspiration and faith. In the meantime, the 'belief in' God and his revelations tends to inspire only inner repression, narrow partisan defensiveness, and even holy war.

For myself, I am at least culturally Christian, and I find the symbols and insights of Christianity much more deeply etched into my psyche than those of any other religion, despite an early rejection of my Christian heritage and about twenty years of engagement with Buddhism. Recently I found this reinforced for me by the words of Jung's *Red Book:*

> *You can certainly leave Christianity but it does not leave you. Your liberation from it is delusion. Christ is the way. You can certainly run away, but then you are no longer on the way.*[1]

What I take Jung to mean by this is that Christ, as an archetype, fulfils a certain function in the psyche, and for those who are culturally Christian, that function is not easily fulfilled in any other way. 'The way' for each individual leads from their starting point to their destination, and if one denies the full conditioning effect of one's starting point, one's way may be lost.

I have dedicated this book to my late father (a Baptist minister) – not because I would expect him to necessarily agree with everything in it, but because he provided me with an early experiential sense of the potential value of Christianity which I am only now beginning to recognise has sustained me throughout my life. My father observed the Christian conventions: but it was always clear, when you asked him about what was most valuable to him, that in his experience God is love. Love is an experience, not a belief.

I have returned to the re-engagement with Christianity marked by this book after the development of a practical philosophy that I believe to be applicable in the context of any tradition: Middle Way Philosophy. Despite its name, Middle Way Philosophy only owes some aspects of its inspiration to the Buddhist tradition, and is not dependent on that tradition. Instead, it understands the Middle Way universally, as a principle of human navigation.

Given our embodied nature and our uncertainty, we can have no justification for choosing absolute beliefs that lie beyond that experience. However, what is distinctive about the Middle Way approach is the equal recognition that we have no justification for *denying* absolute beliefs. This creates a radical agnostic alternative that also steers us well clear of relativism, postmodernism, atheism or any other positions that are widely interpreted as being based (explicitly or implicitly) on such denials. If we don't know, we need to follow through the implications of *not knowing* even-handedly.

Agnosticism has been very unfairly treated by a popular tradition – both religious and atheist – that has failed to understand its potential. There is nothing wishy-washy, indecisive or necessarily vague about the agnosticism I will be recommending in this book. Indeed, it takes considerable resolve to avoid the magnetic pull of absolute affirmation or denial, together with the social institutions that entrench that duality. These opposed social institutions could most obviously be the institutions of the church versus secular humanist movements, but might just as easily be illustrated by the entrenched opposed sides arguing about abortion, or about whether Islam is or is not an intrinsic threat to liberal democracy. Nor is agnosticism only about God: wherever there are absolute beliefs on either side (for example, about freewill and determinism, mind and body, or any kind of absolute categorisation or boundary) agnosticism offers a challenge, in the form of a brave flag of peaceful resistance raised in between the lines of the warring armies.

It has taken me a long time to realise what a profound part agnosticism plays in Christianity, and helps to explain all that is best and most inspiring about it. No, 'Christian agnostic' is not a contradiction in terms, and I will be exploring some of the many ways that Christianity is and can be agnostic in this book. These begin with the basic recognition that we, as humans, are not God: that God is infinite and beyond us, an object of holiness and awe. They can continue with the responsibility for our own lives indicated in the story of the expulsion from Eden. Since we live in a post-Eden world, we live in an experience of uncertainty in which meaning is not written on the heavens – rather it is found in our bodies and brains. The intense pain and conflict created by that state is symbolised by Christ's crucifixion: an event that could hardly have the same sting for us if it was merely the unfolding of a set of pre-determined events, part of a story staged by a heavenly father. It is perhaps only if we feel the abandonment that Christ himself expressed on the cross, being prepared to let go of all reassuring 'belief', that we can find the resurging hope symbolised by the resurrection.

The Middle Way in Buddhism and in Christianity takes an apparently very different form, but an underlying similarity can also be found. In Buddhism the Middle Way is exemplified by the investigatory process that the Buddha (a man who lived in India about 500 BCE) went through: first going forth from a privileged life of merely conventional morality to a homeless life of spiritual searching. He is there said to have encountered spiritual teachers and ascetic practitioners from whom he learnt much, but whose absolute beliefs he eventually found inadequate and moved beyond. It was only after experiencing these two extremes that the Buddha is said to have discovered the Middle Way, relying instead on his own experience to find a more balanced and adequate path of spiritual progress that avoids both absolute and relative assumptions.

Christianity, on the other hand, does not primarily represent the Middle Way through a quest, apart from Jesus' more limited withdrawal to the wilderness, which does have some resemblances to the Buddha's quest that I will be discussing. The main way Christianity represents the Middle Way, instead, is through the symbolism of the incarnation. Instead of *finding* the Middle Way, Christ *is* the Middle Way. In the Nicene Creed he is described as both wholly divine and wholly human, a categorisation that shows the Early Church apparently struggling to confine a living experience into the box of a conceptual certainty. Instead of going through a process of discovery, what Jesus does is to constantly challenge our pretended certainties and their associated positions of power. He challenges the rich and powerful, challenges the complacent, challenges legalism and challenges our failures of love. Instead of a long career of carefully balancing different interests, such as the Buddha seems to have had, Jesus had a short and explosive career culminating in dramatic demonstrations of his ambiguous nature.

Christianity is primarily a faith. 'Faith' has often come to be a euphemism for absolute belief, but on the contrary, I want to suggest, faith can involve the positive avoidance of absolute belief and the positive embrace of uncertainty. One does not have faith because one expects certainty in the future, but rather because one recognises that the human state is one of uncertainty. Faith by its very nature needs to be provisional: a recognition of aspirations whose meaning may be infinite and vastly significant for us, but nevertheless cannot result in absolute belief, because any such belief is recognised to undermine rather than to support that faith. In a state of faith, we are orientated towards a meaningful God whom we experience: a God who offers an archetypal foretaste of an integrated self and an integrated world. But such a God could only be meaningful to us in such a way if we remain uncertain even about his very existence, let alone about such claims as that he created the world or sent Jesus as his son.

Such faith, then, I want to argue, excludes belief in revelation. To believe that God sends us messages requires an absolute presupposition that God exists and is of a particular nature: a presupposition that in our uncertain and embodied state we are not entitled to make. In a post-Eden existence, we are also required to take responsibility for our own interpretation of whatever texts or other sources of information we encounter, and the granting of absolute authority to any such text, or even to a believed-in historical figure, involves an avoidance of that responsibility. It is us that give authority to the Bible or to any other source through the values we attribute to it. Scriptures may offer us inspiration, but do not, above all, licence us to give absolute authority to words that have actually been interpreted by us, and thus by stealthy bad faith claim absolute authority for ourselves. It is that kind of bad faith that, above all, has led me to keep my distance from Christianity for many years, and I do not think any better of it now. But I do not think such bad faith is essential to Christianity.

There are thus no arguments from the authority of scripture, or from the authority of historical events, in this book. Rather, there is acknowledgement of *inspiration* from scripture or historical events, and of our responsibility for interpreting them and justifying our view of them. To *appeal to* a source of this kind, we assume that claims that we interpret them as making must be true because of that source, rather than subjecting any such claims to critical investigation. In the process, we probably confuse the meaning and inspiration of the source for us with an appeal to its authority: but it can be deeply meaningful to us without being appealed to. There will be much discussion, for example, of the gospels in this book, but not an *appeal to* them. There can be no justified authority that is not earned, directly or indirectly, through the experience of those who heed it. No matter how reliable a source is, it also never becomes absolute.

This book, not being based on them, is thus also not amenable to criticism on the grounds of the authority of scripture or of historical events. If a scholar or cleric tells you that Jesus did not actually say this or that, or that a particular stance is not 'Biblical' or not 'Christian' (according to his or her definition of 'Christian'), then I do not care, and I suggest that you should not care either. The importance of Jesus in our lives does not depend on who he actually was, whether he actually existed, whether he was actually the son of God, or whether the stories told about him are true – rather, it depends on how we choose to interpret those stories, interpret his advice, and interpret his traditional status as the son of God. It depends on the way Jesus' teachings and example actually affect our lives.

My sole justificatory criterion in this book is the Middle Way: that is, based on what moves people helpfully towards positions that can be recognised, justified, applied and practised in experience – and thus what avoids the dogmas that interfere with that process. If you need more detail on that approach than I can provide in this book, then I must refer you to my 'Middle Way Philosophy' series, in which it is presented in considerable detail with reference to philosophy, ethics, psychology, neuroscience, and spiritual practice. The approaches here are genuinely open to criticism, but in relation to that framework. If, rather than appealing to authority, you can show me that I am not helping people to engage with what is most meaningful and genuinely helpful to them, once it has been understood in that wider context, then I hope I will reconsider.

The Christian tradition of the last two hundred years or so has proved to be a remarkably fragile tradition. So naïve was the faith of many Christians that it has been decimated by scientific progress in astronomy, geology, biology and psychology, with this damage then compounded by the even more profound effects of consumerism in distracting people from the religious life itself. But the fragility that made that damage possible is caused by absolute belief: belief that must discontinuously either be held fast or broken. In many cases belief in Christian 'truths' has been broken. In others it has been retrenched into a fundamentalist version that is no less fragile, but maintains itself by actively ignoring and repressing alternatives: relying on the vacuum left by a religious education that, where it exists at all, often either inculcates or impotently compares absolute beliefs. That the 'new atheists' can often get away with their assumptions that Christianity as a whole must be rejected because it must be defined by absolute beliefs, is a further indication of this fragility.

But Christianity offers a lot more than these fragile 'beliefs'. The more I consider and re-read the most inspiring Christian figures from the past, the more it seems that they offer. Of course, much of what is written by or about them makes regular reference to Christian belief. Amongst those who stress it most, one is more likely to find those who are often labelled as narrow-minded oppressors, inquisitors, crusaders and bigots. But alongside this there is a whole culture of Christian meaning. That culture is one in which loving, creative and courageous action is inspired by the integrative spirit of God and of Christ, engaged in the resolution of conflicts both within and beyond ourselves. I see it especially in the mystical saints of the medieval period, in the artistic tradition that peaked in the Renaissance, and in the more mystical but socially active tradition of the Quakers. But there are countless other Christians in whom one can find it to varying degrees: saints, churchmen, social reformers, missionaries, and lay people in every walk of life.

One of the major thinkers to point out and develop an alternative to fragile Christian belief has been psychologist Carl Jung. Jung famously said that he *knew* God but did not believe in him: which I take to be his way of saying that he found God overwhelmingly meaningful but this meaning did not imply belief. The recent and long-delayed publication of Jung's 'Red Book', in which Jung recorded his visionary experiences around the time of the First World War, offers an extraordinary resource for those who want to support a more robust, more adequate, agnostic Christianity. Jung offers us an approach to God as an archetype representing aspects of our own experience. However, most importantly in the Red Book, he makes it clear how the archetypal explanation is not just an intellectualisation or 'explaining away' of God. On the contrary, it is the gateway to a fuller and more awe-inspiring experience of him. In the Red

Book, Jung constantly wrestles with God and his nature much as the earlier Christian mystics did, not despite but because of his recognition that God is an expression of his own inner experience. In experiential terms, an archetypal God is not an inch 'unreal', but rather 'more real' than any projected external version.

There have been many attempts to reform and renew Christianity, from Martin Luther to the Iona Community. These all in some way protest, as Jesus did, against rigidity, formalism and the abuse of power – offering instead a community of the living God or living Christ as they experience it, often linked to ecclesiastical, social or political reform. If these reforming movements wish to succeed in the longer term, however, my argument is that they need to find the Middle Way. It is by consciously avoiding the negative absolute (where absolute beliefs are taken to be false) as well as the positive absolute (where they're taken to be true) that cycles of reaction, rigidification, and polarisation can be avoided.

Another important reason why Christians need the Middle Way depends on its universality. Christianity as mere belief, as appeal to revelation, is as divisive as any other absolute belief. It does not matter if that absolute belief is a belief to which the idea of 'peace' is attached: the result will nevertheless in some respect be conflict, if there is no possible way for experience to intercede between those who hold those beliefs and those who deny them. As long as Christians cling to absolutes, their message of peace and love will also transmit the virus of absolutism which will directly undermine that message. Whatever denials are made, the Crusades, the Inquisition, the division of communities in Northern Ireland, the Catholic clerical abuse scandals, and many other abuses will remain on the Christian conscience, because the underlying cause of them in narrow-minded over-confidence will still be harboured in the Christian tradition. But on the other hand, an interpretation of Christianity in harmony with the Middle Way will allow them to join with those of many other traditions, each of which can also be interpreted in terms of the Middle Way, for a shared and genuine engagement with the roots of conflict. It is not that all religions are already one, but rather that the unnecessary barriers between them can indeed be removed, if they are prepared to go through a balanced process of experiential self-scrutiny.

Christianity is above all a religion of divine love. As St Paul wrote, "I may have faith enough to move mountains, but if I have no love, I am nothing. (1 Cor 13:2)" But love is also seemingly the quality that most quickly becomes forgotten or formalised in Christian practice. I want to argue that love is inextricable from wisdom, just as emotion is inextricable from reason. We genuinely love others, not when we merely aspire to feel goodwill towards them, but when our beliefs about them are open and provisional enough to recognise good qualities alongside bad, a friend in every enemy. The avoidance of absolute belief is not just about doctrine, but about people too. All those who want to practise the religion of divine love, I would argue, should practise the Middle Way in the way they interpret that religion.

2

Faith without belief

a. Belief and meaning

My case is against Christian *belief* but in favour of Christian *faith*. The two are, of course, not synonymous in the way I am using them here. To make this case clear I will need to begin by exploring these terms and their meanings, in the process including psychological and brain perspectives as well as philosophical ones.

What is belief? I will define it as any representation of the world or of ourselves, implicit or explicit, that we hold firmly enough to affirm or enact.

Though there is a widespread association of the word 'belief' only with religious belief, beliefs are much more varied than that. I believe that it will rain tomorrow. I believe that London is the capital of the UK. Such beliefs are *explicit* when we consciously refer to them or reflect on them, but a lot of the time they are implicit, merely being assumed in the background as the basis of our actions. The Prime Minister of the UK doubtless continues to believe that London is her capital, but I'd be rather surprised if she explicitly reflects on this point very often, even though a great many of her actions take it for granted. She has other things to think about. The same goes for many of our other beliefs in everyday life. I believe that the chair will support me and not collapse when I sit on it, but am unlikely to explicitly reflect on this point unless it shows signs of breaking.

My perspective on belief here is developed from embodied meaning, an approach to meaning developed on the basis of substantial linguistic and psychological evidence since the 1980's (by George Lakoff and Mark Johnson[2]), which clearly up-ends many of the traditional assumptions about belief as well as meaning. Under embodied meaning theory, the meaning of words (as well as other symbols such as visual art and music) is most basically formed by the development of synaptic links which at least mildly re-enact our active, embodied experience when stimulated by symbols that become associated with those experiences.

According to embodied meaning theory, at the basic, initial level there is a direct association between an experience (let's say that of seeing, touching or climbing a tree) and a word ('tree'), or a more schematic experience (say of one thing going inside another) with a word like 'in'. As we go on, though, our vocabulary expands through metaphorical extension of these basic categories and schemas, so that we can categorise more generally or specifically ('oak', 'plant') and talk in more abstract terms that implicitly relate other situations back to this basic one ('dendritic drainage' dependent on 'tree', 'field of study' dependent on 'in'). Our metaphors can become the basis of whole *cognitive models*, in which a set of inter-related ideas are all dependent on the same metaphorical structure: e.g. the metaphor of medicine as warfare inspires 'bodily defence mechanisms', 'attack of fever' etc, and in this way the meaning of even the most abstract terms can be recognised as dependent on associations with bodily experience.

Contrary to this approach, analytic philosophers (along with their theological and scientific allies) tend to define belief in purely explicit terms, and meaning in terms of the conditions for true belief. For them, meaning is subsidiary to belief: a position that starts from a basically disembodied perspective in which a rational observer makes claims about the world without any particular role for the body in which that observer is placed[3]. There is also a Wittgensteinian variant on this view of meaning that reduces it, instead, to socially-mediated use: but such an account only tells us about the social origins of linguistic conventions, not why those conventions are meaningful to us[4].

Meaning in this deeper sense is a matter of experience, not either of social usage or of truth-conditions. These disembodied ways of thinking about meaning are well entrenched in Western thinking, but I would argue that that they have a basic incompatibility with the Christian recognition of the human body as a positive thing in the image of God (see 4b below). Instead, if meaning is dependent on bodily experience, belief must be understood in turn as formed out of that meaning.

Meaning and belief are thus distinct only in their degree of entrenchment and their practical importance, the boundary between them being vague. Meanings can be associated with individual words or symbols as well as with sentences that make claims (propositions), but it is only when the meanings attached to claims are strong enough for us to act on them (whether we actually do so or not) that we can start to call them beliefs.

One important implication of this new approach to meaning and belief is that art and music can be recognised as fully meaningful in the same way that words and sentences are. No absolute distinction needs to be made between 'cognitive meaning' (the meaning of words as you look them up in a dictionary) and 'emotive meaning' (the 'emotional' associations of words), and both art and music can be credited with a degree of cognitive meaning as well as emotive – for a musical phrase (for instance) can be associated with particular bodily experiences just as the word 'tree' can. For Christians, this means that Bach's cantatas or Michelangelo's paintings in the Sistine Chapel can speak of God as directly as any theologian, if not more directly.

It also implies that stories (whether or not the stories are 'true') can be strongly meaningful to us without that meaning being dependent on belief. Philosophers trying to account for our relationship to stories on the basis of the traditional account of meaning and belief have to introduce clumsy mechanisms like 'suspension of disbelief', which are really not necessary when we recognise meaning as prior to belief. Instead, we find stories acutely meaningful because of the strong associations they evoke for us. Our reading of the situation of characters in a story evokes similar bodily sensations in us as those we would expect them to be experiencing. At the same time, that imaginative meaningfulness falls short of what would be required for us to act as though the story were 'true' in the way that we take our everyday environment to be. For example, if I read from Tolkien's fantasy *Lord of the Rings* that Gandalf rode to Edoras on the noble horse Shadowfax, I can fully imagine the character of Gandalf, the environment of Edoras and the appearance of Shadowfax, thanks to Tolkien's vivid accounts of them elsewhere. The embodied meaning of these things creates an imaginative experience, so that I can, in a limited way, experience the associations involved in riding across the plains of Rohan towards the ancestral halls of King Theoden. But I do not *believe* in them in the sense that I could expect to meet Gandalf in person, to ride Shadowfax, or book a holiday to Edoras. Nor do I disbelieve them in the sense that I would write to the publisher protesting at the 'lies' I read in *Lord of the Rings*. I find the story highly meaningful – meaningful enough to re-live it through my synapses, but I neither believe it nor disbelieve it. No 'suspension of disbelief' is necessary.

This, again, has massive implications for religion. We live in a society where the topsy-turvy view of belief as prior to meaning has become so engrained that the word 'myth', once a highly significant archetypal story embedded in a cultural tradition, has often come to mean 'falsehood'. To remark that the Bible is full of myth and story, I must emphasise, *is not* to say that those stories are necessarily untrue. Rather it is to point out that their truth or falsity is not and should not be the main way in which we relate to them. I read of Gandalf riding across the plains of Rohan, and this is neither to be believed nor disbelieved, just highly significant. When I read of the expulsion of Adam and Eve from the Garden of Eden, or the trial and crucifixion of Jesus, these stories are likewise highly meaningful. But just as I do not expect to meet Gandalf or book a holiday to Edoras, and thus do not 'believe' in Rohan, I likewise do not expect any archaeologist to find the graves of Adam and Eve or the site of Eden. Perhaps the chances of finding more historical confirmation of Jesus' crucifixion are greater, but this would be a side-issue from the fact that its significance to Christians does not depend on any such historicity. They don't find the crucifixion meaningful because they believe in it: they believe in it (if they do) because they find it meaningful.

So what does happen when Christians adopt a 'belief' in facts or events which do not have immediate practical application: a belief that say, Jesus is the Son of God, as opposed to a belief that their chair will not collapse when they sit on it? Obviously such Christians feel just as strongly about such a belief, if not more so, than they would about an everyday matter. They might be offended if you tell them that their house does not 'really exist', just as if you tell them that their god does not 'really exist'. But such a belief would have no force for them if it did not in fact have a practical application that constantly reinforces it, even though this practical application is less direct than is the case with everyday beliefs. Instead of an immediate direct practical application, I want to suggest, such beliefs have practical importance as verbal formulae shared in the Christian group. It is important to be able to say "I believe in God's saving grace sent through Christ", for example, because the sharing of that belief is a badge of group-membership, and often a perceived condition of acceptance and status in the group.

These kinds of beliefs are special, and marked out for that specific purpose in group membership, because they are absolute. Absolute beliefs are distinguishable from provisional ones in a variety of ways. They assume the traditional account of meaning I mentioned above in which belief is prior to meaning (which I call *representationalism*). They can only be true or false rather than justified to a degree. They are constantly opposed to the opposite belief – that which declares what they believe as true to be false or what they take to be false as true. They are closely associated with a group that constantly reinforces those beliefs as the price of acceptance, as already mentioned. Absolute beliefs also repress all alternatives apart from the opposites that they recognise and oppose. Such alternatives tend to be denied or ignored, or perhaps ridiculed or dismissed if they insist on making themselves known. Because no alternatives can be considered, absolute beliefs are not capable of modification in the light of new experience: as long as they remain absolute they are fragile, allowing only a dramatic conversion to the opposite.[5]

The belief that 'God exists', or that 'Jesus is the Saviour' is a classic Christian example of this type of absolute belief. These beliefs are absolute, firstly, because they assume a view of meaning whereby such statements gain their meaning by lining up with reality rather than having an impression on our wider bodily experience. Indeed, their meaning is assumed to be independent and eternal regardless of us or our bodies: God, it is assumed, would exist quite independently of us. These beliefs can only be absolutely true or false: God cannot partially exist and Jesus cannot be a saviour to a degree. They are opposed to opposites who deny them: for example, atheists who deny the first or Muslims and other religionists who deny the second. They are closely associated with the Church, which provides full acceptance and status as Christians only to those who accept these, together with the other absolute beliefs expressed in the Creed. Finally, these beliefs repress all alternatives, as can be seen by their treatment of agnosticism, which is consistently misunderstood, ignored or even ridiculed (a good sign that agnosticism is a far bigger threat to the rigidities of Christian orthodoxy than atheism has ever been).

The relationship between absolute beliefs and groups can be readily seen in the series of cognitive biases that psychologists have identified through experiment as identifiable features of groups. These are social proof, ingroup bias, groupthink and false consensus. Social proof is the tendency to believe that a claim is true merely on the basis of it being accepted by others in the group[6]. A belief that is emphasised by the group but has no other justification beyond it (an absolute belief) is clearly subject to social proof. This is compounded by ingroup bias, which makes us judge those beyond the group by different standards from those within it (thus enabling agnostics to be dismissed)[7]. Groupthink means that judgements in the group are made on the basis of peer pressure[8]. False consensus makes us overestimate the consistency of both favoured beliefs within the group and opposed ones beyond the group[9].

Such biases, constantly reinforcing the relationship between absolute beliefs and group conformity, do not necessarily mean that we are doomed only to act unreflectively as a herd, nor that group association itself cannot take them into account and avoid them. Human beings are social animals, and even the most solitary of us needs the support and solidarity of others. The approaches and methods of how we can more broadly avoid absolutisation as a response to cognitive bias is one I have discussed in more detail in my Middle Way Philosophy writings. It is practice of various sorts, formed on the basis of anticipatory awareness of our likely errors, which can gradually help us turn a conformist group into a relatively critical one: but prime amongst these is incrementality of acceptance, that we do not set up acceptance of absolute beliefs as a discontinuous hurdle to acceptance into a group. Rather we need to base our group solidarity on experience of each other – on mutual trust which is always to some degree conditional rather than unconditional. Only God's love can be unconditional, and we are fooling ourselves if we pretend to have it in human relationships.

Nor, if we hold absolute beliefs, does that necessarily make *all* our judgement inadequate. As already noted, the vast majority of our beliefs are practical ones involving direct interaction with our environment. Because I believe God exists and say, hold fast to a fundamentalist group, does not mean that I cannot have adequate beliefs about, say, geography, or car mechanics. The problems arise only when the group's beliefs become the basis of judgement, and because of the need to remain accepted by the group, we absolutely oppose the opposite, or repress any alternatives that may actually be more adequate. If the absolute beliefs of the group required me to believe that the earth was flat, I would make sure to interpret all the evidence in those terms, and if I ever had cause to fly around the earth would make sure there was a rationalisation handy that would not imperil my group membership[10]. Also, of course, if these beliefs were threatened by someone claiming that the earth was round, I would oppose them. But most of the time, a belief that the earth is flat need not impact on my relationships with neighbours, my conduct of my job, or my upbringing of my children.

Nevertheless, absolute beliefs are unhelpful, and there always remains a likelihood that their rigidity and inadequacy will start to have a direct practical effect on my actions. When the environment changes, as we saw with the impact of nineteenth century science on contemporary Christianity, the fragility of absolute beliefs prevents us from adapting. The core problem is not just 'absolutism' or 'extremism' – token words which are widely used to differentiate ordinary religionists from unacceptable ones without further investigation of what they mean. Instead, fundamentalists are merely those who are most obviously dominated by absolute beliefs that we all have. Nor, on the other hand, are absolute beliefs only a problem for Christians or other religious believers, but they can rather be found in many other contexts, such as politics, science, ethics, health, views of ourselves, views of others and so on. The new atheists constantly neglect this point in singling out 'religion' for special censure.

Nevertheless, the vast majority of Christians still tend to think of their religion in terms of absolute belief. As I shall argue throughout this book, this is both unnecessary and unhelpful. So far, perhaps, I have offered some initial indications as to why it is unhelpful, but the evidence for this will continue to mount as I go on. As to why it is unnecessary as an interpretation of Christianity and what it offers the world, this will be my focus from chapter 3 onwards.

b. Faith and religious experience

To recap, then: I am in favour of Christian faith but not Christian belief. My objection to Christian belief is that it is absolute – not uniquely, but nevertheless unhelpfully so. Christian faith is often used as a synonym for absolute Christian belief, but I obviously want to treat it differently, in harmony with a more experiential strand in Christian thinking. What, then, is faith?

At the basic level, I want to suggest that faith is simply a term for the more embodied and emotive aspect of belief. In this sense it is similar to 'confidence' and 'trust'. I believe that when I sit down on it, my chair will not collapse beneath me: but I do not reflect on such a possibility at every turn. I am simply confident that the chair will not collapse, not as a result of an explicit calculation, but as a result of an embodied relationship with the chair, based on past experience of this and similar chairs, unconsciously processed. If I had never sat on a chair before, I might be much more careful, not knowing what to expect from this kind of object: just as one is more careful with a stranger, a foreign city, or a strange car with different controls. One could thus say that I have faith in or that I trust the chair, just as I trust and have faith in my partner, through a long embodied relationship.

Christians often describe their relationship to God like this: that he is like a person whom they trust. That suggests that the relationship with God and Christ involved in Christian faith, at least at its best, is an embodied one based on experience rather than one based on absolute beliefs. However, the very basis on which I have objected to absolute beliefs is the fact that they are *not* embodied, and indeed involve the denial of embodiment. This embodied relationship found in Christian faith can thus hardly be derived from the abstracted beliefs of 'God exists' and 'Christ is the Saviour'. Instead, I think we need to look at the *meanings* and the *provisional beliefs* associated with Christian belief.

God and Christ, as I have already argued, can be highly meaningful without being objects of absolute belief. I will say more in the next section, 'God as archetype' about ways that this meaningfulness can be positively explained in psychological terms. However, the key point for the moment about God as meaning is that God *is an experience* to which we attach meaning. We can also then hold provisional beliefs about that experience which have a strong emotive and embodied dimension: faith. When I have faith in God, in other words, I have a confidence and trust based on experience, that God as I have experienced him will not let me down. The gap of uncertainty between my experience and any possible reality gives that faith an edge of risk. I may have it wrong, but at the same time I choose to put a positive construction on the direction of my life's experience.

In the next section it will become evident that in some respects people may be experiencing God even when they don't speak in those terms, but for the moment let us focus on experiences of God that people identify as such. 'Religious experience' is a term loaded with controversy and tendentious interpretation: on the one hand from those who require 'genuine' religious experience to be supernatural (perhaps even certified as such by the Church), and on the other by those who want to define it in 'neutral' descriptive ways that can then be reduced to a naturalistic explanation. But let us here just take 'religious experience' to mean any one of a variety of kinds of experiences that Christians say help kindle or to maintain their faith, from a vision of the Virgin Mary right down to an experience of unexpected generosity from a neighbour. What these have in common is the significance that the experiencers give to them.

Such experiences may be far more common than is generally acknowledged, as indicated in David Hay's research[11]. When interviewed in private he found that 62% of people claimed to have had an experience of 'being aware of a presence or power', and even more conventional public polling has revealed between 30% and 48% of people claiming to have 'religious or mystical experience'. Whether or not these experiences can be related to any 'external' power, what they tend to have in common is the encounter with a meaning or potential greater than the limited concerns of the current self.

Such experiences, whether or not they take a specifically Christian form, nourish Christian faith just as they nourish other kinds of faith, by increasing confidence that there is a larger framework of meaning in the context of which one can place the significance of one's normal desires and beliefs.

However, there is a wide variety of research suggesting that, far from supporting any type of abstract or rationalised belief such as the belief in God, such experiences on the contrary give us access to a wider experience of meaning associated with the body. Religious experiences can be induced by meditation – but meditation is based on body awareness and physical relaxation as the starting point before any other development. Religious experiences, far from being abstracted, often involve very positive, indeed blissful, emotional states which are felt throughout the body. The research and direct experience of Jill Bolte-Taylor suggests that religious experience can be closely associated with the disabling of the left brain hemisphere and the dominance of the right, which is open to sensual and bodily experience[12] (I will come back to the brain hemispheres later in this section). Other research has associated the longer term effects of religious experience with *deautomatisation*: that is, with a wider sphere of awareness enabling us to change our normal habits[13]. Other research has identified religious experience as involving stimulus of the temporal lobe, which helps to unify our awareness over time and space[14].

If we are to understand the implications of such research in terms of embodied meaning, it becomes clear that far from supporting or stimulating *beliefs* based on settled cognitive models and petrified metaphors, religious experience is highly meaningful because it engages our experience prior to such beliefs. It opens us up to wider possibilities, and for this reason is often associated with positive changes and new directions in one's life. Such experiences provide a basis of faith precisely because they lead us to *question* beliefs that were previously taken to be absolute. The interpretation of religious experience in terms of beliefs, again, is an outcome of the dominant philosophical model in which belief is prior to meaning rather than the other way round.

Christian faith, then, is a kind of confidence based on access to regular positive and expansive meaning in experience. Some 'religious experiences' may be slighter or more secret than are likely to register on research such as that done by David Hay. However, if they have genuine Christian faith rather than merely narrow dogmatism based on identification with absolute belief, there will be some such experience informing that faith. Such experience and such general faith is universal, but what may make such experience distinctively Christian will probably be its expression in terms of symbols specific to Christianity: probably in terms of God the Father, Jesus Christ and the Holy Spirit. It is to the more specific meaning of such symbols that I will now turn.

c. God as archetype

So who or what is God, if he is not an object of belief, a claimed supernatural entity? One answer to this is simply 'an experience', as outlined in the previous section. But this experience also has a symbol attached to it – one that is meaningful, not just in association with one particular individual's experience, but in relation to a whole Christian (and wider theistic) culture. In identifying an experience as 'God' and interpreting it in terms of God, one draws on this whole wider significance.

In understanding the wider meaning of God, I think inestimable help can come from the Jungian concept of archetype. The concept of archetype has been subject to various misunderstandings and can be clarified, in its turn, with reference to embodied meaning. For an archetype is simply a meaningful symbol: one which happens to have a similarity of meaning across cultures because of the similarity of the psychic function that it fulfils for every person, regardless of culture. Jung's talk of 'collective unconscious' here I find unhelpful, because it is so prone to misinterpretation. The archetypes don't necessarily require some mysterious special link between the bottoms of everyone's psyches, but only a genetic similarity in brain structure that helps to account for our very similar needs to those of other humans.

If one interprets the archetypes primarily in terms of their basic function, rather than in terms of the varieties of form they can take, there are four basic archetypes. Each of these represents a variant in two basic qualities of our own experience that we can project onto what we encounter: self and other on the one hand, and attraction and rejection on the other. Every animal has these basic functions: of feeling that it knows what is self and what is other, what is attractive and what is repulsive. As humans, though, our over-hasty, absolutising prejudice allows us to categorise things in these terms without full enough investigation: that is, to *project* these qualities onto objects that, on closer investigation, only show them in superficial or mixed fashion. Unconsciously projected archetypes, then, are also a way of thinking about certain types of bias: particularly those applied to people. They are a manifestation of what cognitive psychologists call *story bias*. We tell ourselves a story about others and impose that story on the evidence.

However, archetypes do not have to be unconsciously projected. If we maintain awareness of them as archetypes we can also appreciate and celebrate them in their own right. If we do that, we can more fully recognise them as part of ourselves and *integrate* the otherwise conflicting desires that may be attached to them.

These points will be more fully appreciated if I go through a discussion of the four primary archetypes[15]. Though these archetypes can take a wide variety of specific forms in different cultures and religious traditions, I will concentrate on the forms they tend to take in the Christian tradition. The culmination of these archetypes is that of God, but the role he plays will be more readily appreciated if we understand God in the context of the other primary archetypes.

Perhaps the most commonly encountered archetype is the Hero. Every story has to have a hero (or heroine) with whom we identify in the course of that story. The Hero thus represents the attractive self, the self as we egoistically idealise ourselves in fantasy. The Hero, like every one of us, has certain desires that are not fulfilled, due to frustrations along the way, but the Hero (in the story we tell ourselves) overcomes the frustrations and achieves his goals. Jung thought that Christ expressed the Hero archetype, at least as far as he was human like us[16]. He faced adversity, including the final adversity of death, but in the end he overcame even this adversity.

The next primary archetype is the attractive other: what Jung called the Anima (for men) or Animus (for women). This is separate from us, but we want to possess it and make it part of ourselves at the same time. If we were to really possess it, the Anima/Animus would no longer be other, and thus no longer attractive. Most commonly, the attractiveness of the Anima/ Animus has a strong sexual element, but it could conceivably take other forms. Whatever or whoever allures us is the Anima/ Animus. For men, the Anima figure can bifurcate into the virgin and the mother, each having a self-contained otherness that we want to possess in different ways. The figure of Mary in the Christian tradition is remarkable for uniting both these aspects of the Anima. For a heterosexual man, to worship Mary in appreciation that she represents this archetype in us could contribute to avoiding its projection (often with disastrous consequences) onto women.

The third primary archetype is the Shadow, which represents the rejected other: everything that we regard as evil, disgusting and hateful. The Shadow is represented in Christian mythology by the figure of Satan, but we continually project it onto enemies and adversaries of all kinds. This archetype is perhaps the most difficult to recognise as our own projection, for our rationalisations continually insist that it's their fault, and that the object of vilification 'deserves it'. Always, however, even in the case of Adolf Hitler, the 'evil' we project obscures a more complex character and blocks our compassion, perhaps at the very point where it will be most needed.

The figure of Satan represents a basic conflict in Christianity, for Satan seems unfailingly to be vilified as pure evil, rather than loved and respected, despite the importance of the love ethic (even as applied to enemies) in the teachings of Jesus. To many, the very idea that Satan should be loved and respected will be preposterous. But Satan is us, and through him our own qualities are rejected rather than integrated. In this regard, the monotheistic religions stand in apparently unhealthy contrast to Hinduism and Buddhism, where 'evil' figures such as Kali the Death Mother, or the wrathful deities of Tibetan Buddhism, are worshipped in awareness that their 'evil' needs to be made part of a bigger whole. In Christianity, instead, we have only the ultimate recognition that God permits Satan and his evil. In traditional Christian terms, then, the Shadow cannot be integrated other than through the God archetype. Milton, who turned Satan into a hero, and Blake, who extolled Milton's achievement in doing so, recognised something of this difficulty.

Traditional Christians may respond here that there *is* such a thing as evil, and we ignore it at our peril. Even if that evil is not a supernatural Devil living in a place under the ground called Hell, evil still dwells in human hearts, moving them to narrow, deluded and destructive thoughts and actions. I agree with them on that point, and even, perhaps, that Satan needs to carry on symbolising pure evil. We just need to be clearer about what that evil is, and that it is not people who are evil, but absolute beliefs[17]. Since absolute beliefs cannot be integrated, but rather remain in entrenched conflict against their opposites, it is they who are the source of narrowness, delusion and destructiveness in the human heart. I will say more in section d below about the ways in which brain lateralisation, and the role played by the two different brain hemispheres, can support this thesis about evil.

These first three primary archetypes set the scene for God as the ultimate archetype. God is other, but the other that encompasses the self: a projection ahead of an integrated psyche. The 'other' of God also encompasses both the attractive and the repulsive, the Anima/ Animus and the Shadow. That accounts for the way in which we find God both wondrous and terrifying, positive and negative, loving and judging. But the attributes of God do not need to be contradictory if we recognise in God the archetype of integration: that is, of the ultimate reconciliation of all conflicts both in ourselves and in the world at large. That reconciliation has not happened yet, but sometimes, with an awestruck shiver, we may glimpse the potential for it: the divine in ourselves.

The God archetype may take a more or less personal form:

as a wise old man or a wise old woman. The depiction of God as an old man with a beard, and the Biblical honorifics for God of 'Father' and 'Lord', may engage with our projection of what an integrated person is most likely to be like: namely a person with considerable experience, but also one who has made use of that experience to engage successfully with conflicts within themselves and find increasingly adequate ways of judging the world. Such a being could just as easily be visualised in female form as a wise old woman. To gain the wisdom of the wise old man or woman, though, we will need to avoid absolutisation, both positive and negative: making God also a symbol of the notional goal of the Middle Way.

The image of the wise old man or wise old woman (as well as the more impersonal symbol of the mandala that Jung also wrote about) suggests that in some respects, people who are not culturally Christians are nevertheless encountering God. Gurus, wizards, prophets, philosophers and Buddhas can all represent the God archetype, because they can have the same function of symbolising an integrated potentiality. But we need to be clear that the wider presence of this archetype is not a justification for attributing any traditionally Christian *beliefs* about God to non-Christians, or even requiring the term 'God' to be used, loaded as it is with negative associations for many. However, it does provide a basis for universality in basic experience and faith.

The archetypal God incorporates the Anima/Animus by representing the reconciliation of the conflict involved in wanting to possess the attractive other. The qualities that we see in the attractive other, whether masculine or feminine qualities, are now represented as our own qualities, as God is both masculine and feminine. To reach God, then, we will have to cease projecting those qualities onto others. The reconciliation of the Shadow with the Hero is also made possible by God: our desires being fulfilled more sustainably not by eliminating the Shadow, but by learning from it and taking its energies into our own. Evil is seen in a bigger perspective as having a helpful function because it provides part of what is integrated. We reach God, not by conquering evil figures, but rather by separating figures onto whom we project evil from absolutisation as the source of evil.

But the God archetype, in the form of God the Father, can also seem distant and alien, his demands impossible and our perverse desires intractable. The most distinctive aspect of the Christian treatment of the archetypes is the role of Christ as simultaneously both Hero (in his human aspects) and God archetype (in his divine aspects). In this respect Christ represents the way in which we move from our current human position to a more integrated potentiality. Here he represents not just the notional end of the Middle Way (which does not depend on belief in a particular goal, but just needs recognition as a direction), but the Middle Way itself. In many ways a person can even symbolise the Middle Way in respects that the metaphor of a path cannot, as we may associate a path too much with a destination, but a person is readily understood to be changing and developing without us knowing their ultimate fate. It is this stroke of archetypal genius that has inspired millions of Christians – those millions who have found genuine faith as explained in the previous section – to try to follow a path towards greater integration.

d. Brain lateralisation and God

Brain lateralisation – the specialised roles of the left and right hemispheres of the brain – has become an extremely fruitful area of research and interest in recent years, particularly stimulated by Iain McGilchrist's extraordinary work of synthesis, *The Master and his Emissary*[18]. I have already mentioned the role that this can play in our understanding of religious experience, and it can also make a huge difference to our understanding of the meaning of God. The reason for this is that the brain is our instrument (or rather two different instruments) for recognising God, and the differences between those two instruments limit our views of God in different ways, like two people looking at the same view, one with a telescope trained on one distant spot and the other scanning widely with the naked eye.

For those over-used to a polarised debate in which appeal to the brain is used as a reductive weapon, it needs to be emphasised that reference to the brain here plays no such part. Instead of denying or undermining the experience of faith, recognition of brain lateralisation can on the contrary provide us with a wider awareness of the conditions of that very experience, enabling us to interpret it with greater adequacy. Scientific research into the brain is, after all, based only on more experience, namely the experience of experimenters. Neither us, directly experiencing the brain from the inside, nor researchers looking at it from the outside, are free of limiting assumptions, and neither has a magical key to an ultimate reality. However, what is most exciting is the way that brain lateralisation research both confirms and clarifies things that we can experience directly.

Brain lateralisation research shows general *specialisations* of the left and right hemispheres (particularly the prefrontal cortex of each, the 'new brain' uniquely developed in humans). These hemispheres nearly always work together in practice, but doing slightly different tasks: not because each is totally incapable of doing the tasks of the other, but because, being less specialised, it does them less easily. The left hemisphere specialises in representations and goals: that is, maintaining a set of beliefs about the world and of what we want from it. The prefrontal cortex of the left hemisphere contains our tool-using and explicit language-using areas, in close proximity to one another. The right hemisphere, on the other hand, specialises in recognition of new information through the senses, the body, and the imagination. The right hemisphere is much more broadly aware, scanning for threats or mobilising new potentialities. The left hemisphere, on the other hand, is intent on its tasks, and wants to complete them and gain satisfaction by doing so: whether that is killing a deer or completing a puzzle. The right hemisphere is open to a wide range of emotions, including negative ones, whilst the left tends to be superficially optimistic, always sure that another move will get it what it wants.[19]

Clearly, each hemisphere needs the other: without the left hemisphere, we would not seek or obtain what we need and want, whilst without the right, we would be constantly vulnerable to new and unexpected dangers or difficulties. The substantial development of the corpus callosum, which links the two hemispheres, is vital in developing our potentialities by allowing quite literally 'joined up thinking'. But, because the two hemispheres do such different tasks, using them both effectively together is not merely a matter of finding a balance between them.

The left hemisphere has been vital to our distinctive development as human beings: our use of language, tools, complex social organisation and ever-more elaborate theorisations, all enabling us to control our environment so as to meet our burgeoning wishes in ever more complex ways. However, the over-dominance of the left hemisphere can be powerfully destructive because it leads us to neglect contextual awareness. We place too much reliance on our plans and make too little allowance for our ignorance. We become slaves to power, and tend to see both objects and people as mere tools to our ends, neglecting all their other aspects except what serves us. We over-manage and bureaucratise. Most of all we absolutise: tending to think that our current set of beliefs are the whole story. Intent on overcoming whatever stands in the way of our goals, we neglect the possibility of alternative goals or alternative ways of reaching them.

The left hemisphere also lacks the direct awareness of time passing possessed by the right hemisphere, but rather deals with concepts that quantify time.[20] That means that it can easily lose awareness of the inconsistency of its own views over time. The fragile condition of absolutisation, which I described above earlier in this chapter, is thus directly attributable to an over-dominant left hemisphere state. Rather than recognise gradual change in its beliefs over time, the over-dominant left hemisphere will snap directly from one state of belief to the opposite, disavowing or even denying the previous one. The story of Peter's disavowal of Jesus after his death is psychologically realistic for a Peter who has become intent on survival in a stressful situation, and temporarily unaware of the wider perspectives his teacher stimulated. But we have all experienced this in ourselves or others: the smoker who throws away their cigarettes in disgust one night but buys a new packet in the morning, or the boss intent on meeting his targets who threatens to dismiss his employees for minor offences one minute, then wants to take them out for a drink the next.

It is the right hemisphere that provides the contextual awareness that can *integrate* the conflicting states of belief in the left hemisphere. It is only with that wider awareness that we can start to maintain more consistency in our attitudes over time, develop more maturity and emotional stability, engage successfully with addictions and find new ways forward in conflicts.

Without left hemisphere goals and representations, there would be nothing to integrate. Up to a point, indeed, we can make our beliefs consistent using the left hemisphere and its facility with reasoning (which merely works out, when one belief is assumed to be true, what other beliefs would also be true). However, reasoning is only ever as good as its assumptions, and on many occasions we are also not motivated to use our reasoning powers. Much more important in the longer term is the integration that can be provided by the right hemisphere. This puts our beliefs in a wider framework of meaning in which we can consider alternatives. We can change the dominant metaphors in which we are thinking, or re-interpret what we took to be the significance of our experience. In the long-term, the right hemisphere is the integrator, the glue that can stick together disjointed scraps of left hemisphere belief, separated by time and/or by unconscious repression, and help them become a greater and worthier whole.

In the light of the roles of the hemispheres, let us now look again at our experience of God. It becomes evident that there are two versions of God, depending on which hemisphere we are relying upon to encounter him. That does not mean that there are two Gods (I'm not suggesting Manichaeism here), only, as I suggested earlier, that there are two ways of looking at him. To re-apply my earlier image, the person looking closely at one distant thing with a telescope represents the left hemisphere with its narrow focus, whilst the person scanning broadly with the naked eye represents the right hemisphere. Both of these could be looking at the same object, and yet have very different experiences of it.

The left hemisphere God is the God of belief – and also the God of unbelief. This God fits into a world view that is taken to be fully and reliably represented in words (or, if he doesn't fit into this world-view, he is taken 'not to exist'). God, if he 'exists' is taken to be an object in this world – albeit a paradoxical one. This God utters revelations, also in reliable words, that are taken to give us true beliefs: or alternatively they may be false beliefs, or false revelations. In relation to this represented God we have clear goals: e.g. to fulfil his will according to his revelations, or to disprove his existence. Theists and atheists alike who are stuck in this view of God will unite in unholy alliance to defend it.

The right hemisphere God, however, is not an object of belief, but is instead open meaning representing *potential*: more adequate goals and beliefs we could potentially form. He (or she, or it) is not limited to one metaphorical basis, but can shift between metaphors like Proteus. One moment he/she/it is a father, the next a young girl, the next a stone in the brook. All that enables them to feed faith is that these God-metaphors are fresh and offer new living potential. When metaphors die, however, they migrate to the left hemisphere: the breath of spirit, the dove, or the living waters all become stale church clichés when they are over-used. The fresh, Protean right hemisphere God is the God of the mystics, the God of sincere prayer, the God of poets like Gerard Manley Hopkins. The right hemisphere God is also the Holy Spirit: the breath of inspiration, and the flame that descended upon the disciples at Pentecost. The right hemisphere God is our glimpse of integration, as already discussed in the previous section – an archetypal form.

We will all have met these two different ways of seeing God before, but most people merely struggle to reconcile them. If they are over-reliant on the left hemisphere, they become either Christian dogmatists or atheists. If they adopt a more balanced and integrated use of the hemispheres, faith in God may have a positive benefit on their lives and help them engage more adequately with the world. But we all have both left and right hemispheres, and as long as they have incompatible views of God, then conflict will result, whether this manifests itself in internal 'crises of faith' or external conflicts with authority figures onto whom we project this conflict.

Let me emphasise again that the solution here is not to reject the left hemisphere. Without the left hemisphere, there would be nothing to integrate. However, the left hemisphere deals in two different types of belief: provisional and absolute. As already explained, provisional beliefs are capable of integration, because they can be compared with alternatives. Absolute beliefs, on the other hand, come with the attached assumption that they are the whole story and that the words that comprise them are capable of truth. Absolute beliefs thus exclude alternatives and are not capable of integration. It is thus only provisional beliefs, not absolute beliefs (in which we must include belief in God) that are compatible with the right hemisphere experience of God, the glimpse of integration.

The conclusion is thus inescapable: the very structure of our brains requires us, if we are to be inspired by God, not to believe in him. The practice of Christianity may indeed lead us into various beliefs, but these will be of a practical nature. I may believe that my church community has a duty to support the elderly in its congregation, for example, or I may believe that worshipping symbols of God has a beneficial and integrative effect on me. Both these beliefs can be supported by experience and probably have a lot going for them – but they can also be contested and modified without fragility.

That this conclusion is deeply in harmony with the spirit of Christianity can also be pointed out negatively with regard to the spirit of evil. As I argued above, no person, nor by extension any group or tradition, can be wholly evil. But evil, or sin, if it is not to be identified with whole persons, can clearly be associated with absolutisation, or over-dominance of the left hemisphere, within those persons. As St Paul remarked, the conflict of incompatible beliefs accompanies sin: "what I do is not what I want to do, but what I detest" (Rom 7:15). Sin is the failure to consider the wider picture: pride, greed, lust, envy, gluttony, wrath and sloth can all be understood in those terms, as an obsessive decontextualised belief in the value of one attribute or experience at the expense of all others. The features that we associate with evil are also all over-dominant left hemisphere features: cruelty, despotism, megalomania, manipulativeness, rigidity, impatience, literalness and false emotion.[21] If we wish to avoid sin and evil, we need to avoid absolutisation, but with an irony which William Blake spotted, belief in the absolute left hemisphere God is itself a sin, and the left hemisphere God has more in common with Satan than with the right hemisphere God[22].

A loving God, however, both creates and absorbs evil and

forgives sin. A loving God can thus only be a right hemisphere God, with his mercy integrating the sins of the left into a larger whole. God can be a stern judge as well as love only through a process of integration. In that process of integration, the framing of the stern judgement (and of its conflict with the judged) is reconsidered through greater awareness and new resources of thought. The reconciliation of God and sinners is at the same time the reconciliation of the beliefs we hold when we sin with those we hold when we seek to avoid sin, which is an integration of left hemisphere representations over time. For example, the traditional sin of gluttony involves a belief that eating more will bring us happiness held at the time we over-eat, which is in conflict with our wider recognition that moderate eating is much better for us in the long term. The loving God of the right hemisphere not only contains that conflict within a positive wider framework of meaning, but also demands that, in our own interests, we resolve it by thinking in a different framework.

The deeper practice of Christianity implies a commitment to the difficult, messy task of avoiding absolute belief whilst cultivating faith. This requires constant vigilance, perhaps training in supportive practices, and certainly ongoing reflection. That's what I mean by the practice of the Middle Way: the maintenance of a process of navigation between the positive and negative absolutisations of the over-dominant left hemisphere – which is also, more positively, a process of integration that is made possible by avoiding those extremes. The Middle Way itself is not a new absolute, but a provisional belief of a very general nature. There are always alternatives available to it, as the extremes will be presented to us at every turn, and those extremes remain meaningful live options. If we wish to live a life of Christian faith, or any other faith, though, my contention is that we should continue to avoid those absolute options.

e. Human responsibility

If the foregoing is still insufficient, I still have one more major argument in favour of Christian faith but against Christian belief. That is a moral argument, an argument about human responsibility. I want to argue that Christian faith has a positive effect on human responsibility and moral practice, but Christian belief, on the other hand, has a negative effect.

However, I will need to begin with the meaning of 'responsibility'. We tend to use the term in two different ways: in terms of 'feeling responsible' or alternatively of 'being held responsible'. Feeling responsible is an experience of valuing particular people, objects or institutions and having clear expectations as to how our own actions will affect them. This feeling provides a focus for our moral expectations of ourselves, which are also often shared with a community that will help to uphold them. For example, if a parent feels responsible for their child, that means that they value the welfare of their child, and expect themselves to contribute to maintaining that welfare, rather than neglecting things they could reasonably do to maintain it. The community may also disapprove if they neglect their child, and may reinforce these feelings, but 'feeling responsible' is not necessarily dependent on what the community thinks.

'Being held responsible' on the other hand, is not an experience, but an implication of social rules. I may be held responsible by the government and punished by the law if I do not fulfil my legal responsibilities, or disapproved of by the community if I fail to fulfil the roles expected of me. A parent who neglected their child could be 'held responsible' for it in this way, even if they did not feel any responsibility at all.

One of Jesus' most important moral messages in the gospels seems to involve the importance of feeling responsible. He criticises those who do good deeds only for show[23], or who get into a hypocritical lather attacking others for breaking rules that they do not really value[24], but uphold out of social conformity. He does not appear to be interested in holding people responsible, but very interested in encouraging them to feel responsible, as particularly illustrated by his response to the woman taken in adultery[25]. Yet one of the major effects of Christian belief is the constant undermining of this message: the constant externalisation, even bureaucratisation, of responsibility.

Absolute beliefs of any kind undermine the experience of responsibility because they narrow judgement to the two extremes of the absolute belief and its contradiction. But we cannot feel responsible if we do not engage in an exercise of choice by weighing up alternatives. When we believe in a God who issues revelatory moral instructions and then judges us according to how well we have obeyed them, the choice is no longer a genuine choice between different goods each offering different (though often uneven) advantages. Rather we are acceding to absolute power, whether for fear or favour, or defying it, and the question becomes only one of whether we have the strength to defy the group – which we most commonly do not. When we defy it because our biology makes it almost impossible to keep (as in, for example, the Roman Catholic prohibition on masturbation), the result is a highly destructive guilt in which we feel the pain of being held responsible but not the actual responsibility.

The classic theological and philosophical responses to this involve an obsession with another pair of opposed absolutes – freewill and determinism – which it is insisted must either be 'true' or 'false', with the possibility of preferable agnosticism normally not even being raised. Theologians from Augustine onwards have argued that 'God gives us freewill' as to whether or not to obey his instructions[26]. However, such 'freewill' is a mere rationalisation of power as long as the options are limited in a way that makes them effectively a matter only of obedience or disobedience. We do not get to feel responsible merely by being held responsible. It may be that governments, in order to control crime, have to hold criminals responsible regardless of whether they feel responsible, but even then the likelihood of moral reform only begins when the criminal also feels responsibility. In moral and religious terms, however, there is no necessity for holding people responsible except in the terms of law or of other formal social undertakings.

The alternative of determinism, which some Christians (especially Calvinist predestinarians) have at times entertained, is just as corrupting of a genuine experience of responsibility, effectively by telling us that ultimately there is no way in which we can be held responsible. The focus remains on the externalisation of responsibility rather than the experience, with that experience now being denied. In the end, though, if we focus on feeling responsible, neither freewill nor determinism are relevant to that experience or the confidence we may have in it, just as the existence or non-existence of God is irrelevant to our experience of and faith in God.

It is the existentialist philosophers such as Jean-Paul Sartre who made a breakthrough here, in recognising that genuine choice must encompass the standards we apply, not simply a yes-no option framed in absolute terms by some other power. This point applies to judgements of all kinds, whether we are accustomed to thinking of them as moral or as scientific or aesthetic judgements. This does not imply a relativism in which any judgement is as good as another, but on the contrary allows us to introduce a standard based on the integration of the judgement itself. We may well consider traditional criteria of judgement, such as the Ten Commandments, but if we are to make a genuine choice for which we feel responsible, then we must choose to value the Ten Commandments, having considered them against alternative sources of moral guidance.

Sartre, following Kierkegaard, famously offered the example of Abraham as an indicator of our responsibility even in cases where we seek to avoid it[27]. When Abraham was commanded by God to sacrifice his son, Sartre argues, it is Abraham who chose to interpret that command as God's, and therefore as absolute. By that I don't think he meant that we, or existentialist philosophers, should *hold* Abraham responsible, so much as that Abraham would undoubtedly have *felt* responsible for such an obviously questionable action as killing his son, but chose to deny or repress that responsibility by passing it to God. This is what Sartre calls 'bad faith': the failure to consult our experience of responsibility, or even to draw on the full range of evidence available to us when making our judgements, but rather to avoid the discomfort of responsibility by pretending that the standards of judgement are not ours to decide.

The moral failure of Christian belief has much to do with this. By adopting absolute beliefs, it has undermined and prevented genuine morality – in its place substituting a power structure of a kind that Jesus could not possibly have approved of. Despite this, some genuine morality is put into practice, because people feel responsible for their judgements and thus their actions, but a good deal of the history of Christian morality is also dogged with formalism, hypocrisy and institutionalised failure. Of course, there are many notable exceptions, too, of a kind that can in each case be correlated with genuine Christian faith rather than adherence to dogmatic Christian moral beliefs. The dogmatism of those moral beliefs, however, is dependent on the appeal to revelation by which they are justified.

In contrast, Christian faith based on a confident relationship to the God archetype, by opening new potentialities of meaning, makes genuine responsibility possible. It is only when we are able to imagine different alternatives between which we choose that we can both feel responsible for our choice and fully recognise that feeling. Faith can open up a meaningful world to Christians, in which the selection of an option associated with the Christian tradition is not seen as essential to Christian identity, but as the contingent outcome of a comparison with other possible identities. One is only Christian to the extent that one exercises a judgement in favour of Christianity in comparison with alternatives.

Such genuine responsibility has become possible in the modern, globalised world in a way in which it may not have been to many of our ancestors, or to many of the less educated still living in largely traditional societies today. Those who are given no access to alternatives cannot compare them, but instead accept the beliefs of their society, probably unreflectively, as the price of acceptance by that society. Those of us who, instead, are able to research any alternative view in moments by a few clicks of a mouse and typing a few words on a keyboard, may not necessarily take advantage of this opportunity to compare alternatives, but the opportunity is always there. In previous ages, genuine faith could still find new meanings, internally or externally, by other means, but when we look back at, say, medieval mystics (whom I will return to in 7b), we find a tension between their open relationship to experience and the dogmas they nevertheless accept unquestioningly from the society around them. Our surfeit of information provides new opportunities for genuine enquiring faith, and thus to take responsibility for our destiny as individuals: even if the more common outcome is an entrenched pattern of distraction.

In chapter 8, later in this book, I will be returning to the question of what Christian ethics might more positively look like if it is not based on appeals to revelation. However, at this point, for the moment, I rest my basic case against Christian belief and in favour of Christian faith. I have argued for it on the grounds that belief in God can be distinguished from the meaning of God, that religious experience supports faith in God but is very far from supporting belief in him. I argued that God can be understood as an archetype without losing an inch of the power of his meaning for us. I also argued that the hemispheric structure of our brains distinguishes belief in God from faith in him, but that absolute beliefs create conflict between the left hemisphere at different times and prevents the right hemisphere from integrating them. Finally I have also argued that Christian belief undermines the experience of responsibility that we need to actually engage in moral action, substituting an ineffective formalisation.

But this case is only the groundwork for this book, trying to show in outline what Middle Way Christianity looks like so as to provide an initial orientation. My main work, which consists of the re-interpretation of key teachings and symbols from Christian tradition in Middle Way terms, is still to come.

3

Respecting God

a. The infinity argument

Before I begin a process of engaging with key Biblical themes, this chapter will offer a discussion of the role and nature of God in general. My overall argument here will be that those who believe in God and believe in divine revelation thereby fail to respect God – and God is worthy of respect, if anyone is. It is far too easy to unreflectively reduce God to our own size, and a positive effort is required to make him into God again.

I am going to start with the whole question of how we define God, and what I shall call the infinity argument. Philosophers and theologians through the ages have generally defined the God of Christianity as infinite, along with his other associated attributes: he is perfect, eternal, omnipresent, omniscient, omnipotent and omnibenevolent. To 'believe in God' has thus classically meant to believe in the existence of a being who has those infinite attributes. Because I think belief in God is unhelpful, however, does not mean that I have anything against this classical definition of what God is. On the contrary, I want to argue that as we find a being with these infinite attributes meaningful, we should not believe in him. The avoidance of absolute beliefs does not imply that we should not have full-blooded absolute meanings: indeed, on the contrary, it requires us to appreciate those meanings in order for them to fulfil the functions that we wrongly thought belief in them could fulfil.

But let me first defend the classical definition of God against those who assume that the problems created by absolute belief require us to change it. If the meaning of 'God' was not that of an infinite being, he would not fulfil the key function that we need an archetypal God to fulfil; that is, of providing infinite potentiality.

We have other archetypes to represent finite potentialities: the Hero to represent the idealisation of our current desires, the Anima/Animus to represent the attractive finite other, and the Shadow to represent the repellent finite other. But if we turn God into something finite, he becomes another object in our world that we either identify with ourselves or not, accept or reject. Rather than a totality of unknown unknowns, God then becomes part of the known, of the world we think we are acquainted with. The function of the God archetype is different from this: it must always be challenging of our current conceptions, models and metaphors.

An infinite God is also a perfect God, because nothing can be added or taken away from infinity without leaving infinity just as it was. He must also be eternal and omnipresent, which are just ways of applying infinity in terms of our frameworks of time and space. If we attribute personality to God, then, just as a person holds beliefs and values that are justified to a finite degree, and is able to perform limited actions in space and time, God must be able to hold these beliefs and values with infinite justification and perform actions with unlimited power and scope. Of course, it is also possible to symbolise God impersonally, but the archetypal God is personal simply because we are personal: to symbolise infinite potentiality for ourselves we need to understand it in terms of the infinite potentiality of a person. Theologies that change or compromise these classical attributes of God, then (such as process theology), are not relevant to the God of faith.

However, infinity is merely an abstract concept with no direct relationship to human experience. However rapturous or world-shakingly insightful our experiences may be, they cannot be infinite experiences because we are finite beings. Nor can we imagine infinity, for we would need an infinite amount of time even to imagine it in. We can only conceptualise infinity, which means that we can build up a cognitive model based on the metaphorical extension of our experience of traversing space and experiencing the passing of time. The idea of finiteness itself is already a metaphorical extension of our immediate embodied experience of what Lakoff and Johnson call the container schema: our experience of things (like boxes or bodies) having boundaries. We know in an immediate embodied way what it is like to have boundaries, but when we extend this metaphorically to finiteness, and then create an even more abstracted idea of what it would be like not to have boundaries, this concept is still dependent in a stretched fashion on our embodied experience. As we get further and further from our core embodied experience, it becomes harder and harder to retain an embodied meaning for such an abstracted term as infinity, but it is only if we can retain some embodied sense of what it means that we may retain a sense of its limitations.

Otherwise, infinity is a concept that is ripe for absolutisation. You can say almost anything you like about it, and nobody will be able to challenge you on the grounds of experience. If you assert that humans have three legs, everyone will laugh at you because they can see that they do not; but if you assert the far more ridiculous claim that humans have infinite souls, nobody has any immediate grounds to gainsay you.

With God, however, there are some more grounds for hope than in the case of infinity. That's because the experience of God is an embodied one, so what people say about God at least has a chance of remaining embodied. If we can say things about God that directly relate to the experience we have had, whilst recognising it as an experience rather than making assumptions about its origins, we stand a chance of avoiding absolutisation. However, when we start justifying beliefs about God by reference to religious experience, the illicit jump from finite experience to infinite claim is very likely unless we are on our guard and maintain critical awareness.

So, the experience of God, and the related God of faith,

requires God to remain infinite. However, maintaining the meaningfulness of that faith requires us to avoid all claims that apply the notion of God's infinity beyond a recognition of the infinity of the archetype itself. For example, we cannot justify a claim that we experienced or imagined God's infinity, let alone that God provided us with a revelation of infinite authority. Our respect for the infinity of the archetype itself as we experience it in our bodies requires that we preserve that embodied sense of infinity rather than trading it in for a mere concept.

The judgements involved in applying this basic respect for God's infinity are subtle and difficult, but they can hardly be avoided just because they are difficult, and they are also not new. Actually, I find signs throughout Judeo-Christian tradition of people wrestling with this problem, of trying to find the best way of respecting God's greatness without traducing and betraying our experience of that greatness. It is to peoples' past experience of engaging with that difficulty that I will now turn.

b. Holiness and awe

A sense of the holiness of God and an accompanying awe seem to have been part of the experience of God from the earliest Biblical times. When Moses first meets God in the burning bush, he is told to take off his sandals "for the place where you are standing is holy ground". Moses then hides his face, unable to look at God (Ex 3:5-6). Later, when Moses has led the Israelites out of Egypt and come to Mount Sinai, God's presence on Mount Sinai makes its holiness dangerous: people apart from Moses are warned not to go up it, or they may perish[28]. Later, when a select group of Israelites do experience an epiphany of God, it again seems that, like Moses earlier, they cannot look directly at him, but the ground beneath his feet is extraordinary enough: "...they saw the God of Israel. Under his feet there was, as it were, a pavement of sapphire, clear blue as the very heavens (Ex 24:10)."

Awe is something akin to fear, prompted by the recognition of acute danger from something much more powerful than you, but at the same time accompanied by positive emotions. We feel awe in the face of outstanding achievements or vast spaces, perhaps because we are reminded of wider meanings and possibilities than those we normally focus on. Awe may indicate a relatively sudden move from a left-hemisphere focused awareness to a much wider one concentrated in the right hemisphere. The infinite potentialities of God provoke positive and negative anticipation in equal measure.

Awe is the characteristic peak emotion for experience of the God archetype, in this respect also showing the ways that the God archetype combines the Anima/Animus and Shadow archetypes. The Anima/Animus stimulates yearning, and the Shadow terror, but integrate these two together and you have awe – a sort of terrifying yearning. Of course, awe is a peak emotion that we are unlikely to be able to maintain over a long period of time, so a more habituated emotional relationship to the God archetype is that of respect: the kind of respect symbolised by Moses' removal of his sandals. If we are inclined to forget our awe, rituals of respect may help to rekindle it, provided these do not just become a way of exerting social power over others.

The sense of holiness, awe and respect are also entirely appropriate for symbolising the infinite, and trying to ensure that it does not get appropriated as a mere left-hemisphere idea amongst finite objects. They are the emotional aspect of the recognition that we are not infinite and cannot even imagine infinity, so that God is unimaginably far beyond us.

However, the dangers attendant on holiness and awe can also hardly be over-stated. An awe-struck person is likely to temporarily suspend any critical awareness, so is vulnerable to manipulation. Any person who inspires awe, because they have the God archetype projected on them as a wise old man or woman, is also potentially in a position of power. Those who represent God, intermediaries such as priests, are in a similar position, even if the awe is not directed at them personally but at the tradition or institution they serve. Awe is too often a prelude to a highly asymmetrical power relationship, in which the recipient of the God projection responds to the openness of the awestruck disciple by introducing absolute claims and instructions. Often these are well-intentioned, and believed to be for the good of the disciple, rather than obviously exploitative, but even so they have the effect of all absolute beliefs: that of shutting out alternatives, and thus reducing the disciple to a dependent relationship in which obedience is linked to approval, rather than an autonomous learning relationship in which the disciple is enabled to make genuine judgements.

These perils are illustrated as well in Exodus as anywhere else. The epiphanies in Exodus are accompanied by a covenant with God resembling contemporary treaties between a Hittite overlord and his vassal. In return for God's favour, the Israelites' commitment to God and his commandments must be absolute. They must have no other gods, and must follow a great mass of commandments that continue from Exodus into the three other law books that follow it. Many of these laws seem to have no other function but the exclusion of alternatives, whether this involves banning the customs of neighbouring tribes (such as cooking a kid in its mother's milk[29]) or the adoption of other gods[30]. Given the strictures under which Israel is laid, it is hardly surprising if they subsequently have trouble in following them, and constantly slip away from their faith in God.

Again, then, we need to distinguish sharply between the experience of God as holy and the faith it inspires, and the absolute beliefs that have become associated with that faith. Though the ancient Israelites were distinguished for their degree of appreciation for theistic faith, the texts that have come to dominate as records of their laws now also seem distinguished for their rigidity. Though what now appears to us as the brutality of their law (which involves a great deal of putting people to death for breaches of purity codes) was probably not much distinguished from the brutality of the era from which it came, what is more astonishing is the tenacity with which the most orthodox Jews have maintained these laws as an ideal. In the process they have left us a profoundly mixed legacy in which the appreciation of God's holiness is also the basis of rigid belief, power and manipulation.

c. The prohibition of idolatry

One of the effects of the recognition of God's infinity, with accompanying holiness and awe, has been the prohibition of idolatry. This is found in Exodus in the first and second of the Ten Commandments, but has been the matter of much varied interpretation in the three Abrahamic religions ever since:

> *You must have no other god besides me.*
>
> *You must not make a carved image for yourself, nor the likeness of anything in the heavens above, or on the earth below, or in the waters under the earth.*
>
> *You must not bow down to them in worship; for I, the Lord your God, am a jealous God.... (Ex 20:3-5)*

On the one hand this 'jealousy' is just a particularly strong example of absolutisation that excludes all alternatives. The apparent ban even on artistic reproductions of humans or animals makes clear the potential conflict between absolute belief and imagination, which may offer alternatives to that belief. The relationship between the prohibition on idolatry and narrow, puritanical beliefs is evident in the destruction it has wrought, for example in the destruction of great works of art by the original Christian iconoclasts in Constantinople, or the destruction of Hindu and Buddhist images by the Muslims who invaded India in the tenth century, and the more recent ones who blew up the Bamiyan Buddhas in Afghanistan.

But let us look more deeply at the faith motivation that may often lie behind the prohibition of idolatry. Like so much of religious tradition, it is double-edged. For the objection to 'carved images' lies in the way that they reduce the infinity of God to something finite, perhaps potentially also turning the holy into something manipulable. At the time of the ancient Israelites that may actually have been the main use to which images were put, with a mainly illiterate people absolutising the powers of images. Now, however, it is not images at all that are most likely to be the objects of idolatry.

The religion that takes this prohibition far more seriously than any other is Islam, and it is the Islamic definition of idolatry that can help us to uncover its positive value. The sin of idolatry in Islam is called *shirk*, but shirk is defined in terms of taking what is not God to be God. An 'idol' in the sense imagined in the Old Testament does just that, giving infinite status to the finite. Muslims extend the concept even further than this, seeing obsessiveness with worldly things, such as a car or a loved one, as further examples of *shirk*[31]. Here it seems that it is the God of the right hemisphere we are dealing with, not the left. Idols are the objects of left hemisphere obsession that assume the same absolute status as God, so that our desires focused on them cannot be integrated with the wider desires that are channelled into faith.

Iconoclasts, including Muslim ones, are mistaken if they think that all artistic representations of people or animals are idols in this sense. Some of them still are: think of glossy pictures of celebrities, or of pornography. However, visual images are on the whole far more likely to be prompts to engage in wider sense experience, enrichers of meaning, or useful expressions of archetypes separated from their projections. Artistic representations today, are, indeed, far more likely to draw us towards faith than otherwise. But we now live in an age of mass literacy in the developed world, where words have a far wider power and appeal. The far more dangerous idols today are words formed into absolute propositional beliefs.

If we are to think in terms of the overall function and intention behind the prohibition of idolatry, rather than in terms of a decontextualised rule, we need to accept that the application of the rule has completely reversed since the time of Moses. For Moses, the written word engraved on stone introduced a moral consistency that had not previously been present. Morality was no longer merely just defined by kings or local customs. One of the starting points for integration, in terms of rational consistency produced through the left hemisphere, was still developing. There are still people today (small children, for instance) who need to work primarily at this level, and learn to consistently obey rules before they can progress any further. For people in this position, images may have a much less positive impact. However, today it is far more likely that images will quite often (though not always) have the liberating effect of helping people see the world in new ways, whilst absolute beliefs, trapping us in metaphors that are taken to be the correct models, are the stumbling blocks to faith. Moses could hardly have envisaged that time.

Today, then, absolute beliefs, including but not limited to Christian and other religious beliefs, are idolatrous. We may bow down before the words every Sunday and take them to be God: or more likely, we will bow down before consumer products, conspiracy theories, idealised relationships, or even drug-fuelled oblivion. But bowing before Christian false idols does not help anyone to avoid the other false idols: rather it just gets us into idolatrous habits.

The resemblance between the prohibition of idolatry and the Middle Way is quite striking, because both, at root, are concerned with the avoidance of absolutisation. Both have also been formalistically misinterpreted by their respective religious traditions, which have focused on the specific beliefs prohibited in the ancient context where these principles were created, rather than the underlying universal principles. In the case of Buddhism, this has meant the interpretation of the Middle Way as the avoidance of 'eternalism' and 'nihilism', opposing absolute beliefs about the continuing self that were prominent in the time of the Buddha. The avoidance of idolatry is not normally put in terms of a middle between two extremes, but it well could be, for there surely is a reverse form of idolatry that consists in obsessive hatred or rejection, giving an infinitely negative status to that which only has a finitely negative (and mixed) status. Between idolatry and obsessive hatred, then, lies the Middle Way. Perhaps Moses and the Buddha have more in common than is initially evident.

d. The delusions of revelation

So far, then, we have seen that there is a serious attempt to engage with the implications of the infinity argument, not only in Christianity but in all three monotheistic traditions. It will be obvious to all, however, that this is not the dominant tradition in those religions. The major reason for this is that, countervailing the appreciation of God's infinity and otherness, is a tradition of revelatory belief that has had a strong effect in the other direction: towards reducing God to a human level and opening him up to manipulation. Before leaving this chapter, then, I want to look a little more closely at what has gone wrong.

Revelation is generally understood as the communication of truth or knowledge from God to humans, which was not known before and is thus 'revealed'. St Thomas Aquinas distinguishes between general revelation, which is communication from God through created nature; special revelation, which is scriptural and goes further, but is still available to all; and individual revelation, which is God's communication to an individual through religious experience. Here Aquinas has identified three powerful sources of inspiration for faith[32]. However, all these forms of revelation are subject to the infinity argument.

The forms of 'nature' from which moral messages are conveniently read off (for example in the Catholic Church's insistence that homosexuality and contraception are wrong because 'unnatural') are not only categorisable in a wide variety of ways, but also finite once they have been categorised. The idea that we can read messages from a finite number of 'natural' demonstrations, but that these messages have infinite authority, completely fails to take into account our responsibility for interpreting them. The phenomenon of confirmation bias alone would be sufficient to show just how naïve 'general revelation' is: observers of 'nature' do, and commonly have, read the theories they wanted to see into the evidence, for example by explaining away homosexual activity in animals as 'dominance behaviour'. Such observations can give us a degree of information relevant to our judgements, moral or otherwise, but can hardly give us complete or absolutely reliable information of the kind that 'general revelation' requires.

Scriptural revelation similarly fails to take into account ambiguity of any kind in loading written texts with infinite authority. It takes representationalism for granted in assuming that verbal propositions are capable of lining up with any kind of 'reality', let alone an infinitely authoritative reality. To insist that texts can represent 'truth' requires a disembodied standpoint in which the dependence of the meaning of words on our bodies (discussed in 1.a) is simply ignored.

Individual revelation fails for similar reasons: not because religious experience does not happen, or that it is not profound, insightful and supportive of faith, but only because it is not and cannot be infinite (again, this was discussed earlier, in 1.b). When religious experience is said to justify an absolute verbal formulation of belief (such as that life after death is true), such a formula also bears no necessary relationship to the experience. There could be many different potential 'revelations' derived from the same religious experience, and they are much more expressive of the beliefs of those who formulate them than anything else. Again, because it's God we're talking about, it is quite permissible to set the epistemological bar very high (in fact infinitely high) by requiring absolute justification of a revelation that claims to have absolute authority. An absolute revelatory claim requires absolute justification of a kind that is simply not available to us.

Christian existentialist thinkers such as Kierkegaard have suggested that revelation can take the form of ambiguous experience sent by God, that we then take a 'leap of faith' to accept[33]. However, as argued in 1.e above, this way of thinking about revelation only formalistically gives us responsibility. Rather than accepting a belief in comparison to alternatives, the 'leap of faith' can involve a mere acceptance of social power as opposed to denying it. If we regard the revelation as actually doubtful and a matter for our own interpretation, there is even less justification for attributing infinite authority to the revelation, even if we go through a 'voluntary' process to adopt it.

Belief in the existence of a supernatural God is not obviously incorrect if one fails to take into account the negative effects of absolute belief, but belief in revelation is so obviously unjustified that it is difficult to account for how and why people have accepted it for so long. The objections that could be made to it could easily fill a book in themselves, and the above arguments are only the ones I have selected as the most powerful. However, if we revert to the explanatory framework offered by brain lateralisation (see 1.d) it becomes easier to explain why people have accepted it.

The representations of the over-dominant left hemisphere tend, Midas-like, to turn everything they touch into abstract concepts that can form beliefs within their favoured framework. This is a useful ability when we are hunting: i.e. when we have goals that we are trying to fulfil, and need to identify every possible resource to help us reach those goals. Revelation, however, is the processing into left-brain belief of experiences that are helpfully understood only with considerable input from the right hemisphere, because they are experiences of alternative meaning rather than of new objects. This applies equally to religious experience itself, to the archetypal narrative and symbolic content of scripture, and to our experience of 'nature'. All of these things are manifold, variable, elusive, and inter-dependent with each other. These sources of inspiration are the very worst possible objects for the left-brain conceptualising treatment. Like Midas turning his food or his servants into lifeless gold, we assume that what we have produced is supremely valuable, but only belatedly realise that it is not valuable for the kinds of purposes we actually need it for.

The process by which the left brain takes over right brain inspirations and turns them into revelations can be described as an appropriation. Of course, practical justifications can be given for the appropriation. People need to have a shared basis on which to work together that is clearly understood. Inspiration quickly fades, but we need guidance throughout our lives. If we are sufficiently over-confident in our assumptions about what the right goals are, we can make revelation apparently fit those goals. However, all of this misses the point of divine inspiration, which is to get you to re-consider your goals. The kind of guidance people need to engage with the practical conditions in their lives is also rarely of the kind generally treated as revelatory, but much more likely to depend on the slow accretion of human experience to solve practical problems effectively. The appropriation of God to the left hemisphere is misplaced and damaging, but nevertheless difficult to resist. We are so much in the habit of reducing every other facet of experience to propositional knowledge that God automatically tends to get the same treatment.

Another reason for the adoption of revelatory belief lies in our political power structures. Until quite recently, political power did not need any genuine justification. Kings ruled because their fathers had ruled, with changes of dynasty often being supported only by the pragmatic argument that having somebody keeping order was better than anarchy. But kingship in general was given absolute status, perhaps through the invocation of divine right. Generally, the will of the king was accepted because he said so. The revelations offered us by the Church have a similar lack of justification and are similarly manipulable. The compositions of the Old and New Testaments were only finalised by the respective councils of Jamnia and Nicaea on the circular grounds that the selected books were in accordance with the church's doctrine. The Pope only became infallible during the nineteenth century. Why is it only ever a few troublemakers on the fringes, or academics in distant universities, who even mention these points, rather than ordinary Christians? Presumably because the acceptance of an absolute authority on the basis of little more than chutzpah has become too much of a habit, and the church has shown little enthusiasm for educating people in critical thinking to overcome that habit.

From the point of view of anyone seeking power over others, revelation is an extremely useful tool. Its absolute authority can be easily appropriated for political ends, and its implications readily re-interpreted to fit changes in those ends. The Bible has been used to support pacifism and war, political authority and anarchy, slavery and the freeing of slaves, feminism and the subjection of women, racism and racial equality.

At the same time, authority has the function of providing useful information and advice from perspectives that we may not have encountered, and of dealing with political or organisational matters that we may not wish to be involved with. But this type of authority does not have to be absolute or unconditional. A doctor of medicine has authority deriving from medical expertise, but our confidence in that authority is strengthened, not weakened, by the recognition that this authority can be questioned, held accountable, and compared with alternatives. The same point applies to democratic politicians. We may have confidence in the words of the doctor or the politician, but we do not have absolute belief in them. Revelation is not a necessary aspect of such useful authority.

We have seen in this chapter how infinity is a requirement for the archetypal God to perform its function, but also how the idea of infinity needs to be confined to meaning and kept out of beliefs about God out of basic respect for him. Holiness and awe are early indications of the recognition of this point in the Bible, and the prohibition of idolatry tries to put it into action, though it has been too narrowly interpreted and not updated. In the light of the infinity argument, the attribution of infinite authority to finite sources in the belief in revelation is not only unjustified, but incompatible with the basis of faith itself. Using traditional Christian language, we are therefore justified in calling revelatory beliefs idolatrous, disrespectful and sinful.

4

God, humans and creation

a. Three types of creation

What does it mean to create? To understand the Middle Way on the Christian account of creation, let us start, not with the customary 'In the beginning...', but instead with what creation *means* for the humans who engage with the creation story. Only then can we cast light on the Judeo-Christian story. Because of the different roles of the brain hemispheres, there are not just two but three different senses of 'creation' for humans.

In the first, or absolute, sense of creation, *nothing* is present before the creation, and *something* is brought into existence.

In the second, or reproductive, sense of creation, some kind of idea, plan, or copy (whether mental or physical) of what is to be produced already exists. A new version of that copy is produced.

In the third, or mimetic, sense of creation, something already exists that may have a closer or more distant resemblance to the thing to be created. The existing materials are recombined so as to produce something new that was not previously combined in that way, whether in the object itself or in the mind of the creator.

The crucial differences between these three forms of creation depend on what is going on in the mind of the creator.

In the reproductive sense of creation, there are clear goals and representations of what is to be created, and the process of creation is merely to reproduce those goals as precisely as possible. The representations may or may not include an actual copy of the thing to be produced already in existence. A construction engineer building a bridge from a set of painstaking designs is creating in this sense, as is a factory production worker who merely controls a machine that is pre-set to reproduce identical plastic parts over and over again. In this sense of creation, the left hemisphere is heavily dominant.

Reproductive creation follows a closed feedback loop in which an idea is fixed on, a copy of that idea is constructed, and then the constructed thing reinforces the idea. However, reproductive creation will only actually succeed to a certain extent. The plastic parts may appear identical, but will have microscopic variations. The bridge may follow the specification as precisely *as possible*, but there will be at least some small divergences from it. However, the mental state accompanying this kind of creation focuses on the goal of copying, and will either be frustrated by a lack of exactness in the copying or will deny that there is any such lack, re-interpreting the creation to fit the idea and pretending in ad hoc fashion that it was intended to be like that all along. Any divergence from the plan, if it is admitted, is a failure. The view of the world adopted is one where it is assumed that it is *possible* to copy exactly because there is an absolute relationship between the specification and the creation. Whilst it may be admitted, on philosophical enquiry, that the copy in the plan is not *exactly* the same as the created thing, the reproductive creator will insist on the absoluteness of the relationship. This relationship can be called *isomorphism* from the Greek for 'same shape'.

In the mimetic sense of creation, on the other hand, there is no expectation of any isomorphism between a plan or a previous model and what is created. Rather it is accepted that both the form of what is created and its meaning to us will depend on various variable factors: the nature of the materials, the mental state and expectations of the creator, or other incidental factors that contribute to what is produced. It is not that the creator will lack plans or intentions, for these will always have to be present to some extent for the activity of creation to occur at all. However, it is accepted that the creation will in some respects have a life that is independent of the creator. Different goals may emerge in the process of creation that were not envisaged at the beginning. A wider harmony and integrity will be sought for the creation which is only partially in line with any wishes the creator may have started with, also responding to the conditions that arose in the process of creation.

In contrast to the self-reaffirming closed feedback loop involved in reproductive creation, mimetic creation involves an open feedback loop, whereby adaptation to a wider environment is allowed by more flexible responses. An idea of what is to be made is put into operation, but differences between the idea and the creation are not seen as failures, rather as new conditions to be learnt from and responded to. In this way the idea of what is being created continually changes along with the thing being created.

The mimetic sense of creation is obviously one that applies to works of art, following the senses discussed by Samuel Taylor Coleridge[34] and Erich Auerbach[35]. It also applies to parenthood – at least if it is pursued with any wisdom rather than with absolute plans for the child. Mimesis is obviously the embodied type of creativity. It is a type of creativity pursued with an active and integrated role for the right hemisphere, taking new conditions into account as well as the left hemisphere's goals and representations[36]. We tend to describe people as 'creative' who have learnt to manage the process of mimetic creation with confidence.

The second and the third senses of creation are the ones that apply to humans, but then we must return also to the first, or absolute sense. This sense is a notional one, but because of its absoluteness it has no relevance to human experience. The activity of God according to orthodox Christian belief is that of *ex nihilo* creation, with nothing existing, and then something. But such a belief is a complete abstraction, like infinity, that can only be made meaningful through a cognitive model that begins with our experience of reproductive or mimetic creation and then subtracts the prior materials from it. We cannot even imagine nothing existing prior to something, because our experience is always of something, and imagination recombines those experiences.

The only way the first type of creation could be relevant to human experience is as a delusion of the left hemisphere. Given the left hemisphere's lack of continuing awareness of time, an unintegrated left hemisphere may forget the prior existent materials before something changes its form, then become aware of the new thing and assume it has created it out of nothing. A mocking Buddhist story tells similarly of a god who arrives first in an empty god-realm, longs for company, and then coincidentally other gods arrive: so he believes that he has created them[37]. Here he is subject to a causal fallacy and an illusion of control, both of which can be attributed to absolutisation of one's creative abilities that neglect other possible causes.

There is a role for reproductive creation in human experience, as long as it doesn't try to supplant mimetic creativity. Absolute creation, however, like other absolute Christian beliefs, is incapable of being integrated. It is reproductive creation that completely denies its relationship to the wider conditioned world that we experience, 'pure' copying from an idea made so abstract that it must supposedly succeed in ridding us of the inexactness of genuine copying.

In any case, though, there is rightly dispute over whether Genesis is intended to portray ex nihilo creation at all. The Babylonian creation myths, by which it was probably influenced, do not involve ex nihilo creation, and indeed all other creation myths assume some sort of material out of which the world was made. If you read the text of Genesis there is, as always, room for multiple readings:

In the beginning God created the heavens and the earth. The earth was a vast waste, darkness covered the deep, and the spirit of

> *God hovered over the surface of the water. God said 'Let there be light,' and there was light; and God saw the light was good, and he separated light from darkness. He called the light day, and the darkness night. So evening came, and morning came; it was the first day.*
>
> *God said 'Let there be a vault between the waters, to separate water from water.' So God made the vault, and separated the water under the vault from the water above it, and so it was; and God called the vault the heavens. Evening came, and morning came, the second day.* (Gen 1:1-8)

Does the first sentence introduce a more detailed account of how God created the heavens and the earth, or does it tell us what God did first before the rest? The latter seems unlikely, because God is described as making the heavens on the second day (and then the earth on the third), which he would not need to do if he had already made them on the first. But before the creation, then, there seems to be an earth, a deep, and water. Only light is lacking. God does seem to magic light into existence from nothing, but everything else is already there and is just reorganised, until God starts creating the plants and the animals.

So, on a more helpful interpretation, Genesis can be understood as not telling us about a process of absolute creation at all. Instead it is telling us about mimetic creation. The light, plants, animals and humans that God creates are presumably made out of the earth, heavens and water. God presumably had some sort of plan beforehand, but does not seem to be in a hurry. He creates each sort of thing one at a time, and then sees that it is good, pausing at each stage for that day. God seems to be responding to conditions, seeing how things work out a bit, rather than pushing ahead regardless with a rigid plan. How else, after all, could one create life, especially human life? Life immediately starts doing its own thing.

Thus the Creator God in Genesis can be interpreted as the

archetypal God, the God of faith. The Creator God is symbolically demonstrating creativity, through a balanced combination of flexible planning and respect for the arising of new conditions. He does not expect to control everything in his creation, but expects it to develop in unexpected ways. He also demonstrates astonishing creativity in creating the wonders of the earth, thus symbolising the ultimate of what human creativity could be like. As always, it is the *meaning* of this aspect of God that is important, rather than what we believe about it. Believing that God actually did these things leads us, at best, into unhelpful distraction from human experience, and at worst into divisive literalism such as Creationism. Recognising our own potentiality in them, however, we may be inspired to apply our creativity in increasingly adequate ways.

Creation can almost be seen as the great archetypal work of art, and the 'design' (with which thinkers like William Paley unsuccessfully tried to prove the existence of God) as a process by which our planning enters into dialogue with the conditions to which it is applied. This kind of mimetic process of design, unlike that of ex nihilo creation, also reflects the way in which the evidence so far suggests that plants, animals and humans actually developed. Rather than suddenly appearing from nowhere, they developed out of previous forms that were similar, but not identical, to themselves. Natural selection, however, also provides a response from the conditions, which destroys many of the new 'creations' soon after their conception, much as an artist may need to discard many drafts. If, as many more liberal Christians claim, God designed the world through the means of evolution, such a process would again be mimetic, not ex nihilo nor reproductive.

Given the tendency of the Genesis text, how on earth did we ever get to belief in ex nihilo creation in the first place? Any historical answer will be a byway in this argument, the main point of which is that creation *can* be interpreted in a way that is fully relevant to human experience. However, it is worth briefly discussing at least a plausible theory about how the belief in *ex nihilo* creation became dominant. The first evidence of such an interpretation in Judaism is extremely late: in the Apocryphal book of 2 Maccabees dated to around 124 BCE[38]. Its source may lie in the influence of Greek philosophy over the Hellenised world in which later Judaism and Christianity spread and developed. Plato believed that the Form of the Good created the world, because specific objects were only made possible by the Forms and ultimately by the Form of the Good (which is the Form of Forms): these are essential ideas of things in the world. For Plato, then, the idea (or Logos) comes first and enables experiential objects to come into existence. The Logos, famously incorporated into the Bible in the opening words of the Gospel of John ('In the beginning was the Logos'), was also the universal ruling spirit of reason for the Stoics. This influential section of Greek thought, then, imported a strong left-hemisphere bias into the very subject of Creation. This perspective expected creation to consist of a 'rational' plan that was then put into effect, and also expected answers to questions such as how the world *ultimately* began: questions that had not occurred to earlier people because they were not relevant to anything. All of this discourse may have been projected onto Genesis. Though the account of Creation in Plato's *Timaeus* is not identical to the doctrine of *ex nihilo* creation, the move from mimesis to reproduction or imitation of a plan is already clearly present in *Timaeus*[39].

Of course, another more general reason why *belief* in *ex nihilo* Creation may have continued to prevail is the enculturation of the assumption that asking 'How did the universe begin?' is in some way a meaningful and helpful question of a kind that could potentially have an answer. Buddhism and other Asian religions that ask no such question, nor expect any helpful answer to it, make it clear that this expectation is a merely cultural one, and thus could potentially be changed.

b. The creation of human beings

The culmination of the process of creation in the Genesis account is the creation of human beings. In the first account of this creation, identified by scholars as coming from a 'Priestly' writer, in Gen 1:26-31, only human beings in general are created collectively, and apparently male and female at the same time. In the second account, identified by scholars as by the 'Yahwist' writer in Gen 2:7-25, Adam and Eve are created individually and in succession, and we are then given the story of the temptation and Fall. Both of these accounts show considerable tensions in their portrayal of the status of human beings and their relationship to God. On the one hand, both accounts could be read as extending the absolutised, left hemisphere God of Christian belief, and lending authoritative support to some of the most disastrous attitudes associated with that belief. On the other, however, both stories can be interpreted as symbolic of the human experience of the tension between the hemispheres, and in that sense to enrich our understanding of the God of faith and of the human experience of finding the Middle Way.

In the Priestly writer's account of the creation of humans, two particular claims about human nature stand out, each of them subject to a wide range of interpretation. The first of these is that God created human beings "in his own image" (Gen 1:27), and the second that God told humans to "Be fruitful and increase, fill the earth and subdue it, have dominion over the fish in the sea, the birds of the air, and every living thing that moves on the earth" (Gen 1:28).

Whatever 'in his own image' means, it tells us something crucial about God: that is, how he is similar to humans, and thus what it is about humans that is potentially divine and thus should be supremely valued. The term might be taken literally to refer to the human appearance of God: which is accurate for the archetypal image of the wise old man in a way in which it is not for the absolute God of belief. More often, though, it has been interpreted as referring to the self-consciousness and 'rationality' that humans share with God but not with the animals: namely, the ability to make representations of the world in the form of beliefs, and to apply those beliefs in new contexts and compare them with one another for consistency. Under Platonic influence, this rationality has also been identified with the soul, as the divine element of human beings beyond the body. A whole rationalistic tradition of thought has sprung from this that constantly conflates the divine with the rational.

However, this is a very left-hemisphere focused interpretation that represents God only in terms of one cognitive model, rather than as a being we encounter through the right hemisphere or in the way that the right hemisphere integrates left hemisphere representations. If God is to be the God of experience and faith, then the key way in which we resemble God must lie in the God that we find within ourselves: that is, as an archetype offering an anticipation of integration and a glimpse of overwhelmingly full meaning.

Nor is left-hemisphere rationality as distinct from that of other animals as Descartes and other rationalists have assumed. Human beings do appear to be distinctive in their capacity for abstract language, and thus for absolutisations, but 'rationality' in the sense of consistency of belief does not depend on that capacity. Other animals can create consistent views of the world through investigation of their environment, and can learn from their mistakes. Much of this can be done implicitly, without abstract language and self-conscious thought. If the image of God involved only 'rationality', then dogs, chimpanzees, crows and dolphins would be due some of it too.

No, if we are to interpret 'the image of God' helpfully, then it must refer to the integrative abilities of the right hemisphere working together with the left. It is this capacity that, in one sense, we give God, by experiencing the God archetype in its terms – as an object of holiness and awe as well as love. In another sense, God gives it to us, as the integrated psyche that the God archetype represents is prior and more basic to us than the ego that more normally forms the basis of our assumptions about ourselves. When we become more integrated, that which we integrate is already there in our psyches: it is only the alienation of one part from the other that means they are not integrated. The potential for integration is already present, and thus in that sense God creates us, providing the resources for an integration by which we fulfil that potential.

There may seem to be an apparent problem in reconciling this interpretation with the text in that at Genesis 1:27, where the image of God is mentioned, the expulsion from Eden appears not to have happened yet, and thus (at least as I shall interpret the symbology of Eden below), no alienation has yet occurred and no integration yet needs to take place. Our interpretation is under no obligation to make consistent sense of the text, but nevertheless we may be able to do so by taking into account the two different sources that make up the early chapters of Genesis. It is the 'Priestly' writer who tells us about the image of God, but who makes no mention of the Adam and Eve story. Even in the English translation, a marked change in language, style and pace, as well as repetition of aspects of the story, can be seen from the point where the 'Yahwist' takes over at Genesis 2:4 and begins the Adam and Eve story. The 'image of God' can consistently be taken to refer to a post-Eden world assumed by the Priestly writer.

God's instruction to humans to subdue the earth and have dominion over it, however, is much harder to interpret positively. For earlier generations, perhaps, this instruction could be confidently cashed: a blank cheque written by God allowing humans to make as much from exploitation of the earth as they wished, in the calm and unexamined expectation that God would provide from nature's inexhaustible stores. As I write in 2016, it seems increasingly clear that this verse has provided ongoing ideological justification for some of the most damaging effects of absolutising Christian belief. We are finite and the earth is finite. The earth's capacity to keep providing non-renewable resources such as fossil fuels and other minerals, and to renew renewable resources such as fish, water, soil and timber, as well as its capacity to absorb pollution and its effects, are all finite. Yet the absolutisation implicit in this divine instruction has allowed us to carry on assuming that these things are infinite, at least to the extent that we feel justified in ignoring the problem.

This instrumentalisation of the earth and all things in it is symptomatic of a highly unbalanced left-hemisphere approach, which is not unique to Judeo-Christian tradition (a number of past societies, Judeo-Christian or not, have managed to destroy themselves through such environmental over-confidence[40]) but is nevertheless not inevitable and not evident to the same extent in all cultural traditions. We are now reaching a point where the full scale of the damage it is likely to cause is becoming increasingly evident, but if you read this later than 2016 it may be more evident still.

There is, of course, also a liberal Christian interpretation of 'dominion', that does not take it to be an unconditional license to pillage the earth. This interpretation takes 'dominion' to refer to a responsibility under God and to God, which is a responsibility to look after the earth and maintain its ecosystems as well as utilising it. Whilst this is a good deal preferable to the 'blank cheque' interpretation, it still limits human responsibility to the obedience or disobedience of God, rather than helping us to become aware even of the possibility of attitudes that offer alternatives to instrumentalism (other than its mere denial).

Christians need to face up to the fact that this failure represents one of the most compelling reasons today for people to turn their back on the Judeo-Christian tradition. As Peter Singer interprets it:

> *The implication is clear: to act in a way that causes fear and dread for everything that moves on the earth is not improper; it is, in fact, in accordance with a God-given decree. This was the thinking of mainstream Christianity for at least its first eighteen centuries. There were gentler spirits, certainly, like Basil, John Chrysostom, and (maybe, though there is no contemporary evidence for it) Francis of Assisi, but for most of Christian history they have had no significant impact on the dominant tradition. According to the dominant Western tradition, the natural world exists for the benefit of human beings. God gave human beings dominion over the natural world, and God does not care how we treat it. Human beings are the only morally important members of this world. Nature itself is of no intrinsic value, and the destruction of plants and animals cannot be sinful, unless it leads us to harm human beings.*[41]

To say that the environmental problems we face today are largely the fault of Christian belief would thus not be an exaggeration. Not only did Christian beliefs rooted in this Biblical text absolutise human dominance and the myth of infinite natural resources, but cultures dominated by those Christian beliefs have been overwhelmingly responsible, until quite recently, for the largely unrestrained despoliation of landscapes, plants, and animals.

Nevertheless, like the other issues that stem from the absolutisations of Christian belief discussed in this book, they are not necessarily an aspect of Christian faith. The fact that this verse has traditionally received a lot of emphasis, and that this has been very damaging, do not necessarily mean that future Christians cannot either choose to ignore the verse, or interpret it in more helpful ways. Christians need to take responsibility for their interpretations of Christianity, and this verse is one of the key testing points.

Here is my attempt at a more helpful interpretation: though, like my other biblical interpretations in this book, it does not pretend to justification on textual or traditional grounds, only those of helpfulness. 'Dominion' suggests a ruler's power over his lands, with the ability to use that power to 'subdue' the lands to his own ends. However, what those ends are depends on the ruler's own degree of integration, as well as the quality of his relationships with his subjects. The more sustainable the ruler's treatment of his lands, the more sustainably those ends will also be fulfilled. For example, if the agricultural lands are wrecked by short-termist agricultural practices that fail to make long-term provision for the fertility of the soil, the ruler will get their desire for wealth from agriculture in the short-term, but not in the long-term. A more integrated desire for wealth from agriculture will support longer-term policies that support the soil's fertility. This can also support a sense of responsibility for the earth of the kind that the liberal Christian interpretation seeks to promote.

The issues here relate to ethical questions about the use of power that I will return to in 9.f. The Middle Way does not justify us in the negative absolutisation that would be involved in rejecting all possible uses of power, regardless of the consequences, but that use of power needs to be justified by greater integration on the part of those using the power. This is applicable to the use of power over the earth as well as over others. The consequences of not using any of our power over the earth would be very negative for us, so we cannot wholly reject "dominion": but that dominion needs to be a balanced and integrated one.

It is only in the Yahwist's account of the creation of human beings that a third issue emerges: that of the separate creations of Adam and Eve in succession rather than together. This clearly seems to offer an aetiological justification for patriarchal dogma, in which men's superior status (enabling them to use power over women) is supported by their priority of creation. There is no justification for adopting this as a belief, not only because the story is the product of the patriarchy (rather than the other way round), but also because there is no evidence that the power of one sex over the other is necessarily or even generally justified, or that it helps societies to address conditions better. On the contrary, there seems to be some evidence that giving greater influence to women reduces conflict and violence in society, providing at least one basic condition for addressing other conditions better[42].

The most we can say about the meaningfulness of Adam being created first is that it has meaning from the male point of view, from which the story was written. For men, male experience is primary, and the recognition of a female view requires a process of recognition and integration of that view into one's own widening perspective. Adam suddenly finding Eve beside him, and thinking she has only just been created, can be compared to the god in the Buddhist story thinking that he has created his companions: a matter of ignorance. If women were to write a counterbalancing matriarchal story, in which female experience is primary, Eve was created first by the Goddess, and Adam then created from one of *her* ribs, this would be neither more nor less helpful, just equally partial.

The creation of Eve in the Yahwist's story is preceded by Adam naming the animals. In this version, contrary to the Priestly writer's version, the animals are apparently created *after* Adam, in an attempt to find a partner for him.'

> *Then the Lord God said, 'It is not good for the man to be alone; I shall make a partner suited to him.' So from the earth he formed all the wild animals and all the birds of the air, and brought them to the man to see what he would call them; whatever the man called each living creature, that would be its name. The man gave names to all cattle, to the birds of the air, and to every wild animal; but for the man himself no suitable partner was found.* (Gen 2: 18-20)

Here we have an indication that the linguistic powers of the human left hemisphere are already being given priority. Adam represents the labours of countless scientific taxonomists, giving labels to things on the earth and thus ordering them in our cognitive models. However, in the end this linguistic, left hemisphere process is not enough. Adam, who has been made from the earth like all the other animals, also has a right hemisphere and a body, with an emotional need for connection. The coming of Eve into Adam's experience provides one of the basic conditions that will be needed later, after the Fall, for Adam's potential integration.

c. The Fall

But now we come to the even more vexed but important question of the fall from Paradise, the loss of Eden. Christian interpretation of the story has hardly been uniform, but it does tend to be used to try to justify a set of absolute beliefs: that humans, though responsible for their disobedience to God, were tempted by Satan; that evil here entered human life, accompanied by suffering and death; and that a subordinate position for women is justified by Eve's crucial role in first yielding to the Serpent's temptation.

The influential Augustinian interpretation of the story blames *all* evil, even the 'natural evil' of non-human events causing suffering to humans, on the sin of Adam and Eve – the 'original sin' for which we all subsequently suffer. The alternative Irenaean tradition of interpretation, recently championed by John Hick[43], is hardly orthodox in seeing the Fall as in some ways a positive event, because suffering creates contrasts and sets us new challenges that are an opportunity for learning and growth. However, even the Irenaean tradition is still absolutising by trying to justify *all* suffering as ultimately positive, despite the obvious dependence of learning on the contingent psychological states of the learner.

If we search for meanings rather than doctrines in the

story of the Fall, and interpret it in recognition of the roles of the brain hemispheres, it can readily be seen as an extremely rich myth. First, there is the symbolism of Eden itself. I want to suggest that Eden represents, not the ultimately integrated state of God, but the pre-alienated state before any conflict has occurred[44]. In Eden there are none of the things that give rise to conflict: for example possessions, shame, toil, pain, animal slaughter, or environmental degradation. There are desires, but they do not conflict with each other because all judgement follows from the ultimately integrated state (i.e. the archetypal God of faith). However, it does not do so because of a hard-won position in which conflicting desires, all making their own mature and developed cases for priority, are integrated despite the difficulties, but rather out of naivety. This apparent but deceptive 'integration' is the innocence of the very young child.

Then there is the tree of knowledge of good and evil. If we take the story to be the basis of belief, God comes across as a sadist setting a test that he knew humankind would fail. However, if we understand it symbolically, it merely indicates the potential for conflict in the naïve state. Adam and Eve necessarily have left hemispheres as well as right (indeed, Adam is depicted by the Yahwist as exercising his by naming the animals), but the left hemisphere has not yet become over-dominant, obsessive, or absolutising.

Enter the serpent: the symbol in many cultures of wisdom, or of power arising from the unconscious. This reminds us of the positive role of the Fall in setting humanity on a path of potential wisdom. It is only by making autonomous judgement and being capable of defying authority that wisdom can begin, with the left hemisphere offering the initial basis of wisdom in rationality before the stage of right-hemisphere integration. Yet the later Judeo-Christian tradition (which arose in post-exilic Judaism) identifies the serpent with Satan. This does reveal another aspect of the temptation: that the over-dominant absolutising left hemisphere is the origin of evil that inhibits integration and assumes its current desires are sufficient. Obviously, though, serpent or Satan is not external to Adam and Eve themselves.

The 'temptation' is a conflict. On the one hand, the fruit is believed to be forbidden by God (perhaps in recognition of the disruptive effect it will have), but on the other, human beings wish to leave naivety and make their own mistakes. The choice cannot be incrementalised (presumably just having a little nibble would still count as eating the fruit) – so it is an absolute choice, and it is this absoluteness with which eating the fruit has been framed that creates the conflict.

The serpent reveals that eating the fruit will make Adam and Eve like God: "as soon as you eat it, your eyes will be opened and you will be like God himself, knowing both good and evil" (Gen 3:4). Again, we may have a mixture of potential moral reactions here. On the one hand, trying to become like God himself is an idolatrous delusion of the kind discussed in the previous chapter: the over-dominant left hemisphere is very prone to such delusions, by projecting the idea of infinity onto a finite state of affairs. On the other, though, knowledge of good and evil can only arise out of moral awareness of a kind that comes from making discriminations.

There can be no particular justification in Eve being depicted as the 'weaker' sex who falls for the temptation, since there is no evidence that women are more subject to psychological conflict than men (if anything, the reverse seems more likely). Even if there were such evidence, though, we would have no grounds for absolutising an incremental, 'on average' difference between the sexes. Like women being created second in the Yahwist's account, we can take this merely as an indication of the male point of view from which the story is being told. Shame and blame are the immediate effects of the fall, as Eve blames the serpent and Adam blames Eve[45], and these are further indications of conflict. Again, a feminist version that depicted Adam as the tempted one would correct the lack of even-handedness, but would not capture the positive meaning any better.

The punishment that God imposes thus also reflects the double-edged effects of gaining the mature capacity for over-dominance of the left hemisphere. The first punishment is conflict between humans and serpents: "I shall put enmity between you and the woman" (Gen 3:15). This is the first incidence of conflict and violence in the story (even before Cain murders his brother Abel in Genesis 4). It can represent conflict between humans and animals in general, but also perceived conflict between human 'head' and 'body'. The embodied wisdom of the serpent will be forcibly repressed by the overweening left hemisphere. "They will strike at your head, and you will strike at their heel" (Gen 3:15).

The punishment given to the woman is "great labour in childbearing" and "You will desire your husband, but he will be your master". Christian belief here is obliged to take pain in childbirth, suffered more by women than other female animals, as a punishment for Eve's disobedience. According to more recent evidence, however, greater pain in childbirth seems to have been as result of increased human brain size due to the growth of the frontal lobes or 'new brain' in humans, together with their assumption of an upright two-legged posture. So, there does seem to be an element of justification in the connection made here between the new mental capacities that accompany human development out of naivety on the one hand, and pain for women on the other. This is not a matter of justice or women deserving the pain, but the conditions that produced what is represented by the Fall are also the conditions of pain in childbirth. Is it worth that pain? Again, the answer must be double-edged. The enlarged frontal lobes enabled the advanced representation abilities that have allowed the left hemisphere to become over-dominant, but the right frontal lobe was also enlarged (to a slightly lesser extent), allowing integrative awareness that potentially unites differing metaphorical models and conflicting beliefs[46]. Pain in childbirth allows evil and conflict, but it also allows greater good through the integration of that conflict. Everything humans have achieved positively would be impossible without that pain: so we perhaps just need to be grateful to our mothers for undergoing it rather than blaming them for eating the forbidden fruit.

Sexual desire and patriarchy are also depicted as part of women's punishment for Eve's sin. Patriarchy, with its use of power by men over women, is clearly an aspect of the over-dominance of the left hemisphere represented by the Fall. Again, then, it is only Christian belief that need take this as 'deserved': Christian faith can interpret it as a symbol of the relationship between the over-dominant left hemisphere and a use of power from which women suffer disproportionately. Sexual desire is perhaps only problematic here because it is in conflict with patriarchy (male sexual desire is not, after all, mentioned as part of Adam's punishment). Sexual desire for someone who has power over you can perhaps cause psychological conflict of a kind that sexual desire for someone you have power over may not. But men, too, of course, can feel conflicted about their sexuality as an uncontrolled bodily process leading them to act 'irrationally'.

Adam's punishment, on the other hand, focuses on alienation from labour:

> *On your account the earth will be cursed.*
> *You will get food from it only by labour*
> *All the days of your life;*
> *It will yield thorns and thistles for you.*
> *You will eat the produce of the field,*
> *And only by the sweat of your brow will you win your bread*
> *Until you return to the earth.... (Gen 3:17-19)*

In the Yahwist's account, work is not newly introduced at this point, as the task of the man in Eden was "to till it and look after it" from the beginning (Gen 2:15). Instead, it seems to be alienation or conflict *about* work that is being introduced. Humans must work in order to survive, but also have contrary desires to be doing something else that does not involve so much conflict and difficulty. This alienation from economic productivity is rightly linked by Marx to the imposition of power[47], but not only the power of one class over the other – also that of one set of desires and beliefs of an individual over another. Such alienation is not inevitable, but arises as a result of absolutisation of either of the conflicting beliefs over the other. Either fantasies of leisure can be absolutised, given qualities that they would not have in experience and a value that is attributed to it simply because it is different from work, or alternatively the need for work itself can be absolutised by being turned into an end in itself, as in the Protestant Work Ethic. Work is necessary, but many of us often do more work than we need to out of a sense of insecurity or a desire to fulfil rigid social expectations. Like the other punishments, then, Adam's is double edged, allowing us to take responsibility for our lives and to apply effort where we choose to apply it. On the other, though, it creates the basis of many absolutisations.

The expulsion from Eden is perhaps most basically a position of responsibility, in which we become aware of the moral weight of our judgements. The way in which our fulfilment of that responsibility depends on our recognition of it in experience has already been argued in 2e. To fulfil that responsibility, we need to integrate the beliefs of the left hemisphere using the right. However, over-dominance of the left hemisphere can create bad faith, in which we are either *held* responsible or wholly released from responsibility (now turned into a mere concept) by absolutised moral beliefs or their denial. The immediate painful impact of recognising that we are fallen feels alienating, as though we are just being *held* responsible for something we did not do. However, if we can find a fuller *experience* of responsibility, the Fall becomes a more positive event, and Irenaeus is vindicated in seeing Adam and Eve's sin as a happy sin.

d. The Tree of Life

The double-edged meaning of the Fall is perhaps especially encapsulated in the symbol of the Tree of Life. The Tree of Life is depicted as being planted alongside the Tree of Knowledge of Good and Evil "in the middle of the garden" (Gen 2:9). However, God is depicted as motivated to expel Adam and Eve, not by vengeance, but by a fear that they would eat from the Tree of Life as well.

> *'The man has become like one of us, knowing good from evil; what if he now reaches out and takes fruit from the tree of life also, and eats it and lives for ever?' So the Lord God banished him from the Garden of Eden to till the ground from which he had been taken. When he drove him out, God settled him to the east of the garden of Eden, and he stationed the cherubim and a sword whirling and flashing to guard the way to the tree of life.* (Gen 3:22-24)

Christian tradition seems to have been at a loss to incorporate the Tree of Life effectively into its structures of dogmatic belief. If Adam and Eve had already committed the great original sin, could they really have sinned twice as much by eating a second kind of forbidden fruit? Given the scale of the punishment for the first original sin, the potential second one seems already paid for in advance. Perhaps that is one reason why some commentators have argued that there was only meant to be one tree: but that would rob us of the potentially important symbolism of the Tree of Life.

I think that, again, considering the roles of the hemispheres can help to understand the archetypal meaning of the Tree of

Life (and thus part of the significance of the Fall) in ways that are distinct from its relationship to established Christian doctrines. The Tree of Life also seems to hold the key to the idea of 'eternal life' often used in Christianity, as God is depicted as saying that Adam and Eve would live for ever if they ate its fruit.

Eternal life, taken 'literally' in our dominant cognitive model, is beyond human experience. To understand it symbolically, though, we need to consider the different ways in which the brain hemispheres experience time. It is the right hemisphere that directly experiences the passing of time in the form of continuous experience. The left hemisphere uses concepts of time, but without adequate links to the right it will reduce time to measurements and temporally relative events. The left hemisphere is thus the source of impatience (where we want time to be over because we are only focused on conceptualised goals) and retrospective bewilderment of the "where did that time go?" type. Zeno's paradoxes illustrate the difference: for example, in the paradox of the arrow, an arrow is thought to never reach its target, because it travels half the distance to the target (taking half the time), then half of the remaining distance and time, the half of the remainder, and so on ad infinitum. From the left hemisphere standpoint, time is infinitely divisible, but from the right, it is not divisible, but just a unified, continuous, gestalt experience (exactly the same points also apply to space). From right hemisphere experience we are aware that arrows do reach their targets, but from the over-dominant left thinking in isolation it seems that, in theory, they shouldn't[48].

When we say something like "the bus took an eternity to arrive this morning", we are thus in a sense correct, for from the left hemisphere perspective, any continuous time is an eternity. It doesn't really matter how short or long the measured time is: from the isolated left hemisphere point of view it is impossible to grasp it passing at all. We have all experienced this directly: sometimes it seems that even ten minutes will never go by, because we are continually measuring it and thinking of it only in terms of the point in time reached. However, as we have become a little more integrated, we have perhaps become a little less prone to impatience than we used to be, because we can more habitually place that left hemisphere impatience within a wider context of right hemisphere experience.

To make an interpretation of the Tree of Life that relates to human experience, then, I suggest that we understand the Tree of Life as referring to an integrated state in which the temporal isolation of left hemisphere goals and representations is unified. If Adam and Eve had eaten the fruit of the Tree of Life, they would have not only been able to absolutise left hemisphere representations, but also to integrate them over time. They would then have experienced the kind of 'eternity' that actually matters to us embodied humans: that is, an awareness of our goals and representations that spans time and no longer fluctuates between one position and its opposite. In this state of eternity, far from being beyond time, we have accepted time as an experience rather than continually reducing it to a concept. Accepting our temporality, the prospect of death will then no longer seem a threat, because our desire to live will be able to be integrated with our recognition of a wider perspective of which death is a part.

Apart from its association with eternal life, there are other reasons for interpreting the Tree of Life in this way. These lie both in the Christian tradition of symbolic association and the wider associations of the symbol. Some Christian commentators have associated the Tree of Life with Christ's cross. St Paul talked of Adam's sin being undone by God's grace offered through Christ, meaning that Adam foreshadows Christ[49]. On this way of thinking, then, the eating of the fruits of the two trees represents first the source of disintegration and sin (along with a degree of rational integration), and then the integration of that source of sin. Crucially, that occurs through the acceptance of limitation, error and suffering, which provides the basis for new and more adequate beliefs and practices to be developed, rather than the denial of sin. The sinner repents; Christ accepts the cross; Adam and Eve accept that they are expelled from Paradise. Life also makes progress in this way, by making and recognising mistakes, perhaps by sacrificing what has been invested in the mistaken. A tree grows in a direction where the light source is cut off, so that branch withers and dies, but new branches grow in a more promising direction. An animal species fits a given evolutionary niche, but then the conditions change, and the animal dies out: but its ancestors will produce a new variation better suited to the new conditions.

The Tree of Life is not only found in Genesis, but also in a wide range of other myths throughout the world. Very often the Tree of Life spans or structures the whole world, as in the Norse Yggdrasil, the tree that has its root in the lower realms and its branches in the higher ones. It's for this reason that Jung identified the Tree of Life as archetypal, an aspect of the God archetype that emphasises the organic and the incrementally progressive nature of integration, together with its dependence on the Shadow.

> *He sees the tree of life, whose roots reach into Hell and whose top touches Heaven. He also no longer knows differences: who is right? What is holy? What is genuine? What is good? What is correct? He knows only one difference: the difference between above and below. For he sees that the tree of life grows from below to above, and that it has its crown at the top, clearly differentiated from the roots. To him this is unquestionable. Hence he knows the way to salvation.*
>
> *To unlearn all distinctions save that concerning direction is part of your salvation. Hence you free yourself of the old curse of the knowledge of good and evil. Because you separated good from evil according to your best appraisal and aspired only to the good and denied the evil that you committed nevertheless and failed to*

> *accept, your roots no longer suckled the dark nourishment of the depths and your tree became sick and withered.*[50]

Here Jung points out the moral distinction between the Tree of Knowledge of Good and Evil and the Tree of Life. The Tree of Knowledge led Adam and Eve to make distinctions and to attribute reality to those distinctions. The Tree of Life, on the other hand, allows us to recognise the contingency of those distinctions, drawing on the 'evil' as well as the 'good' by questioning what we have previously assumed to lie in these categories. In the process, however, the Tree of Life offers a more adequate ethics, one in which incremental progress is the only criterion ("the difference between above and below"). We can experience how the crown (i.e. highly integrated states) is clearly distinguishable from the roots (less integrated states), just as we can distinguish a grown person from a toddler, yet there is no absolute dividing line anywhere, only a gradual process of integration encountered through the integrating means of the right hemisphere.

The Tree of Life thus also makes a potent alternative symbol for the Middle Way. The Middle Way avoids absolutes and finds value in the experiential space between them, but the Tree of Life spans the absolutes represented by 'above' and 'below' and organically combines what is integrable from each in the process. To combine the two visually, think of the Middle Way as a horizontal gap rather than a vertical one. It is only in the space of the Middle Way that the Tree of Life can grow – continuously and organically, taking sustenance from the earthly conditions addressed by negative metaphysics, and attracted by the light of truth represented by positive metaphysics, without ever quite reaching the source of that light.

The Tree of Life thus potentially bridges some of the cultural gaps between Biblical expressions of archetypes and those of other traditions. However, its use as a positive image in the

Biblical context faces one big problem: that the Tree of Life is forbidden. If the Tree of Life represents an organic process of growth towards integration, why does God, the archetype of ultimate integration, forbid it, even guarding it with the cherubim and a sword?

This problem takes us to a final twist of interpretation of the Genesis story: that the forbidding of the Tree of Life must be a delusion induced by eating the fruit of the Tree of Knowledge of Good and Evil. God is depicted as concerned about the possibility of humans becoming like him, not only in making distinctions but in integrating them, just as he is depicted as 'jealous' in the forbidding of idolatry we examined in Exodus in the previous chapter. But if God is genuinely integrative, he can have no such jealousy, nor could he be in any way opposed to the achievement of integration by humans. No, the problem lies in the way humans would seek to appropriate the Tree of Life by eating its fruit. The fruit is not the Tree of Life itself, though it depends on it, just as left hemisphere ideas of 'eternity' are not the experience of 'eternity' itself – and indeed radically misjudge it as something much more abstracted than it needs to be. We could see God as forbidding the fruit of the Tree of Life because, if we try to appropriate integration in that way (by turning it into an easily plucked and tempting fruit), we will actually undermine it. Its power would be appropriated and abused, then abandoned, like a small child getting hold of a gun or driving a car. But the archetypal God does not really want us to be unable to access the Tree of Life. Rather, as long as we maintain an instrumental view of it based only on our 'knowledge' drawn from the first tree, we see God's forbidding of premature access to it in terms of a total prohibition. Thinking discontinuously in terms of having or not having access to the Tree of Life, we take our limited, embodied engagement with what it symbolises to be a prohibition merely because it is not a totality.

The first three chapters of Genesis are an astonishingly rich engagement with central concerns of human experience. They engage our experience of creativity, of innocence, of moral maturity, of alienation, of conflict and of integration, all dealt with in a thoroughly archetypal way. The projection of such archetypal representations onto 'reality' by interpreting the story either as historical or as supernatural, however, merely obscures what it has to offer us. Even to take Genesis as telling us 'truths about human nature' is to rigidify symbols that can only be understood fully in relation to our changing experience. To interpret the story archetypally, however, is to relate it to recurring and dynamic features of universal human experience, and to a faith that can grow out of and remain compatible with that experience. There is no other standard of 'correctness' for the interpretations I have offered than that of how far they are helpful in the context of such experience and faith, and there may be better ones in that regard. Whatever interpretation we favour, however, we need to be clear and decisive in leaving behind absolutising elements in our interpretation. It is only in this way that the interpretation of Genesis can provide an appropriate platform for an equally experiential reading of the role of Christ.

5

Jesus: Integrated teacher?

a. The dualistic contradictions of the Old Testament

The inability to be God, the failure of our finiteness, is an ongoing issue for human beings. One of the important effects of the Fall seems to be the development of the aspiration to be perfect. We are capable of having a concept of perfection, and even symbolising that concept, even though we cannot even imagine perfection directly. This capacity develops with the use of the dominant left hemisphere to abstract, and hence to idealise, together with the capacity to judge the idealised self as good and the experienced sinful self as evil. By eating the forbidden fruit of the knowledge of good and evil, we have gained a knowledge of God as a perfection remote from our experience, together with the potential to be dissatisfied with our own state by comparison.

Throughout the Old Testament (Hebrew Bible), the Israelites struggled with this gap between the divine and the human. Yahweh appears to Noah, Abraham, Jacob, and Moses as a stern lawgiver whose divinity is enshrined in the holiness of law codes that seem beyond human capacity to keep fully. When the laws are not kept, Yahweh punishes with every sign of anger and little sign of proportionality or restraint, sending the Flood, the plagues of Egypt, and later the invasions of Israel and Judah and their takeover by foreign powers. All of these seem to be signs of the absoluteness of God, and of the impossibility of ever satisfying him. Yet God also maintains partial positions: making a special covenant with the people of Israel and providing them with special favours and revelations because of his love for them. Rather than viewing God entirely as a perfect and absolute force, the Israelites flip frequently between the divine and the human in their view of Yahweh, just as they flip between left hemisphere idealisations and a more balanced recognition of the imperfection to be found in experience. In this they follow the common pattern of those who maintain absolutising beliefs.

This dualism of the divine and the human does not only reveal itself in 'flipping' between beliefs about God's perfection, but also in associated absolutes that go with that perfection. Philosophers and theologians later identified absolute goodness, omnipotence, omniscience, omnipresence and eternality as necessary attributes of God, but for the Israelites and other early monotheists who began to construct those attributes implicitly, such attributes operated inconsistently with more limited, partial, and located attributes.

Yahweh was, perhaps, absolutely or ultimately good for the Israelites, but it would be hard to make a case that he was even ultimately good for the Amalekites or other ethnic groups that were slaughtered indiscriminately in the conquest of the Promised Land. He appears omnipotent in his ability to overcome rival gods and recalcitrant political rulers, but unable to prevent Israel's own slide into sin, injustice and disloyalty (raising the long-standing philosophical issue of how God's omnipotence is compatible with human freewill). He appears to have the foresight to inspire prophecies of doom if Israel does not reform, and even (according to traditional Christian interpretation) to predict the coming of Christ centuries before it occurs, yet he unnecessarily delays the remedy (in the terms of Christian belief) that he must have known people would need – namely the coming of Christ. He is said to be available everywhere, even in foreign countries, but nevertheless fails to make himself manifest to foreign nations.

The Old Testament offers a conceptual model of God and his will that is dependent on an appeal to rational consistency within a single cognitive model. The law books are remarkable for their insistence on such rational consistency in an age when the will of rulers was far more important. The covenant also suggests that God must be consistent in fulfilling his undertakings to the chosen people, in return for the people's consistent loyalty and obedience. Yet there is no such consistency in the Old Testament view of the world, rather a series of flips between a world made consistent by human rules that are attributed to Yahweh, and an archetypal view of Yahweh reflecting people's response to the demand for integration within themselves.

If one interprets the Old Testament in terms of 'belief', then, these beliefs must be thoroughly contradictory, depicting a God who is absolute one moment, but partial and imperfect the next. The use of the Old Testament as a source of direct instruction, then, is dangerous. Yet both these contradictory tendencies also reflect aspects of human experience, and the contradictions do not offer any justification for dismissing the Old Testament. If we can only think of it as a source of contextual information and patchy inspiration rather than of consistently justified beliefs of any kind, then we can make helpful use of it.

Positively, though, the Old Testament provides us with a record of what seems to be humankind's first sustained symbolisation of projected total integration. As noted in the last chapter, we see this related effectively to the experience of creativity. Throughout the Old Testament, the experience of God is one of profound spiritual, moral and political challenge, put together with the confidence that arises from faith that responds to that challenge. The Israelites are given the confidence to escape from slavery by that ability to symbolise something deeply felt that nevertheless lies beyond their current desires and beliefs. The prophets constantly repeat that challenge as a moral and political demand – a demand to look beyond the limitations of current assumptions and see a bigger story. The Psalms illustrate a spiritual response to that challenge, and what it is for a cramped human ego to try to stretch into it.

However, the length and scope of this book require me to

be selective in passing over much further discussion of the Old Testament. We need primarily to merely note the dualistic tensions that the Old Testament left unresolved, and that the New Testament writers believed could be resolved by the new covenant offered by Christ (with the rabbinic tradition in Judaism also subsequently seeking to resolve the same tensions). We focus primarily on the New Testament's attempted resolution in order to go to the heart of the distinctive approaches offered by Christianity.

b. Jesus finds the Middle Way

It's not always easy to distinguish Jesus from Christ. Broadly, Jesus is a historical individual, and Christ is an archetypal symbol, but we'll also need to note the limitations of making any such distinction. Jesus the historical individual has been presented to us through the four gospels in a way that is already selected and interpreted in terms of his symbolic role as Christ. Even if the historical Jesus turned out to be quite different from the one we have been told about, in many ways 'Jesus' would continue to mean that legendary figure that already combines history and symbol, and is thus embedded in the most basic meaning constructs of those in Christian cultures. For that reason, I'm content to discuss Jesus in the terms of that traditional story rather than asking historical questions about its correctness. Rather than being diverted by scholarly questions, I want to ask, which is the most helpful way of interpreting the traditional gospel accounts today.

In those terms, 'Jesus' is the legendary character I read about in the gospels, whereas 'Christ' is the figure who has evolved in a symbolic role throughout the history of the Christian church. It is Christ who is the Son of God, and whose crucifixion and resurrection have central symbolic power in Christianity. It is Christ whom Jung constantly encounters internally in his *Red Book*, and whom it might be suggested many cultural Christians would likewise find large in their psyches. Christ is a part of us. But Jesus, despite the influence of Christ on his interpretation, is still the object of a story in a historical setting. Before going too far in our exploration of the meaning of Christ, it is as well to begin with Jesus.

My own view of Jesus has shifted substantially during the past fifteen years. My Ph.D. thesis, 'A theory of moral objectivity', written in 2001, includes (amongst much other material) my first attempt to interpret Jesus in terms of the Middle Way, and at that time I reached much more negative conclusions than the ones I am going to offer now[51]. At that time I saw Jesus' apparent commitments to his own divinity and to eschatological beliefs as absolutes that fatally undermined his integrity, and that may well have been connected with the apparent alienation and fatalism that led him to embrace the cross. What has changed since then? Well, I increasingly see the power and value of taking responsibility for one's own interpretations, and of making those interpretations positive ones that allow me to integrate the meaning of Jesus with the Middle Way, and thus with everything else I find of justifiable value. What I previously interpreted as the absolute beliefs of a historical Jesus in the Kingdom, I would increasingly see as archetypal aspects of the meaning of Christ that have become associated with Jesus. If we see the crucifixion, not so much as a gory Roman form of execution, but as a symbol of the pain of confronting our own limitations, Jesus' view of it begins to seem more appropriate, and the ambiguities also begin to stand out more. At every point we need to resist the reifying and historicising tendencies of our culture and instead ask of ourselves "Which bit of me is that?"

This approach to Jesus runs against not only the traditional orthodox accounts of him, but also some of the assumptions of more recent liberal ones. For example, the approach made by the liberal scholars of the 'Jesus Seminar' is that of isolating a historical Jesus from the texts of gospels that are largely judged to be unreliable products of later Christian attitudes to Jesus[52]. The Jesus isolated by that process is firmly human, shorn of inexplicable supernatural capabilities and eschatological expectations, more of a cynic philosopher than a Jewish prophet. Whilst I find the Jesus isolated by such methods attractive, I am not going to adopt any of these textual methods, because my approach to Jesus is interpretative rather than historical. The Jesus Seminar, like any other such undertaking, can be readily criticised for applying criteria that have been chosen to ensure results that fit the preferred liberal Christian picture of Jesus: in other words, of confirmation bias and ad hoc moving of the goalposts. Instead, I reject no text that has been accepted by the Christian tradition, but seek to interpret all texts in terms that address our complex experience as human beings rather than offering us absolutising shortcuts. In the end, the question 'Who was the historical Jesus?' is of little significance (especially given its great debatability) compared to the bigger question that I think should be much more of interest to Christians, namely 'Who is the helpful Jesus?'

Let me begin my more positive interpretation of the gospel account of Jesus with the Temptation: an episode that on close examination closely parallels the early period of the life of the Buddha. As the episode is narrated by both Luke and Matthew, it is preceded by Jesus' baptism in the Jordan by John the Baptist, after which a voice from the heavens says 'This is my beloved son, in whom I take delight' (Mt 3:17). If we simply leave aside all questions about literal events, we can recognise this as involving Jesus' own recognition of a special status or mission. In the parallel case of the Buddha, the special status comes first (in the idea that he was the son of a king) followed by a mission that leads him to go forth from the assumptions of that social context. Jesus, too, goes forth, but his origins are humble and his special status is recognised later. Like the Buddha, he goes forth into the wilderness to reflect, to find a better way that would fulfil his sense of mission without being overtaken by the egoistic power of high social status.

While the Buddha's encounter with ascetics and need to move on from asceticism to the Middle Way are an articulated part of the Buddhist story, in the gospels the temporary nature of Jesus' asceticism (in 'forty days' of fasting) seems to be taken for granted. There is no suggestion that asceticism might have become an end in itself for Jesus, so implicitly in one sense he is already practising the Middle Way when he returns to civilisation. However, in the gospel account all the attention is given to the temptation by Satan: an episode that also has a parallel in the life of the Buddha, just before his attainment of enlightenment. The Buddha's tempter is Mara, who represents the distracting forces of fear, obsessive desire, and lack of confidence in the Buddha's mind. Satan, who is depicted as tempting Jesus, can be taken to represent the narrow and obsessive ego in a similar way. Here, though, rather than distracting the spiritual hero from the achievement of a goal that would supposedly take him beyond the power of that ego, the tempter is drawing him on into obsessive identification with his elevated status as 'Son of God'.

We should perhaps pause to consider the relationship between being 'Son of God' and being 'enlightened' or 'awakened'. Archetypally and psychologically, I see no distinction. In either case, the individual encounters the possibility of their total integration in the psyche, and this forward glimpse into a unified self has a powerful effect. In either case, too, though, the status of being 'enlightened' or being 'Son of God' can easily be appropriated by the ego. A live experience of potential in the form of a meaning can easily be turned into a flat, dead, conceptual belief that can then be manipulated for other ends. The 'Temptation' thus consists of the ego attempting to reduce the experience of integration back to its own narrow terms.

Of course, the other parallel of temptation is with that of

Adam and Eve. Adam and Eve were 'overcome' by temptation, and thus had to live with the dominance of the ego. Jesus, on the other hand, 'resists' the temptation, suggesting that the live connection with integrated potential remained open for him and he continued to derive energy and confidence from it.

The tempter subjects Jesus to three tests. The first two of these (at least in the order given by Matthew) each begin with "If you are the Son of God..." (Mt 4:3 & 6), and then challenge Jesus to perform a miracle to prove his status (by turning stones into bread, or by getting angels to save his fall from a height). The egoistic temptation here, then, is clearly to gain social status from the power of integration, yielding to the anxiety to please others and reducing the subtle flexibility of personal integration to an easily demonstrable piece of social capital. In the third temptation, Satan shows Jesus "all the kingdoms of the world in their glory", and offers them in return for Jesus' worship (Mt 2:8-10). Here the egoistic appeal is more obviously that of power, directly representing the narrow left hemisphere focus on instrumentality. To become a ruler, of course, Jesus would have to 'worship Satan' in the sense of being taken over by narrow left-hemisphere states.

In his responses to Satan, at each stage Jesus quotes Old Testament scripture and invokes God: human dependency on the words of God, not putting God to the test (in the sense of demanding material benefits from God in return for worship) and worshipping God alone. All the scriptures that Jesus quotes come from Deuteronomy, so can be taken as invoking the holiness and awe of the Torah's encounter with God, and the intention behind the Jewish laws of maintaining the ultimate respect due to integrated religious experience and not reducing it to more limited conceptual beliefs.

The equivalent of Jesus' invocation of scripture in the story of the Buddha's enlightenment is perhaps the Buddha's calling on the earth as a witness to the efforts he had made towards it, which is a response to Mara casting doubt on the Buddha's 'right' to awakening. In both cases, it is a disruptive 'doubt' of a narrow and obsessive type that is being put into context by obliging us to look at a bigger context. Both the Buddha and Jesus are able to proceed with confidence because they have put their narrow egoistic conflicts aside and got back in touch with a consistent wider awareness.

The idea that Jesus can be seen as encountering the Middle Way during his period in the wilderness can be supported by a number of other elements in Jesus' subsequent approach to teaching. In coming to understand these more fully, I have been very much inspired by R. John Elford's 'Eight themes and emphases of biblical morality'[53]: except that his points are more about Jesus' teaching than about the Bible in general, and not to be confined to the category of 'ethics' as distinct from any other aspect of Christian teaching. In the next section I will explore the various ways in which Jesus' teaching can be understood as synthetic, universal, sceptical, provisional, compassionate, integrative, and balanced. This interpretation should provide an inspiring picture of Jesus for anyone who cares about the Middle Way, but it will also leave out a lot of objections. The addressing of such objections, that is, how we can reconcile a Jesus of the Middle Way with Jesus the miracle worker, Jesus the son of God, Jesus the righteous expeller of money-lenders from the temple, and so on, will be left to the following section.

c. Jesus teaches the Middle Way

The reconciliation of ideals on the one hand and practical demands on the other is central to the Middle Way, as it is to what Christ symbolises in the Christian tradition. However, it is also to be found in the teachings of Jesus themselves. In explaining this I want to start to put Jesus's teachings in a new light by relating them more fully to language that has rarely been used in relation to him. Though I am very much inspired by Elford, I am going to put his points in very different language and reduce his eight themes to seven points. The language in which I will put these points will already be familiar to anyone who has read my work on Middle Way Philosophy, and if it initially seems unfamiliar or tendentious used in relation to Jesus, you will need to bear with me. The objections and limitations to such an interpretation of Jesus' teachings will be considered later.

The seven points of the Middle Way approach that can be found in Jesus' teachings are as follows:

1. **Synthesis:** religion, spirituality and ethics (and by implication other positive values) are inter-dependent and inseparable
2. **Integration:** previously separated approaches are brought together and their conflicts mediated
3. **Universality**: applicable to every human situation
4. **Scepticism**: established assumptions are always open to question
5. **Provisionality**: an openness to new solutions
6. **Love**: love, not bargaining, is the emotional starting point
7. **Balance**: ideals are constantly balanced against the conditions we experience

1. Synthesis

Jesus taught an overall way of living – and thus of making judgements – that united religious and ethical considerations: not by reducing or subordinating one to the other, but by facing up to the uncertainties involved in their connection. On a number of occasions Jesus challenged the narrow or legalistic interpretation of religious rules advocated by Pharisees, priests and Levites, who had an interpretation that would involve the dominance of ethical experience by a narrow interpretation of religious duty.

In one of the best-known of these episodes, Jesus supports

his disciples in picking ears of corn on the Sabbath day, saying "The Sabbath was made for man, not man for the Sabbath" (Mt 2:27). Wider human experience is apparently invoked here, with religious requirements needing to take their place alongside ethical experience rather than subordinating it. The common reaction to narrow legalism illustrates our wider ethical experience. We recognise that a rule with some general value (observing the Sabbath so that enough time is given to relaxation, contemplative and communal activity in society) is being obsessively and disproportionately pursued when it is applied to activities that are only very marginally 'work' (picking ears of corn for personal consumption) and on a very small scale. More than anything, it is the left hemisphere dominant mentality that is being challenged here, with its assumption that a rule could completely describe right action and could be completely observed.

Similarly, when Jesus tells one of his disciples to "let the dead bury their dead" (Mt 8:22) rather than delaying their journey to bury his father, he is apparently urging the neglect of a religious duty (to bury one's parents) that was taken very seriously by the Jews of that time. But further reflection might lead us to become aware that the particular observances of burial, whilst being an important rite of passage for communities, should not necessarily overwhelm all other moral considerations. If we imagine the disciple's life as transformed by the insights he gained by following Jesus, his decision to place value in following him rather than in following communal obligations is one that values empowering experience over unquestioned rule. We cannot justifiably draw a new rule from that, or even cite this case to give us an excuse to neglect the burial of our own parents, but nevertheless it gives us an inspiring example of the ways in which people can sometimes discover an ethical priority in their own experience that may be at the expense of a religious prescription.

If we take the synthetic approach that Jesus adopted here to ethics and religion and apply it in other respects, we should also avoid drawing similarly absolute lines between other fields of evaluation: for example between ethics, science, economics and the arts. Perhaps some of the modern-day Pharisees that Jesus might criticise would be those who take scientific or technological development to be independent of ethical considerations, believing that we should not try to stop scientific 'progress' however destructive some of its effects might turn out to be. The autonomy of economics is another piece of modern Pharisaism, taking the form of the belief that the market will always produce the best results, regardless of contrary evidence about the effects of untrammelled market activity on the environment, social justice or individual alienation. Note that in both these cases, the problem is not science, technology or markets themselves, but rather their absolutisation: the belief that they offer the whole story or the whole solution.

Those who adopt absolutised aesthetic or anti-aesthetic positions are subject to a similar criticism of their narrow assumptions, and this can be illustrated by Jesus' response as recorded in the gospel of John when Mary the sister of Lazarus anointed Jesus' feet with costly perfume. Judas objected, asking if the cost of the perfume could not have been given to the poor, but Jesus evidently recognised hypocrisy and narrow puritanism in his objections[54]. Such a generous and beautiful act has a direct value in experience, which of course should not be taken to overrule all other considerations, but equally should not be dismissed on the basis of narrow puritanical assumptions.

2. Integration

Along with Jesus' synthetic way of relating to the world came a belief that conflicts between different models and perspectives could be resolved. He did not reject the world-views of those around him, but rather objected to their absolutisation, because this absolutisation interfered with the development of love. As long as people are capable of adapting their beliefs to new circumstances, new integrated forms of appropriate belief can arise.

Perhaps the clearest indication of this can be found in Jesus' explicit attitude to the Biblical law: "Do not suppose that I have come to abolish the law and the prophets; I did not come to abolish, but to complete" (Mt 5:17). The term translated as 'complete' here (πληρωσαι) can also be translated as 'fulfil' or 'give full meaning'. In other words, if there is a conflict between that law and the wider moral purpose behind it, we should refer back to that fuller meaning as better able to adapt to a wider variety of conditions. He then goes on "Anyone therefore who sets aside even the least of the law's demands, and teaches others to do the same, will have the lowest place in the kingdom of heaven" (Mt 5:19). In other words, to be in touch with the integrated possibilities represented by the kingdom of heaven, we should not avoid the demands of explicit rules in our social and political context, but rather seek to make them adequate. There is a distinction between taking a rule or principle as a challenge to the objectivity of our judgement (facing up to what that rule or challenge demands of us) and taking it as a complete and final account of how to act. It seems clear that Jesus is recommending the former attitude. If we do not take rules or principles as absolute, then we must also admit the importance of alternative perspectives and integrate those perspectives with the ethics we have understood from the principles (this point is discussed further in 9c below).

Jesus' attitude to forgiveness also illustrates the way that he seeks to avoid the absolutising of wrong, but it becomes crucial here not to read his references to 'the Father' as any kind of external authority from which we are alienated. Take this passage:

> *For if you forgive others the wrongs they have done, your heavenly Father will also forgive you; but if you do not forgive others, then your Father will not forgive the wrongs you have done.* (Mt 6:14-15)

What does it mean for your heavenly father to forgive you? Surely that your desires and beliefs will become integrated with a greater whole within your own experience. If you cannot forgive others, he is surely saying, then you cannot become integrated. Later, Jesus also advises that we should forgive others "up to seventy times seven" (Mt 18:22), in other words, any number of times. Endless forgiveness does not require a failure to recognise others' moral shortcomings, nor a failure to apply social rules or laws, but it does mean that we will never absolutise those shortcomings, or use them as the basis of an absolute judgement on a person's character. They can always reform. However negative our view of a person (or of a tradition, or a nation, or an organisation) may become, there will always be another voice that offers alternative possibilities. An integrative solution involves always leaving the door open for a person to come out of their more limited perspective into a bigger one where they start to learn from other perspectives.

The medium in which Jesus finds his integrative perspective is that of prayer. In prayer, we pause our normal goal-oriented consciousness, whereby we encounter one thing after another and relate to them primarily in the terms offered by our desires. Instead, when we pause we are able to be more receptive and open to right hemisphere perspectives. Right hemisphere perspectives, in contrast to left, offer a wide range of possibilities as well as a wider and more profound type of awareness, all of which can be associated with God. Jesus seeks to make prayer into a genuine communion with wider awareness rather than merely a set of words, which suggests that we need to stop thinking about others' view of our prayer and focus on the experience of prayer itself. "When you pray, go into a room by yourself, shut the door, and pray to your Father who is in secret" (Mt 6:6).

But Jesus does not expect most people to be capable of engaging in formless prayer or meditation, so he nevertheless offers them a verbal form of prayer in what has become known as the Lord's Prayer.

> *Our father in heaven,*
> *may your name be hallowed;*
> *your kingdom come,*
> *your will be done,*
> *on earth as in heaven.*
> *Give us our daily bread.*
> *Forgive the wrong we have done,*
> *as we have forgiven those who have wronged us.*
> *And do not put us to the test,*
> *But save us from the evil one.* (Mt 6:9-13)

This can, of course, be read as invoking a supernatural divine authority and anticipating his rule, but if we put it into the context of 'secret' prayer, it is no longer about power or prediction but about access to a wider integrative awareness. That integrative awareness is directly addressed by the invocation of sacredness and by the father and the kingdom. The recognition that the father's will should be done involves the acceptance of conditions that we cannot change. Awareness of our daily bread in the context of wider gratitude also works against us being too narrowly focused on the gaining of that bread, but allows us to recognise that it is also due to a variety of conditions that are beyond the scope of our own control. Forgiveness as an integrative process, already discussed above, is invoked. In all of these, specific ideas that might be associated with a more or less integrative effect for Jesus' audience become the focus of prayer as a broadening of awareness.

The final two lines of the Lord's Prayer focus more negatively on what this awareness tries to avoid. Putting us to the test (or 'leading us into temptation' in an older translation) would be subjecting us to narrow and obsessive left-hemisphere dominant states of the kind that can also be associated with 'the evil one'. Alongside the connection with wider awareness here, then, there is also a recognition of the dangers of narrower awareness, and of how that cannot be effectively addressed only by challenging one evil with another equally narrow one, but rather with a wider integrative context represented by God. As Jesus says elsewhere, "Every kingdom divided against itself is laid waste, and a divided household falls. And if Satan is divided against himself, how can his kingdom stand?" (Lk 11:17-18)

Not only God himself, but the kingdom of God, to which Jesus makes frequent reference, can be understood as a symbol of integration. A ready connection with the Tree of Life (discussed in 4.d above) can be made by particularly focusing on the organic metaphors of growth than Jesus uses for the kingdom of God. For example, he says "It is like a mustard seed which a man took and sowed in his garden; and it grew to be a tree and the birds came to roost among its branches" (Lk 13:19).

3. Universality

Jesus' teachings are equally applicable to every human situation. This can be seen in his attitude to groups, and also in the implications of forgiveness for our moral thinking.

His challenges to any kind of ethnic or national relativism can be seen in his encounter with a Samaritan woman[55], as well as in his parable of the Good Samaritan[56], both of which challenged Jewish exclusionary assumptions against Samaritans. Although obviously rooted in a Jewish background and conversant with Jewish scriptures, he challenges these in a way that takes us beyond any justifiable limitation of values to a particular group.

Jesus is also well-known for his inclusive attitudes to the poor, the disabled, and to those otherwise rejected or restricted by society. He constantly portrays the poor as rewarded by God[57], perhaps to challenge the unquestioned power of the rich. He stays at the house of the socially disapproved tax collector, Zacchaeus[58]. He encourages children to come to him[59]. Wherever there is a group with boundaries and biases, even when defended by social or political power, Jesus will question those boundaries.

The further implication of this attitude to groups is also that no claim exclusive to Christians as a group can be consistent with Jesus' basic insights. The oft-quoted basis of Christian salvational exclusivity in "no-one comes to the father except through me" (Jn 14:6) is dependent on a literalistic understanding both of God and of Christ as supernatural figures rather than as aspects of experience; it could indeed be read in the most general terms as "no-one comes to the integrated psyche except through the Middle Way."

However, perhaps the most radical universality to be found in Jesus' teaching comes from the implications of indefinite forgiveness. If we never give up on others, always seeing a person (or a group or tradition) as being capable of improvement from wherever they start, then moral and spiritual progress is just as possible for one who is a 'sinner' as for one who is not. Indeed, the experience of having 'sinned' may well offer an advantage in broadening our experience and making us aware of the full consequences of sinning. This is one crucial respect in which Jesus' teaching follows the Middle Way: that is, in being a direction of travel that one can begin from any starting point, rather than a particular path requiring any particular prior condition. The path taught by Jesus is thus never a discontinuous path requiring a particular beginning and a particular end (unlike the Buddhist concept of nirvana). Rather it is a highly flexible path dependent on our experience of balance and stretch between a demanding God and our human limitations.

4. Scepticism

Given the negative direction in which the term 'sceptic' has evolved in the West, it may surprise many to see Jesus as a sceptic. I am using the term in the Pyrrhonian sense of a position in which both positive and negative absolute claims are avoided, and where there is thus no negative implication of scepticism: it is not a threat to justified beliefs either in science or in ethics, but only to absolute claims of truth or falsity. By objecting to absolute assumptions of both a positive and negative type, a sceptic leaves us in a position of needing to re-examine our experience: including, in the case of Jesus, our experience of God.

We have already seen Jesus' sceptical challenges to the Pharisees and to conventional views of limited forgiveness. He also questioned the assumptions of the rich, and the attachment of his disciples to their possessions, families, and social positions, but not apparently to take an opposite position, only an ambiguous middle stance. Often, rather than taking a position, he merely prompts those with strong beliefs to reflect on them, as in the episode of the woman taken in adultery[60]. Even when standing before the Jewish authorities, he refused to either confirm or deny their question as to whether he was the Son of God, saying only "It is you who say I am" (Lk 22:70).

As John Elford writes:

> *So many of his replies to questions were enigmatic to say the least, to such a degree that we cannot but conclude that they were meant not as alternative solutions in themselves, but as pointed challenges to his hearers with but one aim: that of imploring them to think again from first principles and, in so doing, to take nothing for granted. In all this, he did not seemingly proffer solutions at all, they were left to be found by those who questioned him in the first place.*[61]

It is this perspective that can help inform the interpretation of

Jesus' saying "Do not judge, and you will not be judged. For as you judge others, so you will yourself be judged..." (Mt 7:1-2). The Greek term for 'judge' here, κϱινω, means 'to distinguish', 'to reach a determination about', 'to judge by separating': in other words, the left hemisphere process of adopting a definite conclusion for or against a claim or a person in terms of the values that relate to our goals. There are, however, varying degrees to which the right hemisphere can inform the left by providing awareness of alternatives and thus provisionality in our judgements. We would not ourselves wish to be judged in terms that reduce us to objects or tools for another's ends, but on the other hand Jesus' approach cannot exclude judgement of a more integrated kind, where more adequate information is taken into account in deciding right and wrong. Like the Pyrrhonian sceptics, then, Jesus seems to be urging us not to make absolute judgements of belief, but not thereby prohibiting immediate practical judgements.

The long-standing misinterpretation of scepticism in Western philosophy also tends to assume that scepticism undermines justifiable prescriptive ethics, just because it undermines absolute ethical claims. But justifiable ethical claims are not intrinsically dogmatic or 'subjective', and Jesus regularly illustrates this point by maintaining clear confidence in an ethical perspective that depends not on a dogmatic substructure but rather on the avoidance of one. Righteous indignation and 'judgement' are evidently not foreign to Jesus, as in the episode of his anger against money-changers in the temple[62]. Here he evidently decided to act so as to challenge the dominant ways of thinking rather than withholding judgement. The justification of such actions will always be debatable, and Jesus' action does not have to be absolutely right because it was done by him, but it becomes clear that such judgements are entirely compatible with sceptical attitudes.

5. Provisionality

The positive implication of scepticism is an active consideration of alternatives to the socially established 'truths' that people hold to. As Elford puts it: "Jesus... seemed to be encouraging his hearers to try something which is not just slightly different from what they are already doing, but... totally different from it."[63]. In questioning the Pharisees' legalism and indeed more general hypocrisy, he implicitly offers an alternative position based on immediate experience rather than belief in the absolute moral truth of scriptural instructions. His first disciples leave their homes and jobs in Galilee to become "fishers of men" (Mt 4:19), an apparently crazy and highly unconventional thing to do, seemingly under the impact of an overwhelming vision offered directly to their experience. His parables seek to constantly reframe, placing familiar judgements in the context of a different metaphor.

Perhaps in the Sermon on the Mount more than anywhere else, Jesus urges us to think the unthinkable. "Do not resist those who wrong you. If anyone slaps you on the right cheek, turn and offer him the other also."(Mt 5:39) "If your right eye causes your downfall, tear it out and fling it away; it is better for you to lose one part of your body than for the whole of it to be flung into hell"(Mt 5:29). More than anything, these kinds of statements get us to re-examine our priorities. We may have taken for granted that the urge to vengeance was 'natural' or 'inevitable', and we may not have faced up to the possible need for tough sacrifices of things that we feel deeply and instinctively attached to (like body parts). If these are interpreted as new commandments they are, of course, thoroughly unrealistic because they would be conveying an ethic of self-sacrifice, asceticism, even self-mutilation, rather than integration – it is not surprising if they have been unhelpfully interpreted in many ways over the centuries, with some Christians assuming that good comes from self-sacrifice itself (and thus that looking after oneself is bad) and others seeing pain as godly and thus undertaking practices such as self-flagellation. However, if they are interpreted as reframing exercises by which we come to recognise and question our priorities, they serve a much more helpful purpose.

Throughout the gospels, Jesus also often expresses a sense that the current organisation of things is temporary, only being like it is before the imminent kingdom of heaven occurs. If the kingdom of heaven is indeed seen as a way of talking about integration, then its imminence can also be seen as a way of talking about provisionality. We do not know when or how the kingdom of heaven will occur, just as we do not 'know', in a narrow left-hemisphere sense, when any unexpected new information will occur. The kingdom of heaven is an 'unknown unknown' just as are future scientific discoveries before they occur. Provisionality thus consists in preparedness for the kingdom of heaven, as graphically described in the parable of the ten girls with their lamps[64]. As this parable concludes, "Keep awake then, for you know neither the day nor the hour." There is no substitute for awareness that allows for possibilities beyond our present assumptions.

6. Love

The centrality of love *(agape)* in Jesus' teaching is well known, but its interpretation is much more contentious.

> *'Teacher, which is the greatest commandment in the law?' He answered '"Love the Lord your God with all your heart, with all your soul, and with all your mind". That is the greatest, the first commandment. The second is like it: "Love your neighbour as yourself". Everything in the law and the prophets hangs on these two commandments.'* (Mt 22:36-40)

It is clear here that love of God is prior to all other loves. If God stands for integration in our own experience, then our emotional relationship to that integration is thus primary. What we have to integrate may be whatever most challenges us or whatever is most subject to conflict: whether that involves identifications with aspects of ourselves, with other individuals, with groups or with social or political goals. The love of God is thus not simply a response to an archetypal form at one moment, but an ongoing engagement with objectivity – with the challenge of moving beyond our current limited identifications.

The love of God in that sense can hardly be distinct from other types of love, just as it is not distinct from wisdom. Yet in Christianity there has been ongoing confusion about what it means to 'love your neighbour as yourself'. Some regard this as a self-sacrificing love, others as a balancing process in which love of self is taken for granted and love of others brought to the same level. But we cannot take 'love of self' for granted given that our view of ourselves and our own worth is constantly changing. A person with very poor self-esteem will hardly love themselves, indicating that if they follow Jesus' command as often interpreted they may also love others very little because that will be only as much as they love themselves. The idea of 'self' also makes no distinctions between our many different ideas of self, which may rapidly succeed each other, or even co-exist in different degrees of consciousness.

Such confusion can be dissolved if we genuinely put the love of God first, while interpreting the love of God as integrative love. Then, whatever version of self or neighbour we may identify with, the spiritual and moral stretch becomes that of developing that identification. For example, if I love an idea of myself as a competent professional, but hate the flabby body I see in the mirror, I might need to start loving my body, perhaps caring about it enough to deal with the flab. If I love an over-dominant partner but despise myself for being dominated by them, it is this aspect of myself that I need to begin to love. If I love an over-inflated view of myself but despise others, it is obviously others on whom I need to focus my love.

The command to 'love your neighbour as yourself' is thus one to remedy our deficiencies in love of people and to generally stretch our identifications, following from our love of God. It can hardly be interpreted in a way that is separate from the love of God, but making it subsidiary to our love of God can also help to make it more psychologically adequate rather than a vehicle for perpetuating crude ideas of self-sacrifice.

The importance of divine love in Jesus' teachings can also be linked to the unconditional and non-reciprocal application of that love. "If you love only those who love you, what credit is that to you? Even sinners do as much." (Lk 6:32) In other words, we should put aside all expectation of reward from our love, just as we should put aside thoughts of revenge when we forgive others. This radically separates universal or spiritual motives from social morality, where there is often an intrinsic expectation of long-term exchange, even in our closest relationships with parents or children (for example, parents expecting that their trouble in bringing up children will be rewarded with care in their old age).

In the terms of the Middle Way, one of the drawbacks of such bargains is our tendency to absolutise them, so that the concept of something 'owed' to us becomes obsessive if we are disappointed by the failure of an assumed bargain. So, surely, we should interpret the non-reciprocity of love in Jesus' teachings not as an indication that our love will necessarily not be rewarded, but rather as an indication of the provisionality with which we should believe that it will be. We don't only love those who love us, but in practice a lot of our capacity for love is indeed taken up with those who love us and from whom some reward may well in fact be likely. If our focus is on stretching our identifications, we need neither be ashamed of having a limited practical capacity for love, nor afraid of the uncertainties surrounding how others may treat us in future.

7. Uncomfortable balance

The final feature of Jesus' teachings is that of a balance between immediate conditions and ideals – between how we are and how we might be, or in other words between the human and the divine. As will be discussed later, Jesus' symbolic role as Christ is also central to this tension as it is understood in Christianity. However, it is also an aspect of Jesus' teachings.

On the face of it, Jesus might not seem like a very balanced figure: after all, he takes disciples away from their families, challenges the religious authorities, and up-ends the social order. But we should be careful not to merely accept conventional accounts of where the extremes are and thus where the balance lies in addressing the conditions of our lives. To take into account the divine element of our lives as well as the conventionally established, we need to question both conventional beliefs and abstract idealisations of the divine at one and the same time, and it is this two-sided challenging process that Jesus demonstrates most strongly. The extremes are opposed absolutisations, not necessarily positions that are conventionally regarded as 'extreme'. Any position that starts by living with the tension between the absolutising extremes of divine and human is in a profound sense balanced: but the process of balancing is always an active and a controversial one, not a neat measurable process of finding a median. For that reason, it is probably best described as an 'uncomfortable balance', to avoid any hint of the self-satisfaction or completion that the term 'balance' may invoke for some.

Of the four gospel accounts, the one that deals most consistently with this tension in the life of Jesus is John, and the modern text that has transformed my understanding of John is Stephen Verney's *Water into Wine*[65]. Verney brings out this tension, and thus this uncomfortable balance, at every stage in John's presentation of Jesus. Even the humble words 'I am' are read by Verney as simultaneously invoking both a divine demand (evoking the words of God from the burning bush in Exodus[66]) and a mere humanity[67]. Almost any episode from the gospel of John as interpreted by Verney can be used to illustrate this tension, but I will pull out two examples.

The first example comes from Jesus' response to being lionised and absolutised, to having the God archetype projected onto him from someone who could conceivably move on from it. In John 1:43-51 Jesus' disciple Philip persuades his friend Nathanael to come and hear Jesus. Jesus compliments Nathanael on his approach and Nathanael immediately concludes "You are the son of God, you are the King of Israel" (Jn 1:49).

> *Jesus answered 'Do you believe this because I told you I saw you under the fig tree? You will see greater things than that.' Then he added, 'Amen, amen I say to you all: you will see heaven wide open and God's angels ascending and descending upon the Son of Man.'* (Jn 1:50-51)[68]

The ascending and descending angels directly reference Jacob's ladder, which Jacob saw in a dream[69], and which Verney explains thus:

> *The angels, God's messengers, were carrying the earthiness of Jacob up to heaven, and were bringing the presence of God down to stand beside him and protect him on earth.*
>
> *Now Jesus says to his followers: "You are going to see the reality of which our father Jacob dreamt. You will see heaven opened, and a ladder joining earth and heaven. I shall be that ladder, and upon me the angels will be going up and coming down."*
>
> *The Greek words he uses for up and down are ano and kato. The angels will be going up from earth, from the order of kato, lifting up to God the needs and egocentricity of humankind, and they will be coming down from the order of ano, bringing to the world the mercy and the truth of God.*[70]

Several aspects of this episode are striking. Firstly, that Jesus responds to a new disciple merely pointing upward by directing his attention, instead, to the dialectical interplay between up and down. The greater thing to recognise, he seems to be saying, is this tension or interplay rather than merely my status who tries to make you aware of it. Secondly, the image of the ladder itself is a dynamic Middle Way image rather than one of the static metaphors of transcendence that have unfortunately gained more prominence in much religious life. It's not that holiness gives us direct access to heaven, but rather that we become aware of the ways that the meaning of heaven can become relevant to life on earth. The image of the ladder, like that of the ship navigating the strait between two extremes, involves a recognition that we will move between the two extremes, and indeed benefit from what they offer, without being entirely in the power of one or the other.

Thirdly, the ladder image provides a potentially useful interpretative key to the vexed problem of Jesus' view of his own status. Jesus often seems to talk in terms of his own divinity (especially in John), but it is impossible to know whether the absolute status this has for many later Christians is being attributed to him at these points in a way that substitutes for a more complex understanding of a mediating role. This is a point that will be taken up below in the chapter on Christ the mediator. If being 'Son of Man' or even 'Son of God' is, instead, an intermediary role such as we could envisage in terms of the ladder, Jesus' apparent view of his own status need no longer be the basis of absolute belief or rejection. Rather, to engage with Jesus' message and trust the person we feel we are meeting means to find the ladder within ourselves, and recognise our potential both to ascend and descend it according to our degree of integration at any moment.

My second example from the gospel of John is Jesus' conversation with Nicodemus, a Pharisee who seems curious and comes 'to Jesus by night'. Once again, the conversation starts with the other person projecting absolute status onto Jesus, but Jesus responds by challenging them to try to engage in an actual spiritual and moral process rather than just worshipping (or rejecting) an idealisation from afar.

> *Jesus answered, 'Amen, amen I say to you, no one can see the kingdom of God unless he has been born from above*[71]*.' 'But how can someone be born again when he is old?' asked Nicodemus, 'Can he enter his mother's womb a second time and be born?' Jesus answered, 'Amen, amen I say to you, no one can enter the kingdom of God without being born from water and spirit. Flesh can give birth only to flesh; it is spirit that gives birth to spirit.'* (Jn 3:3-6)

As Verney explains:

> *The primary meaning of anothen is "from above"; but the word is deliberately ambiguous, and in a secondary sense it can mean to be born "again". To be born again from ano is to become part of a new order where ego-centricity has been transformed into love.*
>
> *Unless man is born out of this womb of ano, said Jesus, he cannot see the kingdom of God – he cannot see men and women being set free to love each other by the Spirit of Love....*
>
> *Water and spirit are the two realities which must meet in us and become one. There must be a marriage between the raw material of human nature and the spirit of God, between egocentricity and love, between kato and ano. The spirit must enter into the water, and the water become alive with spirit, each preserving its own distinctive nature, but becoming one in the interaction between them. Then there will be a new order, a new earth and a new heaven – the kingdom of God on earth as it is in heaven.*[72]

The idea of being born again has become such a tired evangelical cliché that it requires some effort to reconnect it to wider experience and re-freshen the metaphor. What Jesus is saying here about being born again, however, does not seem to be simply a matter of accepting an absolute belief that will then magically transform your life, even if there are still unfortunately many Christians who do understand it in those terms. Instead, we can interpret the rebirth as a sudden recognition of an alternative perspective beyond the over-certainties of the dominant left hemisphere. Far from adopting new absolute beliefs, one is born again 'from above' by moving beyond such beliefs into a wider perspective, accompanied only by the confidence (or faith) required to do so.

Water is metaphorically associated with flexibility, through the idea of fluidity, as well as with immersion (a total embodied experience) and with at least a slight danger and unpredictability. The relationship between water and spirit then seems to be that we need to become more fluid in order to access the even less bounded experience represented by spirit. The role of water (which is of course symbolically important in baptism) is thus that of a mediator between the solidity of human normality and the otherness of the spiritual. Engaging with experience beyond our normal assumptions may at first seem wholly other and thus frightening and alarming, but first being 'born again from water' gives us an intermediate step in which we let go of some of our fixed beliefs.

These teachings by Jesus have a naïve audience in the shape of Nicodemus, who can apparently only understand the idea of being 'born again' in entirely literal terms. In this sense, despite his relative openness to Jesus' teachings, he is still a Pharisee: still stuck in absolute ways of representing the world. We are not told anything more about whether he comes to understand Jesus, but his reappearance in John 19:39 after Jesus' death suggests that perhaps his view of the world was broadened in some way that changed him.

The more we try to engage with this uncomfortable balance

between the divine and the human, however, the more in effect we must move beyond Jesus' teachings and instead into Christian symbology and personal experience. I think I have said enough here to show how the Middle Way can be directly detected in Jesus' teachings, at least as they are presented to us in the gospels, not only in Jesus' response to this tension between divine and human, but also in the synthesis, integration, universality, scepticism, provisionality and love to be found in Jesus' teachings – all of which provide us with alternative routes in understanding the Middle Way. But before I go on to further positive exploration of the nature of Christ (and of course of the crucifixion and resurrection), I must face up to some of the likely objections to the case I have made about Jesus so far.

d. Was Jesus an absolutist? Authority and fulfilled prophecy

In arguing as I have above I am confronting, not only the voices of secularists, but my own assumptions from the past. Surely, all these voices argue, Jesus, far from finding the Middle Way, was both extreme and absolutist? Am I guilty merely of cherry-picking text (in a well-worn Christian tradition) to support my own tendentious interpretation?

The doubts likely to be raised by such voices deserve to be confronted fully, at least by looking more directly at the other side of the coin. But first I must point out that my basic position is compatible with such doubts. As I have already stated, I am not claiming to have found 'the correct' interpretation of Jesus, whether in a historical or a revelatory sense of correctness. Rather I am aiming to create a *helpful* interpretation of Jesus, meaning one that inspires people to overcome internal and external conflicts and thus address conditions through better judgement. If I have succeeded in this, such criticisms become irrelevant. It would be quite possible to be historically incorrect yet helpful, to cherry pick and yet be helpful, and indeed to be tendentious and yet helpful. It is only if one does these things but at the same time claims to be offering an absolutely correct position that such an approach becomes unhelpful.

So, let me concede that it's quite possible that Jesus was an absolutist. Nevertheless, it seems to me that the teachings I have discussed in the previous chapter nevertheless show a great deal of ambiguity. I am more deeply convinced (from a long process of study, thought and practice) that absolutism is unhelpful than I could ever be convinced by the authority of any supposed revelatory source, so the possibility of interpreting Jesus as an absolutist and also relating to his teachings positively is effectively closed to me (as I believe it also is to many others). I am left with the alternatives of interpreting him as an absolutist and treating it negatively (an approach I have taken at times in the past), or not interpreting him as an absolutist at all. The latter option seems to me so obviously helpful and positive, that it is my responsibility to explore it. If we accept an interpretation of Jesus as teaching the Middle Way, though, it must be in a way that is in harmony with the Middle Way: that is, with provisionality and scepticism. I do not *know* that Jesus taught the Middle Way, but I am increasingly confident of it.

So, what is the most obvious evidence that Jesus was an absolutist? All of the following may be suggested, but all of them can also be interpreted in more helpful ways.

1. His belief in God and his divine authority
2. His appeals to Old Testament scripture
3. The apparently supernatural aspects of his miracles
4. His apparent certainty about his own death and resurrection
5. His belief in the imminent coming of the kingdom of God

There is a great deal to discuss here, so in this section I will confine myself to the first two points. The subsequent sections will take up the last three points.

Jesus' belief in God and the source of his authority

When interpreting anyone's statements about potentially absolute things, it's important to do so with a recognition that the words used are unlikely to completely capture the meaning of that absolute thing for the person concerned. The statement "I believe in God" for example, may involve anything from a dry metaphysical claim motivated mainly by social conformity, to the spontaneous sharing of a living personal experience of faith. Rather than going only on the words used in the claim, it may often be more informative to look at the *function* of the claim in its context. Is it used so as to absolutise some claim about the 'truth' of 'falsity' of an ambiguous state of affairs, and thus to contribute to the fulfilment of narrowly-focused goals? Or is it used more to increase our awareness of a wider insight or of a new condition affecting us?

So, that's exactly the approach that I think needs to be used when we consider Jesus' belief in God. There's little doubt of Jesus' *faith* in God, particularly of a direct relationship of trust with something he found within his own experience, but I can see little evidence of Jesus making metaphysical claims about God, or of invoking God's power and authority to support his own or his group's goals. It is thus the sources of Jesus' authority that we should look at most when considering what 'belief in God' should be understood as meaning to Jesus.

When Jesus refers to God he overwhelmingly tends to use the term 'Father', which emphasises a directly experienced relationship, particularly one to be directly entered through prayer. He also often uses the terms 'word of God' and 'Kingdom of God', but does not enter into anything requiring philosophical discussion of the existence or nature of God. The term 'kingdom of God' can easily be interpreted in terms of provisionality, as discussed in the last chapter, and 'word of God' can also be understood in terms of meaning or the impact of that meaning for faith. The parable of the sower[73], in which the word of God is compared to seed, is entirely understood in terms of meaning that produces fruitful results rather than in terms of a specific belief justified by appeal to God.

It's also striking that on occasions when Jesus could have invoked divine authority to support his own, he tends to draw back, either giving ambiguous replies or enjoining secrecy. The "Messianic Secret" in Mark and to a lesser extent in Luke and Matthew, was first identified by D.W. Wrede in 1901[74], and is found in a set of passages in which Jesus instructs disciples or other witnesses not to tell anyone about an exorcism or a healing[75], or not to mention claims that he is the Messiah[76] or not to tell anyone about the transfiguration[77]. Wrede interpreted this as an indication that Jesus historically did not claim to be the Messiah – a claim that of course is disputed by other scholars. Leaving aside all historical claims and focusing only on our choice of interpretation, we can interpret the 'Messianic secret' quite differently as part of a coherent but also practically preferable view of Jesus: one that shows him as a man that sought to avoid absolute shortcuts to authority that were based on a reputation for supernatural power. Jesus is often depicted as speaking and behaving with authority of a kind that stems directly from the confidence of his character, and it is this kind of authority that was more likely to bring him followers that were actually interested in spiritual discernment as opposed to ones that merely wanted to be associated with his power. The superficial popular response of those who followed him because of 'signs' that indicated power may well have been one he recognised as counter-productive in the long run.

Of course, we get a very different attitude to the 'Messianic secret' in the gospel of John. Here we are given a series of 'signs' that John seems to regard as indications of Jesus' divinity, and Jesus says many things that can readily be interpreted as claims of divinity – even though, when closely examined, they are never unambiguous about this[78]. But we do not need to set up a dichotomy of Mark in favour of the 'Messianic secret' and John discarding it. Instead, we can see John as moving decisively towards the *meaning* of Jesus where Mark offers reasons for caution in our beliefs about him. The Jesus depicted by John can be less guarded because he is much more archetypal, and the 'signs' are indicative of the Middle Way itself in the ways richly explored by Stephen Verney. So although it is clear that the Jesus of John believes both in God and his own authority given by God, both of these are also equivalent to a divine path between above and below.

Even the Jesus depicted in John, however, also shows a wish to avoid the use of 'signs' as a basis of metaphysical power. "Will none of you ever believe without seeing signs and portents?" (Jn 4:48) he grumbles when asked to heal an official's son. I will discuss below some of the possible reasons why Jesus may have provided healing miracles and the like despite a wish not to use them as proofs of absolute authority, but his attitude here suggests that, whatever his reasons for healing, he would prefer people to develop faith based on grounded confidence than absolute belief founded on miraculous demonstrations.

Jesus' appeals to the Old Testament

There are a number of points where Jesus quotes Old Testament law (as during his temptation, already discussed above) or where he is said to act in fulfilment of Old Testament prophecy. As an example of the latter, in Matthew's account of Jesus' entry into Jerusalem, Jesus tells his disciples to find a donkey with a foal for him to ride, apparently in deliberate fulfilment of a prophecy in Zechariah[79]. It may seem in such accounts that Jesus is absolutising the authority of the scriptures, and his deliberate fulfilment of scriptural prediction also raises troubling issues either of determinism on the one hand or manipulation of people's expectations on the other. If Jesus thought the fulfilment of prophecy was inevitable, how do we reconcile this with his stress on moral responsibility? On the other hand, a deliberate manipulation of prophecy seems like charlatanry.

However, as always there are other ways of interpreting Jesus' attitudes. Constant allusion to the Jewish scriptures was simply a basic part of the culture in which he lived. He could no more avoid references to scripture (particularly when discussing spiritual issues) than a modern English person could avoid using words or turns of phrase found in the King James Bible and Shakespeare. If the Jewish scriptures shape the cultural and linguistic landscape in this way, it is hardly surprising if they also shaped Jesus' attitudes: but it is what he does with this legacy that is more important.

A Middle Way use of such a cultural legacy would be to avoid absolutising it either positively or negatively – that is, neither using it as a form of absolute authority nor necessarily rejecting it. Thus, when Jesus cites the Old Testament we should not be surprised, and the test of whether he is absolutising it should not be whether he cites it but whether what it says could be justified in alternative ways. When he cites scripture to Satan in the temptation, everything he says could be argued in other ways, as discussed above. When he adopts a flexible interpretation of the law without abandoning the law, as also discussed above, he also strikes the Middle Way.

In episodes that are interpreted as fulfilling prophecy, whether apparently deliberately or not, it is important to look closely at the meaning of the scripture being fulfilled. In the case of the passage from Zechariah fulfilled by Jesus entering Jerusalem on a donkey, the original scripture probably intended to contrast a peaceful king mounted on a donkey with a more conventional warlord mounted on a horse. For Jesus to ride, not just a donkey but the foal of a donkey (apparently unridden before that time) involved a kind of comic lowering of expectations, indicative of his wish to take the messianic expectations of the Jews and subvert them for new ends. A modern equivalent might be a foreign dignitary turning up for a reception at Buckingham Palace in a clapped-out mini. He can thus be interpreted as not absolutising the prophecy so much as adopting a subversive element that was already there in the prophecy, and using it to communicate provisionality and scepticism in political matters.

e. Was Jesus an absolutist? The miracles

The miracles recorded in the gospels are a well-known feature of Jesus' ministry. There are a number of miraculous healings, resurrections of people who were recently dead (Jairus's daughter, the widow's son, Lazarus), exorcisms, and so-called 'nature miracles' such as walking on the water, turning water into wine and the feeding of the five thousand. I have already considered above the question of whether Jesus used such miracles as the basis of absolute authority claims, but there is a more basic problem underlying this for many modern readers. Did Jesus, simply by 'breaking the laws of nature', performing apparently supernatural or magical acts, prove divinity in a way that should inspire absolute belief?

I do not want to become embroiled in fruitless naturalistic arguments about whether 'miracles' actually took place which 'broke the laws of nature'. Scepticism requires that we recognise that there are no absolute laws of nature, and thus that no event should be absolutely ruled out as impossible; but this point should not, on the other hand, be exploited to support belief in highly improbable events. Since scientific beliefs are no more than highly probable general beliefs, there is no conflict between science and the *possibility* of miracles. Nevertheless, I think it is entirely against the sceptical spirit of Jesus' message to place weight on such mere possibilities as the basis of positive confidence.

Instead, an agnostic approach is needed to the question of

whether 'miracles' actually took place. Because they are possible, we have no grounds to assert that they definitely did not, nor that they definitely did. As David Hume persuasively argues, based on common human experience there is a greater probability that the gospel writers were mistaken than that the accounts of miraculous events are correct[80]. But Hume's argument does not justify us in dismissing miracle stories: rather in remaining agnostic about 'supernatural' claims whilst searching for the significance of miracles elsewhere.

It is only in the post-enlightenment context that the significance of 'miracles' has primarily come to mean the breaking of 'laws of nature', in the wake of Hume's influential discussion. If we think about their broader significance across time, it is rather as astonishing events that tell us about the attitudes, social influence and symbolic significance of Jesus. All of these can be understood as leading back to Jesus as a Middle Way teacher.

As indicators of Jesus' attitudes, the healing and resurrection miracles are perhaps the most obvious. They are acts of compassion. For example, when meeting the funeral of a dead man who was the only son of his widowed mother, we are told:

> *When the Lord saw her his heart went out to her, and he said 'Do not weep.' He stepped forward and laid his hand on the bier; and the bearers halted. Then he spoke: 'Young man, I tell you to get up'. The dead man sat up and began to speak: and Jesus restored him to his mother.* (Lk 7:13-15)

We could attribute Jesus' ready compassionate response to his genetic character, or to his degree of integration, or to a combination of the two, but in either case we are given the impression, not so much of divinity, as of humanity. However inexplicable Jesus' power to resurrect may be, his *attitudes* here arise not from a 'God's eye view', but rather from a human perspective that has been developed by questioning assumptions of separateness. A thoroughly God's eye view would offer no grounds to choose one dead person to resurrect rather than another, or indeed for 'God to break his own laws' at all. Are people not subject to death for good reasons? Would an unending life not be a torture to us, embodied as we are? Jesus' intervention is messy, and obviously the result of an inconsistent but nevertheless highly developed human perspective that should be celebrated in its own right rather than confused with an absolute divine one.

But many of Jesus' miracles seem to come not primarily from him being touched in this way, but rather from the faith of the people he encountered. A centurion is confident that Jesus only has to say the word and his sick servant will be cured[81]. A group of men carrying a paralytic, unable to reach Jesus due to the crowds, lower him into the room where Jesus is through an opening in the roof[82]. A woman suffering from chronic haemorrhages is cured simply by touching the hem of Jesus' cloak, without his prior knowledge[83].

Such faith, again, is not an abstract belief in Jesus as having a certain absolute status, but rather an immediate response to the person they encountered. Often Jesus' presence seemed to be so overwhelming, at least to people who were sufficiently receptive to it, that they immediately invested immense trust in him. This cannot in any way have been a calculation of the left brain about Jesus' status, but rather a right brain led response to an embodied human presence bearing the attributes of trust that these people had already encountered in others whom they related to – but to a much greater degree.

Jesus' response in these situations also supports the interpretation that these people had effectively healed themselves. For example, in the case of the woman with haemorrhages, he says, "Daughter, your faith has healed you. Go in peace." Here it is the changing mental states of the people concerned, and their complex but mysterious interaction with bodies, that evidently produces healing. We do not have adequate explanations for how such healing works, scientific or otherwise, but we do know that it depends on the power of embodied meaning for the person concerned, rather than the abstract acceptance of a proposition, let alone supernatural interference. With good reason, we do not talk about 'belief healing', but rather about faith healing.

The exorcisms also provide an impression of Jesus as integrated and thus as able to help others achieve integration when they are subject to the horrific internal conflict we now tend to call mental illness. Perhaps the most striking example of this is the exorcism of 'Legion'.

> *Jesus asked him, 'What is your name?' 'Legion,' he replied. This was because so many demons had taken possession of him. And they begged him not to banish them to the abyss. There was a large herd of pigs nearby, feeding on the hillside; and the demons begged him to let them go into these pigs. He gave them leave; the demons came out of the man and went into the pigs, and the herd rushed over the edge into the lake and were drowned.* (Lk 8:26-33)

The multiplicity of conflicting identities may be associated with what we might now call schizophrenia or multiple personality disorder, and the personification of these identities as 'demons' is not irrelevant to modern understanding. As discussed above[84], the archetype of the Shadow can be associated with Satan, as it can with other devils or demons: beings that are constituted by the narrow hatred of our rejection of them. The less integrated we are the more demonic our experience becomes, as it becomes more dominated by qualities like power, obsession, craving, defensiveness, impatience, literalness and despair, and these qualities either take us over or are temporarily rejected and then reassert themselves. Iain McGilchrist also discusses the links between over-dominant left-hemisphere states and schizophrenia[85].

The ending of the demonic possession is presented as an exorcism – i.e. a conflict between Jesus using divine power and the demons as separate, negative supernatural entities. However, there are many hints in the narrative that can help us interpret it in a way that simply reveals Jesus' integration and the overwhelming effect that could have on others. One such hint is the way that the demons immediately recognise Jesus and are overawed. They recognise that here there is a perspective far beyond their conflicted world, but, given their limitations, fear is the dominant response. Integration, to a demon, looks like conflict in which absolute force is used against them. So the demon cries, on first seeing Jesus "What do you want with me, Jesus, Son of the Most High God? ... I implore you, do not torment me" (Lk 8:28). Another indication is the way in which Jesus does not simply destroy the demons or 'banish them to the abyss'. Instead, they are allowed to go into the pigs. Whatever we may think of this from the animal welfare point of view, Jesus is here using his influence to challenge absolutised conflict, and avoiding a merely negative absolutism in response by providing an alternative for the demons. The demons then destroy themselves rather than being destroyed by Jesus. In the same way, whatever our demons may be, we cannot merely destroy them or banish them. The Middle Way suggests that we should be deliberate about not adopting their narrow assumptions, but that we should provide their energies with alternative directions in which to flow.

Supposed 'nature miracles' also often tell us about Jesus' integration. Let us take the calming of the storm as an example.

> *One day he got into a boat with his disciples and said to them, 'Let us cross over to the other side of the lake.' So they put out; and as they sailed along he fell asleep. Then a heavy squall struck the lake; they began to ship water and were in grave danger. They came and roused him: 'Master, master, we are sinking!' they cried. He awoke,*

> *and rebuked the wind and the turbulent waters. The storm subsided and there was calm. 'Where is your faith?' he asked.* (Lk 8:22-25)

Here we can see panic seizing the disciples. Their amygdalas are putting them on hyper-alert, but Jesus probably realises that this state of frantic fear does not help one deal effectively with this kind of crisis. Rather than panicking, one's best chance when dealing with a new unexpected condition is to maintain a wider awareness so as to see it in perspective and stop the reptilian red-alert function taking over our brains. One is then able to consider coolly how best to act. Due to his level of integration, Jesus seems to be able to avoid panic, and thus seems to the disciples to be in control of everything when they are not. He has maintained 'faith' – in this case confidence at dealing with unexpected conditions. Beside this central point about Jesus, the question of whether he can actually change the weather is an irrelevant distraction about which we are in any case likely to remain ignorant.

Beside this indication of the personality of Jesus, the whole passage can be interpreted as symbolic of a spiritual journey. 'Crossing over to the other side' of a body of water is a common metaphor for spiritual progress to a point where things look substantially different because we have gained a bigger perspective. In Jainism, the founder of the religion (Mahavira) is entitled 'Tirthankara' meaning 'ford-maker', and in medieval Christian tradition, St Christopher was said to carry travellers across dangerous rivers. However, getting 'to the other side' is not always an easy process. We may fall asleep (lose awareness), and be surprised by threatening new conditions (the storm). Within the terms of such a metaphor, the storm is internal, even if there is one externally as well. If we respond effectively to the storm and sink and lose our lives, then that's just the effect of the conditions: but if we encounter an inner storm as well as an outer storm, losing confidence and wider awareness when we most need it, then we may lose our lives unnecessarily due to our lapse in awareness.

Such symbolic interpretation is probably the most helpful response to miracles like walking on water, turning water into wine, and feeding five thousand. Water represents a basic condition of ordinary human life, as well as a condition of slightly greater fluidity or flexibility in our ego-bound state, as already discussed. In relation to that fluidity, dense solid objects sink, just as rigid attitudes sink when they come into contact with new conditions, but when Jesus walks on the water we see his ability to ride that fluidity and accept it in its own terms rather than being over-ridden by it.

Turning water into wine also represents a transformation from a more fluid ego-state to a more developed state of integration, as beautifully explained by Verney[86]. The feeding of the five thousand, on the other hand, concentrates on the symbol of bread, with ordinary nourishment being likened to integration:

> *'Amen, amen I say to you, it is not because you saw signs that you came looking for me, but because you ate the bread and your hunger was satisfied. You should work, not for this perishable food, but for the food that lasts, the food of eternal life.'* (Jn 6:26-27)

Jesus here makes explicit that the significance of feeding the five thousand does *not* lie in its status as a miraculous 'sign'. Instead, it is the satisfaction of a deeper hunger. Our desires cannot be satisfied as long as they remain in conflict with each other, because when our desires change, the goals we previously sought are no longer relevant, and the satisfaction of previous ones seems meaningless or even shameful. The long-term, adequate satisfaction of hunger thus depends on integration ('the food of eternal life').

The feeding of the five thousand is especially relevant today given the conflicts that rage in our attitude to food, and the attendant eating disorders and obesity of the rich accompanied by malnutrition of the poor. Jan Chozen Bays identifies seven types of hunger[87]: of the eye, nose, mouth, stomach, cells, mind and heart, which is a way of analysing our tendency to eat in an alienated and distracted way, absolutising one belief about food, one emotional response to it or one overwhelming response to a sense experience, without a wider awareness of whether our 'hunger' is really part of our wider experience. It is only the more fulfilling fare of integration that can make us sufficiently mindful of our hunger to be genuinely satisfied when we eat.

This point is brought out in John's account of the miracle:

> *Then Jesus took the loaves, gave thanks, and distributed them to the people as they sat there. He did the same with the fish, and they had as much as they wanted. When everyone had had enough, he said to his disciples, 'Gather up the pieces left over, so that nothing is wasted'.* (Jn 6:11-12)

The account does not tell us how much food each person had, but rather that they had as much as they wanted. If we understand this in terms of their receiving 'the food that lasts', then it seems that it is the change of *what they wanted* that could have been the genuinely significant effect of the miracle. Again, we do not know whether or not the food actually increased in quantity in a way we would consider 'miraculous', but we can be inspired by the integrative process of a crowd that has changed its mental state sufficiently to be content with little.

The gathering up of leftovers is also significant. Firstly, that the crowd were not afraid to leave leftovers, because they were evidently not anxious about eating when there was food available but only about fulfilling their immediate integrated hunger. Secondly, Jesus is nevertheless concerned that the food should not be wasted, even though he doesn't want to make the people anxious because of this. Both sets of conditions are addressed here – that we should not waste food and that we shouldn't overeat due to anxiety about not wasting food. This is very much the Middle Way in action in a very practical sense.

Again, then, in the feeding of the five thousand as in other such miracles, the traditional interpretation that Jesus used supernatural intervention to 'break the laws of nature' can be left aside, because it conflicts with a wider understanding of Jesus as teaching the Middle Way. But we do not need to leave aside the story as a whole – far from it. It tells us more than anything about the integration of Jesus as a character, the strength of his judgement, and the remarkable ways in which people were affected by that integration.

f. Was Jesus an absolutist? His predictions

In this section I will take up the final two points on my list of possible reasons for thinking of Jesus as an absolutist. Both of these are concerned with Jesus' predictions, either about himself or about the coming kingdom of God.

Jesus' prediction of his own death and resurrection

There are a number of points in the gospel narratives where Jesus appears to know about his death and resurrection in advance, and also to be certain about both the inevitability and the rightness of those events. These points have always created difficulty for me, because they appear to show a deterministic Jesus with definite beliefs about how events will turn out, as well as a belief that God is in charge of events – apparently discounting contingency and mystery. Let us examine one such typical passage, from Mark:

And he began to teach them that the Son of Man had to endure great

> *suffering, and to be rejected by the elders, chief priests, and scribes; to be put to death, and to rise again three days afterwards. He spoke about it plainly. At this Peter took hold of him and began to rebuke him. But Jesus, turning and looking at his disciples, rebuked Peter. 'Out of my sight, Satan!' he said. 'You think as men think, not as God thinks.'* (Mk 8:31-33)

Of one point we can ourselves be clear: even if Jesus believed clearly that such things would happen, the vehemence with which he maintains that belief here must be mistaken. Such a belief can only possibly be an absolutisation, given that the actual responses of the Jewish leaders and Roman authorities alike were only predictable in general and fallible terms at best. Even if he had firmly decided to confront both religious and secular authorities in Jerusalem, how could he be so certain that he would not manage to convince them of a more integrated path, in the way he had done with so many other people? There may also be an absolute value associated with this – the value he associates with acting in this way, whether it is associated with self-sacrifice or with a particular unassailable belief about the good he would achieve.

Peter's rebuke seems apt, and Jesus' response to it inapt. Perhaps Jesus felt that Peter wanted to stop him accepting the conditions that would afflict him in this way, and thus thought that Peter was working on the basis of narrow assumptions that would place the bodily welfare of one loved leader before a greater purpose. We could interpret 'as God thinks' to be a more integrated state from which Jesus may have felt he could better predict events than Peter could. But that hardly excuses Jesus' over-reaction.

There thus seem to remain two other alternatives in interpreting passages such as these. The first of these is that we could read them as reflecting an inaccurate view of Jesus that has been projected retrospectively back onto him by the gospel writers. More significance is attached to an event by presenting it as inevitable, and more pathos is attached to Jesus' acceptance of those events if we assume that Jesus knew of them fully and precisely beforehand. Jesus' predictions thus serve the purposes of the early church in promoting an absolute view of Jesus that could more easily unite the group. However, this type of solution may rightly be accused of an *ad hoc* tendency. It is too easy to rationalise one's rejection of texts one finds unhelpful by attributing historical inaccuracy to them, and much more honest to simply recognise that one finds them unhelpful.

The second and probably better alternative, then, is to interpret such passages as indicative of an unintegrated aspect of Jesus. We seem to have plenty of evidence so far that Jesus' integration was powerful and striking to others, but if we are to avoid absolutising it, we must also recognise that integration is always a matter of degree, and can be incomplete and asymmetrical. Indeed, the idealising of figures such as Jesus and the Buddha so that they have to be morally and spiritually perfect in order to fit later dogmas about their status is the biggest hurdle we have to face in reaching a view of them that is inspiring without being absolutising. Let's face it: Jesus had his faults.

The faults exhibited here also make sense if we think about Jesus' background and situation. He was obviously immensely committed to practical integration as well as having a sceptical view of the 'truths' in institutions around him, but he lacked any of the education or training, formal or informal, that might have helped him question his own assumptions. Fatalism is also a very common assumption in the ancient world, which even the well-educated frequently adopted. It would be surprising if Jesus could question it. Added to this, he finds himself in a position of authority in which he is very vulnerable to the guru's mistake of over-confidence in his own intuitions. If he listened to Peter or anyone else who questioned his assumptions, his authority might be at stake. That it is possible for someone who was astonishingly integrated in some respects to also fall unwittingly into such absolutisations should not surprise us: it is what humans tend to do. More broadly, I have always found it a matter of dismay that there seems to be no instance at all in any of the gospels of Jesus admitting that he was mistaken, and that again suggests some of Jesus' weaknesses.

'Out of my sight, Satan!' thus seems to be an instance of Jesus' personal fragility. But there may be a positive aspect to this. For Jesus to over-react in this way suggests that he was unconsciously aware of such a vulnerability but repressed that awareness. That at least indicates that Jesus had some awareness of the possible drawbacks of absolutised determinism and self-sacrifice – enough to make him feel conflicted about it. We should also put this in a larger context so as to avoid the nirvana fallacy. Jesus, like the rest of us, is on a journey. We should no more reject what he has to offer because of imperfection than we should anyone else. Rather, our appreciation of what he has to offer can be positively strengthened by our response to its humanity.

Jesus' belief in the coming kingdom of God

The kingdom of God (or 'kingdom of heaven' in Matthew) is an oft-recurring theme in all the gospels, often as an apparently expected future state. There has been much dispute in the Christian tradition, firstly as to whether it refers to a present or future state, and secondly whether it refers to an inner or outward state. Is the Kingdom of God a new state of the world we should look forward to, a political change we should bring about, or a change in the individual brought about by faith?

Whether it should be one of these or all of them, it seems clear that the kingdom of God is central to Jesus' understanding of how finite humans can relate to infinite God. In many ways the ambiguity is appropriate, because it reflects the ambiguity of the subject. There are many ways that humans can encounter or recognise that state of potential integration they call God, and these can be both present and future, as well as both inward and outward.

Nevertheless, Jesus' view of the kingdom is often interpreted in terms of cosmic justice beliefs (indicating that all good actions are necessarily rewarded and all bad ones punished) or in terms of an imminent intervention by God that would save him personally. Either of these would unavoidably be absolute beliefs if Jesus held them. Albert Schweitzer understood Jesus as dominated by eschatological expectations of a kind that he expected to be fulfilled at the time of his crucifixion[88], so that his 'Cry of Desolation' on the cross ("My God, my God, why have you forsaken me?" – Mt 27:46) is interpreted as one of a disappointed hope of dramatic supernatural intervention. However, Jesus' cry can just as well be interpreted as that of a man afraid of losing touch with a larger integrated awareness because he is overwhelmed by pain.

When Jesus talks of eschatological scenarios, such as those of judgement, elsewhere, there is obviously a cultural weight of earlier Jewish tradition in the terms of which he speaks, where eschatological expectations were already established. Nevertheless, our interpretation of the judgement does not have to be eschatological, but can just as well refer to the necessity of integrated judgement in us. To be practically adequate, after all, we cannot cease from judgement, which means using the evidence and value criteria available to us in experience to distinguish between better or worse actions in ourselves or in wider society. At one and the same time Jesus urges us against premature and unintegrated judgement ("Do not judge, and you will not be judged" – Mt 7:1) but gives us a paradigm case of integrated judgement in what have often been interpreted as 'final' or eschatological judgements.

Let's take the famous passage of the judgement between the

sheep and the goats:

> *When the Son of Man comes in his glory and all the angels with him, he will sit on his glorious throne, with all the nations gathered before him. He will separate people into two groups, as a shepherd separates the sheep from the goats; he will place the sheep on his right hand and the goats on his left. Then the king will say to those on his right, "You have my father's blessing; come, take possession of the kingdom that has been ready for you since the world was made. For when I was hungry, you gave me food, when thirsty, you gave me drink; when I was a stranger, you took me into your home; when naked, you clothed me; when I was ill, you came to my help; when in prison, you visited me.... Anything you did for one of my brothers here, you did for me." Then he will say to those on his left, "A curse is on you, go from my sight to the eternal fire that is ready for the devil and his angels. For when I was hungry, you gave me nothing to eat...[et seq.]...Anything you failed to do for one of these... you failed to do for me."* (Mt 25:31-46)

The Son of Man (a phrase deriving from Daniel, also translated "one who is like a human being") here sits in judgement in the same sense that we all do, but his glorious throne and his comparison to a king are ways of representing the integrated state in which a fully justified and thus genuinely authoritative judgement can be made. The presence of all the nations reminds us of the universality of the moral judgements we might make. Unavoidably, when we make a moral judgement, by implication we separate those who have acted well in accordance with that judgement from those who have done badly – the sheep from the goats. However, that need not stop those who are sheep in some respects being goats in others, and vice-versa.

The basis of the judgement here is that of practically applied love, so that our awareness of God is no longer distinguished from our awareness of our neighbours. By loving our neighbours in this way, we love God – which means that we love our integrated selves by loving others represented in our own minds at the same time. By doing this, we 'take possession of the kingdom that has been ready for you since the world was made', namely an integrated awareness that has always been a potential for us throughout our lives. If we fail to do this, however, we go to the 'eternal fire' – that is, the torment of frustrated and unfulfilled egoistic states, which seems to us eternal in the worst sense through our impatient desire to be free of them.

Note also the way in which this passage uses the terms 'right' and 'left', bearing in mind the association of the right side of the body with the left hemisphere of the brain. Those who have been positively judged can only be judged in the judging hemisphere, the left, which represents what it approves of as being on the right. But, strangely, enough, it is the goats who pass the shepherd on the left that suffer through being most entrenched in a narrow view of this 'rightness'.

On a reading of this kind, the kingdom of God is not *solely* within us, but it is by recognising its role within us that we undermine the projection of judgement in the terms of externalised power, so that when we do apply our judgements to the wider world we still recognise that these need to be integrated judgements. No, we cannot be sure that Jesus did not primarily have such an externalised eschatological judgement in mind, and the possibility remains that Jesus was either confused in his account of the kingdom, or that his interpreters were, and that they added the eschatological elements. But if we want to find a helpful teaching in Jesus we cannot interpret such passages as these in terms of an externalised power that contradicts almost everything else that Jesus stands for. Could he really recognise the redeemable complexity of human moral experience whilst advocating the literal condemnation of whole people to eternal hellfire? No. Could he really forgive sinners seventy times seven and then sit on a throne and condemn them utterly for all time? No. If we are not to merely reject Jesus, he must remain an integrated figure, which means that we cannot accept the scenario of him suddenly moving from human to divine status as opposed to being a human who engages astonishingly with the divine.

6

Christ the Middle Way

a. Christ the mediator

At this point we move from Jesus to Christ, though the boundary between them is far from clear cut. So far, I have been asking whether the Jesus represented in the gospels can be understood as teaching the Middle Way, but to ask about Christ as the Middle Way is to start at a different point. Christ, as he has developed in the psyches of millions of Christians, is not a represented historical figure but an archetype. To discuss Christ from that point of view does not require me to entirely abandon my discussion of biblical interpretation, but it does require that interpretation to be approached archetypally rather than in terms of what it may claim to teach. I have not yet discussed Jesus' crucifixion and resurrection because I regard these as having an overwhelmingly archetypal significance.

In 2.c, I have already explained the ways in which God can be understood as an archetype, and at least briefly touched on the archetypal role of Christ. There I suggested that in some respects Christ is a hero figure. We can certainly see that side of him in some aspects of the life of Jesus in the gospels: he is the rebel who defies the Pharisees and other authorities and the heroic healer who exerts astonishing powers to help others. Like many great heroes, he faces pain and suffering, even death, with equanimity. In his resurrection, he defies death. In all of these stories, we identify with him. His achievements become associated with the identifications in our ego just as our own do. We root for him just as we do for Sir Percival, Oliver Twist, or Harry Potter.

However, in other respects Christ is also a representation of the God archetype, one of the Trinity. He is the divine logos, the Pantocrator, the Son sitting at God the Father's right hand. When he performs miracles or achieves resurrection, we may see his power as supernatural and hence divine. When he speaks with apparently divine authority or offers 'signs' in the gospel of John, we are dealing not so much with an exceptional man as with a God in human guise.

Both of these archetypes are universal, but what is distinctive about Christ is the way in which he combines these two archetypes, or rather represents a path from one to the other. It is in this sense that "Christ is the way", as Jung wrote in the passage I quoted in the introduction. Christ is a mediator in a sense that is dialectical – that is, in taking elements of the integrated self (the divine) that can be combined with the limited or egoistic self, and in doing so synthesising what previously seemed irreconcilably opposed. In this sense he is identical to the Middle Way. Thus we can regard Christ as most profoundly representing an archetype that is neither heroic nor divine, but a third archetype, that of the Middle Way itself.

As with all archetypes, however, the Middle Way archetype can have integrated and unintegrated forms. Unintegrated archetypes are mistaken for their projections, as we assume that a person that we have attributed archetypal attributes to simply consists in those attributes. Another way of putting this is that we *absolutise* the archetype, assuming that the archetype is the whole story when we have projected it onto a person. Thus, for example, we can project the Shadow by attributing only hateful characteristics to someone we have had conflict with, or project the anima/animus by falling in love and thinking of the beloved person only in terms of their attractive other features. The Middle Way archetype, like the others, represents a process in our own identifications, but it remains unintegrated when we assume that it is fully instantiated in someone or something beyond that process.

The Middle Way is such a tricky process to engage with in

experience that there are multiple ways to project unintegrated versions of it. I want to suggest that there are at least four of them, all of which have formed traps for Christians that have distracted them from the Middle Way function of Christ:

1. We can identify the Middle Way with the hero, assuming that the dialectical path is simply a matter of effort
2. We can identify the Middle Way with the divine, assuming that it is some kind of ultimate person or reality
3. We can flip between the heroic and the divine without any dialectical engagement, and assume that the Middle Way only consists in such flips
4. We can identify the Middle Way only with a concept, and assume that the concept rather than any practical process completes the dialectic

All of these processes can also be identified with *belief* – a left hemisphere abstract construction that operates as a kind of shortcut, trying to integrate the divine and the human by an easier method than the arduous and incomplete ones that are actually possible in experience. They substitute belief for the embodied faith or confidence that is needed to actually engage in the process of the Middle Way.

The first of these ways, identification with the hero, in Christianity may take the form of obsession with the idea of Jesus, or with "Jesus' sacrifice for us". I will be discussing the doctrine of atonement later in this section, but without awareness that one's own integration is a process, Christians may try to become like Jesus just through dwelling on the idea, and blame themselves for not being like Jesus. A widespread popular conception of Jesus as 'selfless' and human beings as 'selfish' may also contribute to this. If we only try harder, it is thought, we can be 'selfless' too. But since the ego cannot be eliminated, and is rather the positive basis of all progress, such a quest is doomed to failure from the start. Christian ethics, when they are a matter of 'will', become institutionalised failure in which we continue our sinful lapses and occasionally console ourselves by shifting to the second unintegrated approach.

The second unintegrated approach to Christ involves seeing him as God and thus as all-powerful and all-controlling. In this way he just becomes a more accessible version of God. The belief that God saves us and that we cannot save ourselves (as in Luther's salvation by faith) may then come to the fore. Rather than saving ourselves, then, we throw ourselves on God's mercy. This may have a temporary consoling effect as we compensate for our inability to change, but it is no more integrated in the longer-term than the first approach.

The third approach is likely to result from the combination of the first and second. Rather than understanding the ways that the human needs to be modified by faith in the divine, and understanding of the divine likewise needs to avoid idealisation by engagement with the human, we instead flip between the two. We will recognise that Christ is both divine and human, but still in practice find this a contradiction rather than a way forward. When reading the gospel accounts we may at times identify with Jesus as a man, and at other times worship him as a God. When considering ourselves, we may also flip between a sense of powerlessness and an idealised sense of ourselves as redeemed.

The fourth approach does involve a recognition that Christ offers a path between the human and the divine, but rather than a practice, this path is still just an abstract conceptual belief. In this approach, Christ seems to be offering us a sort of magic. Such magic may be especially associated with the ritual of the eucharist, which I shall also discuss further in 8.c. By taking the eucharist (or perhaps by some other ritual associated with Christ) we invoke a path between the human and the divine, but the symbolic expression becomes a token that substitutes for the difficulties of actually following that path.

My thesis is that, on the many occasions Christians have failed to effectively engage with the Middle Way through Christ, they have become caught in one or more of these types of unintegrated approaches. They have done so, not because the Christian tradition and scriptures cannot be interpreted in ways that support an integrated approach, but because humans are too often over-dominated by left brains that like shortcuts, these shortcuts have become socially established and thus been reinforced in interpretation, selection and custom, and so in many cases Christianity has come to seem almost necessarily a shortcut. However, it is up to us what we make of Christ.

To integrate Christ, on the other hand, we need to recognise that he is both inward and outward. The inward is not an end in itself, but without recognising the inward, our outward attempts to follow him become mere projections that elide the full experience. Inwardly, Christ is me – both me the hero, with the capacity for idealisation and effort, and me the divine, a potentially integrated being in which conflicts are resolved and energy is united. For a dialectical mediation of those two archetypes, I need not just to bring the ideas together at one moment, but to bring them constantly into contact with each other. Every effort needs wider awareness of the full resources that can be brought to it, if it is not to be self-defeating, whilst every ideal also needs awareness of the conditions of its non-fulfilment, if it is not to become a matter of mere substitutive form.

As with the Tree of Life discussed in 4.d, an organic metaphor is perhaps the best one for showing how inner and outer experience can be unified in growth from human soil towards the divine. In the gospel of John, Jesus provides a similar image:

> *I am the true vine, and my father is the gardener. Any branch of mine that is barren he cuts away; and any fruiting branch he prunes*

> *clean, to make it more fruitful still. You are already clean because of the word I have spoken to you. Dwell in me, as I in you. No branch can bear fruit by itself, but only if it remains united with the vine; no more can you bear fruit, unless you remain united with me.* (Jn 15:1-4)

We are the branches, but the Christ archetype is the vine: not separate from us, but a way of talking about the roots and stem that heroically grow out of the ground and unify the energy that flows up into the fruit. The God archetype is the gardener, again not entirely separate from the vine and its branches, but providing a wider awareness of conditions to make sure that the vine remains watered and pruned. The vine is dependent on the gardener, just as the Middle Way archetype is dependent on the God archetype (and vice-versa). The vine, as Stephen Verney points out[89], turns water into wine.

In the chapters that follow in this section, I shall be applying this view of Christ to all the crucial symbolic events that give Christ that archetypal role both in the Bible and in Christian tradition: his incarnation, crucifixion, and resurrection. In all of them, I am going to suggest, we can find interpretations that show him as a mediator and thus support us in the Middle Way. I do so, not because Christ is a unique expression of the Middle Way, but because by doing so I can bring symbols of great meaningfulness into fruitful contact with it.

b. Annunciation and incarnation

It is a matter of great wonder that the God archetype is found in human experience, and still more that a way can be found towards that total integration from the limited and deluded ego. It is in that spirit of wonder that I suggest we approach the narrative of the incarnation. We do not know anything about its historicity: let us set that aside. What we do have is the meaning of the annunciation and birth of Christ as absorbed and re-created by twenty centuries of Christians, in art, music and literature. Each of those Christians is able to re-create the meaning of Christmas anew for themselves from archetypal experience. Never once, however, in a childhood of Christmases, do I remember it being seriously suggested to me that the birth of Christ might lie in myself. What a difference it might have made to my understanding if it had!

I have always found the annunciation the most meaningful of the stories associated with Christmas, because of its encounter between the innocent human bafflement that comes from narrow horizons, and the strangeness and beauty that comes from a sudden recognition of new potentiality. This is a quality that is brought out most strongly by the best artistic representations of the encounter between Mary and Gabriel. But the story is only found in Luke:

> *In the sixth month the angel Gabriel was sent by God to Nazareth, a town in Galilee, with a message for a girl betrothed to a man named Joseph; the girl's name was Mary. The angel went in and said to her, 'Greetings, most favoured one! The Lord is with you.' But she was deeply troubled by what he said and wondered what this greeting could mean. Then the angel said to her, 'Do not be afraid, Mary, for God has been gracious to you; you will conceive and give birth to a son, and you are to give him the name Jesus. He will be great, and will be called Son of the Most High.....' 'How can this be?' said Mary, 'I am still a virgin.' The angel answered 'The Holy Spirit will come upon you, and the power of the Most High will overshadow you....'* (Lk 1:26-35)

Whether the idea of Mary's virginity came about through a mistaken translation of a prophecy does not matter, for in Luke's hands it becomes primarily a device for registering our astonishment at having God within us. We may protest that we are spiritual virgins: that we have no idea how this marvellous potential for integration found its way into our ego-ravaged self. But nevertheless, there it is, however unworthy we may feel we are. We may also recoil in fear, as Mary does, but rather than denying it and going back to more familiar territory, as we may be tempted to do, she acknowledges it.

The psychological power of the annunciation is also wonderfully reflected in Jung's Red Book. The key difference between Jung's account and Luke's, however, is that Jung is entirely aware of the embryonic God within as a representation under his own control. In his previous vision, he brings back the sick God Izdubar to his own home, but then finds he is too big to fit through the door: so he squeezes him down to the size of an egg to fit him through[90]. This, if you like, is the impregnation. But, gazing at the egg, Jung then continues with incantations:

> *Christmas has come. The God is in the egg.*
>
> *I have prepared a rug for my God, an expensive red rug from the land of morning.*
>
> *He shall be surrounded by the shimmer of magnificence of his Eastern land.*
>
> *I am the mother, the simple maiden, who gave birth and did not know how.*
>
> *I am the careful father, who protected the maiden.*
>
> *I am the shepherd, who received the message as he guarded his herd at night on the dark fields.*
>
> *I am the holy animal that stood astonished and cannot grasp the becoming of the God.*
>
> *I am the wise man who came from the East, suspecting the miracle from afar.*
>
> *And I am the egg that surrounds and nurtures the seed of God in me.*[91]

Mary's perspective is included here, but it becomes one of many synthesised perspectives. The simple fact of potential is unavoidably one that requires multiple perspectives: for by having God within, I can take on all these perspectives, appreciating the meaning of the archetypal event through multifaceted imagination. Jung makes powerful use of the Biblical stories, but presents them entirely in terms of his live experience.

The Middle Way on the incarnation, then, is not to 'believe' that God took on human form, but nor is it to contradict or dismiss it on the basis of historical doubts or any of the contradictions involved in the very idea of incarnation as an object of belief. It is not Jesus who is God incarnate, but you – for you are Christ. The story about Jesus' birth is told to celebrate the same archetype as the one that is your function (as well as that of all other humans). This story sets you at the beginning of the path – as you may be again at any moment. From the very beginning that path may bring you face to face with difficult conditions. You may end up being born in a stable. But as long as you welcome the shepherds and the wise men and have confidence in the new perspectives they offer, you may set off aright.

c. Crucifixion and provisionality

At the root of provisionality is our response to suffering. Most of the time we pursue self-reinforcing cycles of behaviour – positive feedback loops whereby the successful pursuit of a reward reinforces the tendency to value that reward and seek it again. But sometimes we encounter unexpected obstructions, and suffer pain (or at least frustration) as a result: our friendly overtures are met with indifference or refusal; the ice-cream is dropped on the ground; or walking down the street, we are unexpectedly set upon by muggers. Whenever we encounter such pain, we have the opportunity to change our values or our tactics: to avoid the unfriendly person or the dangerous street, or to be less attached to the pleasure of ice-cream.

Provisionality is the ability to respond to the new information that accompanies such suffering, and modify our beliefs and values accordingly. Rather than getting stuck in one inappropriate pattern, we have the capacity to reassess the situation and try another. This may not only be to your advantage, but also to that of others. For example, the person who treated you with apparent indifference may actually want to befriend you but be reserved by temperament. Find another way of befriending them and it will help them too.

Why was Jesus crucified? The conventional Christian answer is that he did it for our sake. However, he did not die to save others in any obvious and immediate sense – unlike, say, a soldier fighting against tyranny. The only way that pain is normally helpful to us is as part of a negative feedback loop, enabling us to learn and adjust our responses. This is also, it seems to me, the only possible positive way of interpreting Christ's crucifixion. Neither his death nor his pain can have been valuable in itself. Rather, he chose to risk all in getting others to re-examine their habitual course.

We do not, and cannot, know whether or not this was Jesus' motivation in the historical events of the crucifixion: for example, we cannot rule out the Schweitzerian contention that Jesus believed he could summon last-minute divine intervention, even though he is depicted as refusing such 'testing' of God at the time of his temptation. It is possible that Jesus was in fact deluded in one way or another about his crucifixion and its effects. However, to interpret the crucifixion as a stimulus to provisionality fits both the Middle Way aspect of Jesus' teachings discussed in the previous section, and the Middle Way function of Christ in the individual psyche. For the Middle Way is defined by its avoidance of absolute positions (whether positive or negative) that produce inflexible positive feedback loops. The alternative to absolutisations that fix us in unchangeable positive feedback loops is to be able to make use of negative feedback loops – which does not necessarily mean seeking out pain, but does entail developing a capacity to learn from it.

There is much in the four gospel accounts of the agony in the garden, trial and crucifixion that can support us in this picture of Jesus' motives. To begin with, the difficulties and conflicts attendant on such a motive are not obscured (at least in the three synoptic gospels). According to Matthew, "Distress and anguish overwhelmed him" (Mt 26:37) and he says "The spirit is willing, but the flesh is weak." (Mt 26:41) In Luke "in anguish of spirit he prayed the more urgently; and his sweat was like drops of blood falling to the ground" (Lk 22:44).

Nevertheless, Jesus acts according to his awareness of an integrated state, setting aside his resistance as he prays "My father, if it is possible, let this cup pass me by. Yet not my will but yours" (Mt 26:39). The Jungian commentator Edinger suggests that the 'cup' here can be identified with the cup of wine used in the eucharist, and thus that Christ, by accepting the 'cup', is symbolically drinking his own blood. Self-devouring of this kind (as also in the *uroboros*, the serpent that devours its own tail) is more widely symbolic of the integration and assimilation of the opposite within oneself[92]. Our struggle to accept helpful suffering in a state of awareness is also symbolised by the sleepiness of the disciples, that Jesus rebukes for not maintaining the vigil with him (i.e. not maintaining awareness).[93]

Christ aims not to use power, but rather to enable learning through a profound shift in those brought to reflect on their own behaviour against him and jolt them from their confirmation bias. Thus he forbids his disciples to use violence against the soldiers who arrest him[94], and (at least in the synoptic gospels) does not even use the verbal power of advocacy to defend himself. Before both the High Priest and Pilate he remains silent or says "The words are yours" when asked if he claims to be the Messiah. In Luke he says only "If I tell you, you will not believe me; and if I ask questions, you will not answer" (Lk22:67-8), showing awareness of the fruitlessness of disputing with those who are already convinced and who will merely interpret everything you say as evidence against you. Only in John, with his sympathetic portrayal of Pilate, does Jesus explain to Pilate that "My kingdom is not of this world" (Jn 18:36).

When on the cross, Jesus only at one point utters the Cry of Desolation that I have already discussed above. He is subject to accelerating taunting and cruelty, illustrating the ways in which the ingroup bias takes off when someone has been condemned by the group. Nevertheless, for the most part he remains in an integrated state, saying in Luke "Forgive them, for they know not what they do" (Lk 23:24). Edinger explains that this

> *...can be understood as a personification of the redeeming nature of 'consciousness of wholeness'. It has nothing to do with meekly turning the other cheek, but rather refers to the fact that the individuated ego can endure the onslaught of the power principle without identifying with it, that is, without succumbing to either defensive violence or despair. The consequence is a gradual transformation of the collective psyche.*[95]

It is quite possible to interpret Jesus' motives as masochistic, but crucial not to do so if we want to avoid getting into an understanding of religion as waging war against the ego rather than integrating it. Nor (we must assume) does Jesus withdraw his awareness from the suffering he is undergoing through repressive alienation: James Hall points out that until the eleventh century, most Christian depictions of Christ on the cross show him as "alive and open-eyed, a triumphant saviour wearing a royal crown"[96]. Rather than being masochistic, passive, or alienated, his actions are significant because they illustrate how to put suffering in a bigger context.

Jesus' crucifixion between two thieves also helps to give a wider symbolic value to the events. According to Luke's account, one of the thieves taunted him, but the other was respectful of him[97], leading to the tradition that one of the thieves went to heaven and the other to hell. Jung points out that this shows Christ symbolically stretched between two irreconcilable opposites[98], a design that fits the later use of the crucifixion as part of a mandala (a spatial diagram of integration).

In short, Jesus reinforces a view of himself as a facilitator using shock tactics to get others to rethink, except for one point, repeated in all three synoptic gospels, and judged 'blasphemous' by the High Priest: "From now on, the Son of Man will be seated at the right hand of Almighty God" (Lk 22:69). This is the point that introduces some doubt about the motives of the historical Jesus. To interpret this charitably, Jesus may just want to communicate that he is speaking from a standpoint of integrated awareness, but lack the language to do so other than in these apparently bombastic terms. But it is difficult to avoid the impression that he was deliberately antagonising the High Priest. Here, perhaps, Christ needs to be particularly separated from the Jesus depicted in the gospels.

The story of the cross is one of great power, and its connection to the courage of the historical Jesus may be of great inspiration, but we will miss the recognition that Jesus evidently wished to get across to us if we focus only on him and not on the crucifixions that occur within ourselves. Rejection by those we love, sudden injury, disappointment, career failure, illness and pain, the loss or alienation of children, bankruptcy, natural disaster, guilt: all such suffering can entrench us in a cycle of rigidity and depression, or it can trigger provisionality and change. Though it may cost us great anguish to embrace that suffering, there is always a Middle Way that leads on from the point we have reached. This relationship of the crucifixion to our own organic experience can be particularly symbolised by its relationship to the tree of life, discussed in 4.d above, which has sometimes been depicted artistically in Christian tradition in the form of the crucifix combined with a tree.

d. Atonement, grace and salvation

As a child in a clerical household I often used to hear the word 'atonement', but had little idea what it meant except that it had some relationship to making up for your sins. Later I learned more about the extraordinary legalistic theology that has grown up around the idea that Christ 'died for our sins', involving a kind of notional equivalence in which we are released from the necessary punishment of original sin if someone else freely takes our place in suffering for it. C.S. Lewis even has the lion god Aslan repeat the exercise in 'The Lion, the Witch and the Wardrobe'. All of this seemed to me, and still seems, mere alienated abstraction: the kind of legalism that Jesus challenged when it was used by the Pharisees.

I only began to grasp what atonement *might* mean at the point when I became aware of its derivation from *at-one-ment*. If one pronounces it in this way (rather than as 'a-tone-ment'), its relationship to integration becomes much more obvious. Atonement is traditionally seen as overcoming conflict in one's relationship with God (becoming 'at one' with God), but since God is an archetype himself representing oneness in us, atonement must be a way of talking about making contact with that oneness, of moving beyond the narrow perspective from which we may presume ourselves in conflict with it.

In what sense, then, can Christ's sacrifice atone for our sins? Sin is something we can experience fully enough: a narrow state of conflict in which our attachment to ill-adapted desires and beliefs brings us into sharp, painful conflict with the wider recognition of conditions. As St Paul puts it, "What I do is not what I want to do, but what I detest" (Rom 7:15). We can only emerge from such conflict by acknowledging the wider conditions, not only in the 'rational' part of ourselves that (at least abstractly) understands the wider conditions, but also in the 'sinful' part. As long as we remain in the positive feedback loop in which our experiences are interpreted in terms that reinforce that intractable conflict, sin and its associated conflict will continue. It is only the suffering represented by Christ's crucifixion that can jolt us into provisionality by making us aware of how out of tune we are with the conditions, starting us on a negative feedback loop in which we can adjust our desires and practical beliefs.

Jesus' crucifixion as a historical event thus did not, and cannot, magically change the cosmic settings so that, even if we carry on pretty much as we did before, all we have to do is 'believe' in his atonement and our original 'sin' will be removed. Sin is a matter we experience, and cannot be removed by magic, however abstracted, legalised, and socially reinforced the spell. But sin as we experience it can indeed be addressed, by the very means that Jesus' crucifixion shows us. It can be addressed by integration (or at-one-ment). Suffering accompanied by reflection can jolt us away from the rigid extremes and back into the Middle Way. Far from being an object of absolutised 'belief', the crucifixion can symbolise the very mechanism whereby we come to challenge such beliefs and find a more integrated faith.

But atonement in this sense is not something that Christ does for us. He merely offers an example. Integration is a *practice* in which we need to take steps to create the conditions of provisionality in ourselves. We can do this by working directly on our habitual levels of awareness (which depends on our states of mind and body) through such practices as meditation, or a variety of physical disciplines such as yoga. We can also do it through the arts, which enrich the range of meaning that we can draw on in our thinking. We can also work on integration of our beliefs through critical thinking and bias awareness. Any or all of these types of practice (which I have written about extensively elsewhere[99]) can contribute to raising the chances that when suffering strikes, we can respond to it positively and adaptively, bringing us back *at one* with others, our environment, and our own long-term interests. I will write more about such practices in chapter 8, and also more about their relationship to traditional Christian practices.

Atonement in traditional, belief-based Christianity is also inseparable from the key concepts of grace and salvation, both very much a product of the early Pauline shaping of Christian thought. The atonement is said to 'save' us from sin, together with its consequences of eternal punishment, by the grace of God. For Catholics, this then gives us the opportunity to earn our salvation by works, whilst for Protestants salvation is more typically attained through 'faith' (by which is usually meant belief) in the atonement. Either way, though, it is God's grace that ultimately saves us from a hell-fire that we would otherwise be taken to deserve.

God's grace, it seems to me, does relate to human experience – that is, of our egos not being entirely responsible for the process of integration. In some respects, 'effort' is required, but if that effort is too narrowly focused on particular goals, it can be self-defeating. Psychology talks of the 'hedonic treadmill' by which a desire for a particular goal can undermine its own attainment, by leading us to neglect the wider conditions that are required to enjoy what we seek. For example, a hard-working businessman who concentrates for many years on building up money for a comfortable retirement, may well find that by the time he gets there he has lost the capacity to enjoy that retirement, so accustomed is he to repressing the desire for immediate pleasure for the sake of an abstract idea of future reward. Instead, our efforts need to be punctuated by relaxation, and our periods of narrow focus balanced by space and time given to wider awareness. At such times, new recognitions can come to us that seem to lie beyond ourselves, and it is these that make integration possible.

God's grace is the energy of that alternative voice coming from wider conditions: a voice of warning, creativity, love, or conscience for example. We may even encounter that grace through religious experience, which may also seem to come 'from without'. But it is important not to confuse a grace that comes from beyond the *ego* – i.e. from beyond whatever narrow goals and identifications we may be focusing on at the moment – with a voice that comes from beyond experience. Even if that voice seems to speak in the tones of others, it is the voice of our own potential: the voice of the God archetype. We must recognise its necessary role in us in order to avoid projecting it prematurely outwards.

God's grace also *saves* us, but we need to beware of absolutised beliefs about what we are being saved from that arise only from a narrow, group-reinforced, left hemisphere predominance. We are saved from hell, but we do not know hell to be a state beyond death, or a lake of fire into which we are cast at the last judgement: these are symbols of what it feels like to be caught up in narrow, self-destructive closed feedback loops, 'eternal' only because of our impatience. We are saved from this by the wider motives we find in ourselves, which may take all kinds of unexpected forms. God speaks to us in mysterious ways.

Such salvation requires both faith (in the embodied sense I have been using the term in this book) and works. If we do not have confidence in the voice of the God archetype, we will not heed it, and shrink with fear back into our narrow ways. Similarly, though, if we do not act, we cannot be saved. That salvation may or may not happen at death or at the end of history – but we can experience it happening at every moment when we become aware of wider conditions, and beside that immediate experience, beliefs about future judgement become irrelevant.

So, Jesus does not save us, but Christ, the Middle Way archetype within all of us, does save us. At every moment it can save us from another hell of our own making, taking us a small step closer to the potential heaven offered by the grace of God. Christ within does this by at-one-ment, by integrating conflict. The positive acceptance of suffering represented by the crucifixion is an important part of this process – but so, as we shall see next, is the hope offered by the resurrection.

e. Resurrection and hope

We do not know whether or not Jesus was resurrected on the third day, but we do experience a more profound and much more common kind of resurrection, when out of every intransigent problem springs hope. Of course, we maintain many kinds of hope, but the most powerful is that which comes out of apparently lost situations, which are only a matter of despair because of the way we have been framing them. The resurrection stands for not only a reframing of death, but a reframing of all other human suffering.

If, indeed, as the gospel narratives insist, Jesus was resurrected, it was an odd kind of resurrection. For the resurrected Jesus, it seemed, delighted in teasing people's plodding certainties when resurrected even more than he did in life. Instead of confronting his disciples directly after his resurrection, he left them to discover an empty tomb and to be told the news by an angel[100]. When resurrected, he appears and disappears abruptly and unpredictably[101]. He is often not recognised at first, but only in retrospect or when he performs a characteristic gesture[102]. He can enter a room with a locked door[103]. He is at pains to point out that he is not a ghost, but a corporeal being who eats, can be touched, and bears the physical marks of the crucifixion[104], but in other respects he hardly follows the normal habits or limitations of an embodied person.

All of this suggests overwhelmingly that the resurrection of Christ is not a glorious certainty that we should believe in as a historical event, but rather a glorious uncertainty. When all seems lost in the old paradigm, when the paradigm shifts to a new way of understanding, we should only expect the unexpected. In amongst the possibilities remains the likelihood that all is lost, but there also remains grounds for hope – that even the most intractable conditions may yield when we are prepared to change our view of them. Incurable cancer may clear up. The certainties of Newtonian physics can give way to relativity. People separated by the entire mass of the earth can communicate instantaneously without leaving their bedrooms. A man from a race once enslaved can become president.

The new grounds of hope arise from the integration of energy associated with possibilities that were previously repressed. That means that, in archetypal terms, resurrection is created from the integration of the Shadow. That process of integration of the Shadow is represented in the non-scriptural Christian tradition of the harrowing of Hell. Between the crucifixion and resurrection, it is traditionally believed, Christ descended to Hell, bound Satan, and rescued the Old Testament prophets who had been damned purely due to original sin, regardless of their personal merits. One can see this, of course, as a medieval theological invention designed to explain away an awkward implication of atonement: that nobody who lived before Jesus could be saved, no matter how good or faithful. However, that development also has a positive symbolic function which we could perhaps interpret rather as removing the apparatus of original sin and damnation entirely: when we engage in the integrative mediation represented by Christ, we are freed from the Hell of the constricted ego.

For Jung, the harrowing of Hell has a close relationship with the psychological function of the resurrection:

> *The present is a time of God's death and disappearance. The myth says he was not to be found where his body was laid. "Body" means the outward, visible form, the erstwhile but ephemeral setting for the highest value. The myth further says that the value rose again in a miraculous manner, transformed. It looks like a miracle, for, when a value disappears, it always seems to be lost irretrievably. So it is quite unexpected that it should come back. The three days' descent*

> *into hell during death describes the sinking of the vanished value into the unconscious, where, by conquering the power of darkness, it establishes a new order, and then rises up to heaven again, that is, attains supreme clarity of consciousness. The fact that only a few people see the Risen One means that no small difficulties stand in the way of finding and recognising the transformed value.*[105]

The prime Christian virtues are faith, hope and love: but all of these are founded, not on absolutising beliefs, but on the recognition of uncertainty. Faith, as already discussed in the second section, depends on embodied confidence. 'Doubting' Thomas was not wrong to seek embodied experience as the basis of his faith, and Jesus treats his need with understanding[106]. We might be better to call him Faithful Thomas. Faith projects that confidence forward into what we have not experienced yet, but hope goes further in offering possibilities that we could not justify faith in. Love (or charity) depends on maintaining a flexible and rounded view of others, who are neither instruments nor obstacles to us, but rather persons. All three of these virtues, then, are dependent on provisionality, and none of them can be practised without the Middle Way. But hope is the most forward of them all, the most alive to mere possibility. Hope springs most of all from the flexibility of the imagination, and is constrained by the iron repression of belief. That is why it is so ironic that the resurrection, so much a symbol of hope, should have become an object of metaphysical belief and thus undermined hope.

f. Pentecost and the Holy Spirit

According to the Biblical account, however, divine inspiration in human affairs did not cease with the final ascension of Christ. In the gospel of John, Jesus is already depicted as talking of the 'advocate' or *paraclete* he will leave behind in his stead:

> *I will ask the Father, and he will give you another to be your*

> *advocate, who will be with you for ever – the Spirit of truth. The world cannot accept him, because the world neither sees not knows him; but you know him, because he dwells with you and will be in you.* (Jn 14:16-17)

Dwelling with us and in us, this spirit (the Holy Spirit) must be a central part of our experience. It is nevertheless a distinct part of our experience from the Father and the Son, and becomes more necessary and important when we are no longer directly in touch with the Son. From the accounts that follow in the rest of the New Testament, it seems clear that the Holy Spirit represents states of temporary integration: inspiration or religious experience that is dependent on certain conditions to arise, but nevertheless provides a powerful reminder of, and motivator towards, integration. It is the "Spirit of truth", not because it tells us true beliefs, but because it puts us in states of wider awareness where we are more likely to overcome delusions and address new conditions.

The relationship between the three persons of the Trinity – Father, Son and Holy Spirit – thus seems to be that between potential integration (the Father), long-term integration (the Son), and temporary integration (the Holy Spirit). In Buddhism this might be put as the relationship between Awakening, Insight and Dhyana. All three of the persons are powerful symbols *because* they represent different aspects of our experience of spiritual and moral challenge. We get glimpses of how we might potentially be in a full state of integration (the Father), but we sustainably move towards this by the Middle Way (the Son). But we also get less sustainable states of integration dependent only on particular conditions that can remind us of integration and give us motivation to practise (the Holy Spirit). When we slip away from the long-term path, putting ourselves in conditions that can encourage a temporary burst of integration can really help us to re-connect.

The Holy Spirit descends on the disciples at Pentecost, often seen as the founding event of the Christian church.

> *Suddenly there came from the sky what sounded like a strong, driving wind, a noise that filled the whole house where they were sitting. And there appeared to them flames like tongues of fire distributed among them and coming to rest on each one. They were all filled with the Holy Spirit and began to talk in other tongues, as the spirit gave them power of utterance.* (Acts 2:2-4)

The wind and the fire are powerful ways of symbolising experiences of temporary integration: religious experience of the kind discussed in 2.b above, most likely involving greater access to the right hemisphere, deautomatisation, and stimulation of a strong sense of meaning from the limbic system. Wind is associated with God as spirit and with creativity, going back to God breathing life in to Adam. Wind is also a core part of our embodied experience because of its close association with breathing, and focus on the breathing is a common and often highly effective form of meditation that widens our attention from the habitual obsessive narratives of the language centres in our left hemisphere's frontal cortex. Fire, on the other hand, is closely associated with energy: the surge of energy we are likely to feel when conflicts in our experience are suspended and the whole of our motive is given to a new unifying focus.

Wind and fire also have a symbolic association with flexibility and thus with provisionality. As one ascends up the four traditional 'elements' (or material states) from earth, to water, to air, and then to fire, one also moves from rigid to gradually more flexible states of relationship with the world. John the Baptist says of Jesus "I have baptised you with water; he will baptise you with the Holy Spirit" (Mk 1:8) suggesting an association between higher forms of spirituality and greater provisionality. Disciples inspired by the Holy Spirit are temporarily able to bring more of themselves: to access more meaning, more energy, more love, more wisdom, because the repressions that more typically block these things have been removed. This may happen spontaneously, or may arise as a result of prayer or meditation that relaxes habitual patterns of obsessive association. In the case of the apostles we are only told that they were "all together in one place" (Acts 2:1), which makes it likely that they were engaged in prayer.

Such temporary integration is very often a private and individual experience, but what seems particularly extraordinary about this occasion is that it was shared, and resulted in a burst of communication that assumed a new energy and universality. We do not really know what "began to talk in other tongues" means, though the following section of the Acts account[107] portrays the surprise of a range of foreigners at hearing their own languages spoken. As in other places where miraculous events are said to occur, agnosticism about the precise historical events is by far the best policy, so as to avoid premature acceptance or rejection of a meaning that relates to our own experience. We do not know whether the apostles suddenly gained the ability to speak languages that were previously unknown to them, but it is easier to understand how a state of temporary integration could equip them with a new inspiration and a new universality in communication.

The experience of such inspiration as being 'other' or as coming from without is also illustrated in Jeremiah: 'Then the Lord stretched out his hand, and touching my mouth, said to me, "See, I put words into your mouth"' (Jer 1:9). The words we find in our mouths at such moments are all the more eloquent, and speak more directly to people because they are not pre-rehearsed or pre-formulated. Rather they draw on the whole range of meaning available to us, including what is intuitive or unconsciously acquired rather than only what fits into a pre-set left hemisphere model. Speaking 'from the heart' (or from our right hemispheres) we are also far more likely to be universal, because we are responding instantaneously to our audience and the particular things they need to hear. The most skilled speakers can give every auditor the sense that they have heard what they most needed to hear because of that flexibility and spontaneity.

A less charitable interpretation of the events of Pentecost is that they consisted of some kind of group hysteria: the very same kind of group hysteria that appears to often pass for religious experience in the more modern Pentecostalist movement. Group hysteria should not be confused with temporary integration, for it does not involve the expansion of individual awareness then shared in a group, but rather a shortcut: the authority of the group triggering a type of shared behaviour through conscious or unconscious suggestion. In such a state of hysteria, the state of energy that people enter into is primarily created by the temporary breaking of barriers with other members of the group in a shared sense of purpose – the same mentality that emerges in a riot. It is characterised by cognitive biases associated with groups, such as groupthink (people repress alternative beliefs not shared by the group), social proof (people take positive cues about what to believe from others rather than experience) and false consensus (the assumption that everyone else believes what the group believes)[108].

Perhaps the most probable scenario, given the complex mixture of human states and motives, is that the original Pentecost, like its more recent imitators, contained a mixture of temporary integration and hysteria. However, in our own judgements it is extremely important to separate the two, and to interpret Pentecost (when it is a source of symbolic inspiration) in terms of the former rather than the latter. Temporary integration can be an extremely helpful support to provisionality, provided only that it does not become an end in itself, and is invested in longer-term integration. Hysteria, on the other hand, is a left hemisphere shortcut that can move people to act in ways that merely reinforce limited judgements. The emotional tone may feel expansive, but the assumptions on which they are based are not. Hysteria does not support or promote the Middle Way values I identified in Jesus' teaching in 5.c: synthesis, integration, universality, scepticism, provisionality, love or balance. At best, hysteria bonds a group around absolutised ideas, but the bonding ends with the bounds of the group and makes it more likely to conflict with other groups.

The Pentecost experience is the prime inspiration behind Christian evangelism to this day. The language of evangelism reflects Biblical metaphors that were once alive, and may still sometimes be experienced with the freshness of right hemisphere experience accessed through temporary states of integration. However, modern evangelism is overwhelmingly associated with dead left-hemisphere language: repeat a phrase like "the living word" too often and it very quickly becomes the dead word, focused only on the instrumentality of winning converts and instilling belief. The mass hysteria whipped up by evangelists at rallies or services can hardly compensate for that deadness, when the living experience of inspiration is only counterfeited in a way that is dependent on the group's presence. Faith, as opposed to belief, can only be cultivated incrementally on the basis of a growth of individual integration – which can only then be shared with the group and supported by it, and the only kind of evangelism that can be of service to the world supports faith, not mere belief. It can only do that through a slow, receptive, and provisional approach to communication.

7

Christian agnosticism

a. The courageous faith of uncertainty

How can a Christian be agnostic? What are the implications? In this chapter I am aiming to bridge the gap between the explorations of the Bible so far and the practical issues discussed in the final chapters. Christian judgements today are not just a question of interpreting the Bible, nor of merely meeting immediate needs. Instead, there are a great many pressures from other approaches: other religions, science, psychology, atheism and feminism, to name only some of them. In addition to this, the divisions within Christianity that have emerged over the centuries have not yet been decisively put aside. Does an agnostic Christian necessarily belong to some denominations or schools of thought and not others? Is agnosticism another manifestation of 'liberalism' or 'post-modernism'? I will be addressing these kinds of issues in the pages that follow.

Let me begin by re-iterating some of the central points about sceptical argument and its interpretation, which I find are usually unfamiliar to most Christians. As I have argued above, God is, for us, a matter of potential, not knowledge, and thus profoundly uncertain. Our response to God is thus closely aligned to our response to uncertainty itself. To respect God's holiness is thus to respect uncertainty. However, what is usually missed in Western philosophical discussions of uncertainty and sceptical argument is the quality of *even-handedness*: the recognition that negative claims are just as uncertain as positive ones, and that uncertainty is in no sense a cloaked form of denial. Instead, we need to identify the recognition of uncertainty as implying provisionality, starting from our embodied position, and seeking better and more integrated judgements that avoid false certainty on both sides.

Even-handedness leads to agnosticism. We see the limitations of an absolute view, but rather than rushing to the opposite – a relative view or an opposed absolute view – we also ask ourselves whether the alternative is subject to the same problems we find in the first view. If we look closely, and pause in a moment of awareness before rushing from one rejected group to the welcoming arms of an opposed group, we are likely to find the same weaknesses in every absolute view, positive or negative. Denying the existence of God gets us no further than dogmatic acceptance of it. Determinism is no less dogmatic than freewill. Materialism is just as dogmatic as belief in the soul. So, we avoid the whole framing of these debates along with the conflicts that come with that framing: we leave them aside and focus on more helpful kinds of thinking. That is agnosticism, recognising that we don't know.

There are several misunderstandings about agnosticism in widespread circulation. One is that agnosticism is in some way confused, vague, or indecisive. This is very far from being the case. Agnostics are courageous enough to face up to uncertainty, not only about God, but about any other kind of absolute claim. Their confidence in their position needs to come, not from any kind of metaphysical abstraction, but rather from the grounding of uncertainty in embodied experience. To be embodied is to lack shortcuts to 'reality', because we have to take our best guess at every turn based on the limited information offered by our senses. To accept our embodiment is to accept that everything we believe is interpreted – which is precisely why it is meaningful for us. To be confident in that embodied experience, we need to be quite clear about resisting claims that have no justifiable relationship to the values we experience – which means refusing either 'beliefs' or their denial when these are based only on dogmatic assumptions. That is agnosticism.

It is the people who go along with the group and its easy

shortcut abstractions that are the ones lacking courage, not the agnostics. It is those who can be seduced by metaphysical talk who are vague and confused, not the agnostics. It is those who cannot make up their minds to stand on their own experience and (where necessary) defy baseless claims of authority that are indecisive, not the agnostics.

Sometimes philosophers of religion distinguish between two types of agnosticism: strong and weak agnosticism (or hard and soft agnosticism). A weak agnostic is waiting for further evidence to confirm absolute or metaphysical claims, and thus does not rule out 'believing' them in future. However, the weak agnostic could be in for a pretty long wait – until doomsday or beyond, in fact. The weak agnostic has not really accepted one of the key conditions involved in agnosticism, which is that there are no shortcuts to justify beliefs that go beyond experience. If you expect certainty in the future, you have not yet really accepted uncertainty. It is only hard or strong agnosticism that has faced up to the power of sceptical argument, and I want to go further here and suggest that strong agnosticism is at the core of faith.

My argument so far should have shown that this recognition is compatible with the insights of Jesus, and that these build on insights that go back to the Pentateuch. It should also show that the spiritual role of Christ, as well as that of the Father and the Holy Spirit, depends on the same recognition of uncertainty, interpreted with even-handedness. That argument depends on a particular interpretation of the Bible and Christian tradition that is justified, not by historical claims, but by pragmatism. It is an attempt to respond to the balance of conditions that affect us as embodied human beings, with practical beliefs and desires and with two brain hemispheres with differing specialisations. The archetypal roles of Father, Son and Holy Spirit emerge directly from that embodied situation rather than only from scriptural authority taken in the abstract, even though the scriptures can give a particular Christian form to these universal concerns.

However, Christian culture, even since the time of the early Church, has clearly contained strong elements of absolutism. Although the absolute status of the Biblical law was rejected, eschatological beliefs took their place as a focus of certainty from early times. From the time of Constantine, too, political and religious authorities became more closely aligned, creeds were developed, and scriptural canons finalised. From that time, then, various combinations of scripture, church authorities, tradition, dogma, and (later) appeals to selective reason and natural law became the basis of Christian absolutism. Absolutism does not depend on political power, but it is a tool of power – a shortcut to group support. Even now that the era of the unquestioned Christian state is largely over, the absolutism that accompanied it is not, because Christian churches still struggle with each other and with all other religions and philosophies to win converts to their 'beliefs' in the private sphere.

It was that absolutism, rather than 'religion' in general, that produced the excesses of the Crusades, the Inquisition, the forced Christianisation of the Americas, the Thirty Years' War and other wars of religion, but that hardly means that these historical examples do not need a Christian response. In every case, violence and conflict would not have occurred without an intractable conflict between absolute beliefs, between groups, within groups and within individuals. This past record of repression offers no grounds for wholesale dismissal of Christianity, but it does contain strong warnings. If Christianity has not been responsible for so much blood-letting in the modern era, this is not because Christianity has ceased to be absolutist, but rather because it has changed its sphere and mode of influence. Rather than operating through the power of the state, the modern model of religion has embedded itself into public discourse through privatisation. It has an interdependent relationship with a model of a secular public space that allows absolute belief as long as it is a harmless 'personal choice'.

For Christianity to avoid this absolutism requires an upending of widespread assumptions about religion – that is, for 'faith' to come to mean a recognition of uncertainty rather than being a cloaking term for 'belief' that actually means an assumption of the truth of a metaphysical claim that can only be discontinuously true or false.

A religion based on uncertainty is no rival with other religions, or with any other view of the world that is likewise based on uncertainty. As long as the Middle Way is the underlying model for the interpretation of religion, there is no clash of incompatible absolutes, but merely a cultural preference of forms dependent on background, like the language one speaks or the clothes one wears. Such religion can be acknowledged in the public sphere without conflict.

In subsequent chapters in this section, I shall be exploring how this understanding of religion can work helpfully with other religions, between different denominations, with science, psychology, atheism and feminism. Before I do that, however, I want to explore the ways in which agnosticism is already deeply rooted in a Christian tradition that runs through almost its entire history – that of mysticism.

b. The mystical tradition

The mystical tradition is one that prioritises religious experience, its cultivation and application, above other priorities such as theology, church organisation, or ritual. That doesn't mean that mystics necessarily excluded themselves from these other activities, or that they were necessarily unorthodox; but it does mean that when they engaged in more 'outward' activity, they tended to do so in a way that valued the flexibility that comes from direct experience of integrative states rather than operating out of a rule book.

Quite a range of great Christians of the past have been called 'mystics', including such contrasting figures as St Augustine of Hippo (who was an influential bishop and theologian), Meister Eckhart (who was put on trial for heresy), St Mechtild of Magdeburg (a humble figure who described herself as "a poor despised little woman") and Hildegard of Bingen (who was a visionary and artist, as well as an abbess). Interestingly enough it most often seems to be male mystics who were inclined to be distracted by metaphysical belief and the accompanying struggles for power that this created (whether they were on the side of the established church or of 'heresy' in pursuing them), whilst there a greater number of impressive female mystics who focused much more completely on experience, and became impressively integrated figures as a result. Some mystics were more mystical than others, but it is in the more mystical ones that we can find a considerable practical reliance on the Middle Way.

I want to suggest seven main ways in which the Christian mystical tradition has at least partially maintained the Middle Way of faith and kept the reductions of absolute belief at bay. Though all these ways are rarely found together in the same individual, they can each offer helpful inspiration, and together create a composite picture of the implications of the Middle Way in Christ.

1. Agnostic views of God
2. A positive view of the body
3. The cultivation of integrated states
4. Integrative understanding of the role of love and wisdom
5. Identification of God and/or Christ with the self
6. A practice of humility
7. The nurturing of creativity

1. Agnostic views of God

One influential early mystic who shows considerable use of the Middle Way is Dionysius the Areopagite, or 'Pseudo-Dionysius', who took the name of a character in Paul's letters but was actually probably a Syrian monk of the fifth or sixth century. Dionysius stresses that we do not know God, and indeed cannot know anything about God: though strangely enough (perhaps to avoid heresy) he also claimed that we can know God's revelations[109]. Nevertheless, this recognition of the significance of God lying in *not knowing* him is the start of what became known as the *via negativa,* or apophatic mysticism. This offers an example of scepticism and provisionality like that of Jesus applied to the interpretation of Christian religious experience.

However, it's ironic that throughout the long history of the *via negativa,* most Christians have been unable to take 'not knowing' at its word as such, but rather have insisted on interpreting 'not knowing' as actually some ultimate type of knowing. It was often thought that to get to some underlying metaphysical truth you might have to purge the distractions of mere appearance, and that is an approach taken by philosophers such as Descartes as well as mystics. God was always apparently seen as a 'reality', perhaps due to a pervasive Platonic influence on Christianity, even if that 'reality' was different from everyday 'reality'. This pervasive belief to this day stands in the way of recognising God as simply part of how we understand and engage with the world, rather than as a 'thing' either in or parallel to 'things' in the world.

Even psychologists who have analysed mystical experience have not been able to let go of the assumption that such experience gives us 'knowledge': thus, for example, William James defines mystical experience as *noetic* (having the quality of giving knowledge) as well as necessarily passive and necessarily authoritative over the individual[110]. Though I'm a great admirer of James' work in some other respects, I can't think of a case where an influential individual has so thoroughly misunderstood what he was studying. Not only is mystical experience the opposite of 'noetic', but rather than 'passive' it requires a balance of effort (an openness coupled with a clear general intention), and rather than being 'authoritative' over them, it greatly empowers the experiencer in confidently making their own judgements.

Christian agnosticism has been under constant pressure from the cognitive obsessions of the establishment throughout its history, whether these came from the church hierarchy or more recently from scientific expectations: so it is hardly surprising if the explicit understanding of agnosticism in Christian tradition is less well developed than it is, for example in Buddhism (particularly Nagarjuna), the *neti neti* (not this, not that) of Vedanta, or the balanced scepticism of Pyrrho and his followers. However, that a lot of the same tendencies are there is testament simply to the structure of the human brain: whether you're a medieval Christian, a Hellenistic Greek, a Buddhist or a Hindu, you will have a right hemisphere capable of developing awareness that potentially questions the cognitive over-assertions of the left.

2. A positive view of the body

One of the key starting points for a more thorough-going agnosticism is the recognition that meaning of all kinds is based in the body, as already discussed in 2.a at the beginning of this book. Our sensual, emotional, and imaginative experiences are not second-class meanings to be judged as dependent for their meaning on the cognitive representations of certain areas of the left frontal lobe. Rather, we experience all kinds of meaning directly. Meaning arises primarily from the limbic system, but draws on many other areas of the brain and body, and is a prior condition for cognition rather than a subsidiary dependency on it. We need to be agnostic precisely because there are many areas of experience whose meaning is best appreciated without reduction to 'knowing' of some kind. A positive view of the human body and its value helps us to appreciate that meaning as worthwhile in itself, even if we do not take on the more intellectual task of formally challenging the cognitive ascendancy in the way that Dionysius did.

In the tradition of Christian mysticism, that positive view of the body is associated with an appreciation of Christ's incarnation: it comes from what has become known as the Christocentric strand of mysticism as opposed to the theocentric. It's only by genuinely embracing the limitations of the human condition, as Christ did, that some integration can be achieved, some movement towards God. Embracing those limitations means embracing our dependency on the senses, our vulnerability, our sinfulness, even our bodily excrescences: for it's only in that context, not in a divine or perfect context, that God can really start to mean something for us.

One example of a mystic for whom this kind of corporeality was important was Angela of Foligno, a lay Franciscan follower of the late 13th century. She wrote of being able to see, feel, touch and smell in new ways because of her identification with Christ's body. More than anything she felt an intense bodily love for Christ[111]. The sexual aspects of the relationship of celibate female mystics with Christ can be understood as sublimations of sexual energy, but are no less embodied for that. This sublimated sexuality was formalised later by Theresa of Avila as 'mystical marriage'.

A more recent female mystic who understood the grace of God in a way that is thoroughly channelled through the phenomenology of the body was Simone Weil. Weil was a philosopher before she was a mystic, developing a phenomenology of the body similar to that of Merleau-Ponty before encountering religious experiences that led her to try to reconcile phenomenology with Christian grace through an understanding of the body communicating a divine 'reality' that abstraction could not. As Lissa McCullough summarises this:

In Weil's thinking, the imaginative body is that actively sentient,

> *perceptively empowered portion of matter that first and continually engages the environ, delineates order, construes and specifies the data of reality, suffers necessity, arbitrates all important decisions pertaining to action, mediates real, existentially necessary relationships for thought to think, and in the process incarnates faith.*[112]

However, this degree of Christian mystical acceptance of the body is unfortunately overshadowed by a strong counteracting body-denying tendency in Christian tradition, which is particularly revealed in ascetic practices such as flagellation, in the denial of sexuality as 'sinful', in puritanism and hypocrisy about the body. Many of these attitudes go back to the early church, but are much more attributable to Platonic beliefs in the proper ascendancy of the 'rational soul' over the body than to biblical attitudes. The over-dominant left hemisphere tends to regard the body as a mere instrument for the will, and thus 'sinful' desires as disobedience to 'reason' – creating a whole cycle whereby spirituality and ethics alike are only understood in terms of the use of power. As I shall discuss further in 7.g, one of the other unfortunate effects of this Platonic element has been misogyny.

The number of mystics with a positive view of the body is thus unfortunately dwarfed and overshadowed by the number who were at war with it.

3. The cultivation of integrated states

The mystics often describe states of ecstasy – which are temporary states of integration as already discussed in relation to the Holy Spirit. These states, as well as longer-term integration, could be cultivated though spiritual exercises. Even though it was appreciated that God's grace was required to go into ecstasy, one could also prepare the ground for it, making oneself receptive to God. Dividing a spiritual path into a number of stages was a common form of mystical writing.

Perhaps the best-known spiritual exercises are those of Ignatius Loyola, the early sixteenth century founder of the Jesuit Order, in the book of that name. Loyola had a military background, so used knightly metaphors of Christian training and service. Thus while he recognised the element of God's grace in all spiritual development, he was not afraid to approach it with deliberate effort and discipline. The *Spiritual Exercises* offer an orderly programme of contemplation and self-scrutiny over forty days[113]. Loyola's mysticism was very practical in intention, and the Jesuits became well-known for rigorous training followed by hard service, often in missionary work to distant places. This 'methodical' approach to the cultivation of integrated states for social service is also characteristic of John Wesley, the founder of Methodism in the eighteenth century.

Of course, the fact that one attempts to cultivate integration in a disciplined way does not necessarily guarantee high levels of success. In the cases of both Jesuits and Methodists, I would suggest that devotion to spiritual progress may often be undermined by dogmas of belief. Unless integrative training includes enough attention to provisionality, allowing balanced effort of a kind that allows integrated states to arise rather than just wilful repressive states premised on a goal, there is a danger that a lot of hard work will simply create a sunk costs fallacy. The more one has worked at something, the harder it is to let go of it. But at least the idea of working at it is present.

4. Integrative understanding of the role of love and wisdom

A great many Christian mystics have put a lot of emphasis on the encompassing experience of God's love. Clearly, mystical divine love is an open emotion, in which provisionality is maintained in the bliss of universal acceptance, temporarily taking the place of narrow judgement of oneself and others.

The experience of God's love was often the basis of ecstasy, but it could also be combined with a huge perspective. Julian of Norwich experienced everything in the world as the size of a hazelnut, vulnerable yet sustained by the love of God.

One of the clearest indications that mystical love was seen as an integrative emotion can be seen in St Bernard of Clairvaux's analysis of four degrees of love, in ascending order:

1. Loving ourselves for our own sake
2. Loving God for our own sake
3. Loving God for his sake
4. Loving ourselves for God's sake[114]

Here we must assume 'our own sake' to mean a narrow view of ourselves, while 'loving God' is a much wider, universal emotion. The four stages show a widening set of concerns. The first move is from a narrow identification to a wider one on the grounds that the wider will eventually serve the narrower (what's often called 'enlightened self-interest'). The second move (from 2 to 3) begins to see wider concerns as valuable in themselves. However, at that point there is a danger of leaving one's more significant feelings behind and merely getting temporarily carried away by unintegrated enthusiasm for the idea of loving God. The final stage is to recognise our own narrow concerns and maintain them, but see them within a wider context at the same time. This final move of Bernard's seems psychologically acute.

Anything we can say about integrative love also applies just as much to divine wisdom. Hildegard of Bingen made wisdom her life's concern, but there seems to have been a general recognition that in the end, there is no distinction between love and wisdom. This indicates a synthetic approach in medieval mysticism similar to that discussed above in relation to Jesus.

5. Identification of God and/or Christ with the self

Christian mysticism clearly shows an approach to God that has got beyond the mere projection of the divine to an object beyond oneself more commonly found in popular Christianity. Instead, God and Christ are functioning as integrated archetypes when they are experienced as oneself or the whole of one's experience.

Meister Eckhart identifies God with the self and with the whole of one's experience. Rather like Jung or a Vedantin, he sees God as a divine spark in the centre of the soul, providing a potential for unity. The 'birth of God in the soul' is brought about by withdrawal and spiritual cultivation. The self can then be absorbed into God, just as God is absorbed into the self[115].

Hildegard of Bingen also talks in a similar way about the identification of the self with God, or as Christ as a creative force in the universe.

> *I, the fiery life of divine essence, am aflame beyond the beauty of the meadows. I gleam in the waters. I burn in the sun, moon and stars. With every breeze, as with invisible life that contains everything, I awaken everything to life.*[116]

6. A practice of humility

The practice of humility has been incorporated into Christian mysticism from the monastic tradition, and, when pursued with sincerity rather than formalistically, can offer a ready basis of provisionality. A genuinely humble person realises that they do not have the whole story, although if they have also subordinated themselves to authority they may at the same time assume that the authority (typically, in medieval Catholicism, the Pope) does have the whole story.

One of the great models of the practice of humility is St Francis of Assisi, whose major achievement was the founding of a new kind of monastic – the Franciscan friars, who were homeless mendicants without the wealth or vested interests of the existent monasteries. In a famous episode early in his life, Francis is said to have exchanged clothes with a beggar and lived as the beggar for a day.

At the same time, the foundation of a new order is not the act of a one-sidedly humble person. Francis undertook a journey to Rome to persuade the pope to support his new venture, which he would hardly have succeeded in without a good deal of confidence. Humility without integration can simply consist in passivity and weakness, but figures like St Francis show that in the Christian tradition it was possible to find a balance, particular to each embodied situation, between the openness of humility and the assertiveness of leadership.

7. The nurturing of creativity

A final sign that the Christian mystical tradition has developed people's integration is the creativity that some mystics have exhibited: they show courageous individuality – which in the case of medieval mystics is often in stark contrast to most of the surrounding society. Such authenticity can develop with integrative practice because more of one's own energies are able to be united in the development of a new plan or project. One takes genuine responsibility for one's creation and thus avoids merely copying or reacting against the work of others. That individuality is shown by mystics in their writings, in their devotion to new initiatives in practical life, and sometimes in art, as well as in the rest of their lives.

The creativity of Hildegard of Bingen is one of the most outstanding examples: her *Scivias* describes twenty-six visions, but also accompanies these accounts with thirty-six miniature paintings. At the same time she founded two new convents and did much travelling and preaching. Her creativity is outstanding but not unique. Nearly every well-known mystic became known because of their writings, and some because they became known in the wider life of the world. St Catherine of Siena tried to broker peace between Florence and the Papacy, and also to persuade the Pope to return from Avignon to Rome – immensely bold political initiatives for a woman of the fourteenth century.

This list of seven integrative aspects of Christian mysticism is unlikely to be complete in accounting for all the helpful aspects of this huge and varied tradition. However, it should give some indication of the huge fund of inspiration that Christians can find for Christ as the Middle Way in the many great figures of their own tradition. None of these figures, whether they have been canonised or not, offers a perfect model: but humanly imperfect models are actually more effective models for faith than idealised ones. We can see each of the mystics as succeeding much more in some areas than others, as illustrating asymmetrical degrees of integration. But that is how humans make progress.

c. Universality and other religions

Somewhat inspired by the example of Jesus, I'm going to start this section with a parable.

An American was visiting Israel for the first time. In fact, it was the first time that he'd been abroad at all. Unlike many of his compatriots (that's an advance apology for stereotyping), this particular American was rather naïve and not very well educated.

As soon as he arrived at Tel Aviv airport, he was welcomed by a distant relative who was a settled Israeli. The Israeli took the American to a local bar for a drink.

"I'll pay for this," said the American generously, and he offered the bartender a $10 bill. The drinks were listed on the menu and came to 8 shekels.

"Sorry, sir, I don't accept dollars," said the bartender. "You'll need to pay in shekels. That will be 8 shekels."

"What do you mean, you don't accept dollars? That's money, isn't it? And what are these shekels you're talking about?"

"Shekels are the currency of Israel" explained the Israeli. "You're

not in America any more. You need to pay in local currency."

"Not on your life!" cried the American. "I'll pay in real money or not at all!"

"If you go to the exchange counter just over there," said the bartender politely and helpfully, "They'll give you shekels for your dollars. It'll only take a minute. Then you can pay me in shekels."

"No way!" said the American. "I'm not exchanging good dollars for bits of paper!" At that he stormed out. His Israeli relative was obliged to pay for the drinks after all.

In the world of international travel to which we've become accustomed, the American seems both ignorant and unreasonable. Different countries use different currencies. For a variety of reasons, both economic and cultural, they don't all use dollars. We accept this arrangement as a matter of course. We would no more refuse to pay in roubles in Russia or yen in Japan than we would use a screwdriver to hammer in a nail.

OK, now for 'currencies' substitute 'religions', and for 'paying for drinks' substitute whatever you consider the goals of religion to be – let's say, for the sake of argument, salvation. Supposing the American had not been in a bar but in a synagogue, but refused to accept that a synagogue was a religious building on the grounds that he was a Christian and that only Christianity was the true religion leading to salvation. Would that be any more reasonable?

Presumably an absolutist Christian should say 'yes' here, and claim that the two scenarios are entirely different and my analogy irrelevant. Religion is different from currency, she will say, because religion is *true* (or false), whereas currency is just a convention, so one does not admit falsehood by using a foreign currency. Alternatively, she might argue that the only thing that's unreasonable in the synagogue scenario is the refusal to recognise religions other than Christianity as religions. You can show basic civility for practical reasons, she might argue, whilst still thinking the other religion is false. The American can do whatever it's polite to do in a synagogue, whilst inwardly reflecting on the falsehood of Judaism.

But even the latter approach is still, if not contradictory, at least productive of conflict and hypocrisy. It faces us with Christians who have friendly relationships with their neighbours whilst apparently believing that they will go to hell. It obliges us to completely ignore all the similarities between religions (and those between Judaism and Christianity are especially obvious) and focus only on the differences, whilst ignoring the huge differences within one religion, so that we can really believe in the efficacy of the label 'Christian' for making all that difference. It also obliges us to ignore all the other things religion does (social, mythic, ethical, ritual, experiential) and the functional resemblances they provide between religions, and focus only on the bit that is magically supposed to produce salvation – presumably the acceptance of Jesus' atonement. Some extremely complex boundaries are made far too simple.

What's the alternative? Well, religious relativism is not much more coherent. If we believe that all religions equally lead to salvation for their own followers, we also ignore differences between religions whereby some may be better than others. There's also a problem of defining 'religion' – does worship of football lead to salvation? Then, what about individuals who leave one religion and join another? Are they saved despite now being in the 'wrong' religion? Or are all individuals saved anyway? (In which case why bother with religion?). In relativism, you have still adopted the over-simplified, essentialised account of religion used by absolutists, and tried to use it relatively – which fails to remove the problems caused by the way religion was understood in the first place.

Instead of this conventional false dilemma between two opposed but counter-dependent sets of assumptions, I want to suggest, of course, that the Middle Way is what we need. The

Middle Way solves the problem of universality between religions without dismissing religion altogether, and without assuming that all religions are of equal value.

To explain how this works, let's go back to the currency analogy. Let's assume that all religions are like currencies, in the sense that they have value for the people in a place where they can use that religion. If they go to another place (mentally or physically, or both) they may need another religion – or they may not. Christianity is thus of value for people we might describe either as Christians in the full sense or (like me) cultural Christians. They might go away and use Buddhism instead for a while (as I did), but they can always come back and use Christianity instead.

However, if you switch between Buddhism and Christianity, or Judaism and Christianity, or any other combination, it's immensely complicated working out what the relationship is. Are they of equal value and it's "just a matter of personal choice"? Well, no, we can't assume they are of equal value. More importantly, we can't assume that different interpretations of a given religion are of equal value either. I really can't believe that a Muslim fundamentalist terrorist is getting as much of spiritual value from his religion as the Dalai Lama, or even as someone more spiritually developed in Islam such as a Sufi master.

As with currencies, the values of different religions (and of different interpretations of those religions) are not only different but fluctuating wildly. To measure them helpfully you need a comparison currency that is at least reasonably stable – that gives a measure of religious value without being a religion itself and thus subject to all sorts of complex factors. That's where the Middle Way comes in. The Middle Way operates as a kind of comparison currency that everyone can recognise and use to assess any religion or religious interpretation. More importantly, it offers a universal basis of value other than absolute appeals to having a sole basis of salvation (or a reduction to a mere social glue).

As I've been suggesting throughout this book, the Middle Way is universal, because it provides a criterion for judgement based on the avoidance of absolutes, whether positive or negative. If we can avoid absolutes, we are thrown back on experience, which is going to be much more adequate to the conditions around us than absolutes – which are just shortcuts involving the use of power and are creative of conflict. It is in experience that we find faith, hope, and love, along with a lot of other virtues that we can justify really valuing. It is in experience that we find flexible principles that work for the moment – but not a rigid Pharisaic law. It is in experience that we can find goals that we've really thought about and related to rather than abstract absolutisations. Avoiding absolutes removes the key blockage to integration, where we positively gather values that are backed up by a wider experience rather than a narrow one.

The Middle Way is universal because we all have the tendency to absolutise, but we also all have the potential of wider experience that we could become aware of – if we could quieten the nervous racket for a while. Absolutisation and wider experience are the products of the very architecture of our brains as humans – you can't get much more universal than that.

But that doesn't mean that the Middle Way is another religion, now competing with the others, which everyone should convert to, because it's got the real true universality now that the others didn't get. It's not as simple as that. The Middle Way isn't a religion, and creating a religion takes many centuries of work by many people. Religions don't just need a set of helpful ideas and practices, but also live symbols embedded in culture that people can relate to. That's why we need religion as well. No, the Middle Way works much better as a criterion for assessing religions and their interpretation, and for justifying their value, than it does as a religion itself.

In this book I have been attempting such an assessment of

Christianity. That means finding equivalents for the Middle Way so as to give the helpful and integrative aspects of Christianity full credit, but also making it clear what is unhelpful. You can see that as like setting a reserve currency equivalent. I've judged Christianity interpreted in terms of some key integrative teachings as rating high on the Middle Way scale, but a more typical belief-based Christianity as rating a good deal lower.

So now I can get to the key point of this section. If you're a Christian, how can you make comparisons with other religions and their value? Well, using the Middle Way as a standard, on the one hand you make a valuation (of the kind I've been attempting here) of the Christianity you try to practice, and then on the other, you also need to make a similar valuation of the other religion (again, based on a specific interpretation). By the time you've done that, you should be able to draw a reasonably confident justified conclusion about the relative merits of the two religious approaches. You won't know whether they'll get you to heaven or save you from hell, but you'll be able to make a confident judgement as to whether they'll help to make you and others more integrated, and thus more practically effective at addressing the wide variety of issues and conditions on this planet.

There is, of course, scope for other books making similar assessments of other world religions using the Middle Way, that might help you with such comparative judgements. I have in some ways already done such a job with Buddhism in an earlier book called *The Trouble with Buddhism* (though I now consider the assessment in it a bit crude in places, and it could do with revision). Someone needs to write books like this one on Judaism and Islam and Hinduism and so on – probably not me.

Any judgement about your involvement in a particular religious group, though, needs to take into account not only a general assessment of the merits of that particular interpretation of the religion concerned, but also your own needs, capacities, and symbolic resonances. Not only what's best, but what's best *for you now*. Particularity is not the same as relativism. There are a variety of options for you now, some of them better than others: they're not all the same. Only you are really in a position to assess your personal situation and discern the best one. But you can still use the Middle Way to help judge that, and thus gain greater justified confidence in the judgement you make.

d. Forks in the path: Christian divisions

There are a great many Christianities: Armenian, Coptic, Syrian, Orthodox, Catholic, Anglican and Protestant. Within Protestantism there is much further division between denominations, and even within the Orthodox Church there is much national differentiation. Perhaps more profound than these formal differences are the gulfs between different schools of thought, between liberal, conservative and fundamentalist forms of Christianity, often cutting across denominations. Very often, though, a great deal of division is a sign of fragility and hence of dogmatism, because Christians have disagreed on points that they took to be absolute and thus were unable to work together. Are the differences between types of Christianity thus a matter of indifference to anyone who seeks an integrative approach to Christian tradition?

Clearly they cannot be entirely a matter of indifference, since there can be no default or neutral account of what Christianity means and implies that does not involve accepting the cultural (and perhaps the theological) assumptions of one group or another. For those who, like me, come from a Christian cultural background, the starting point is also not neutral. 'Christianity' to me, unavoidable means predominantly the types of Christianity that I am most familiar with: which means the Baptist Church of my father, similar non-conformist churches such as the United Reformed Church and the Methodists, the Quakers (with whom I've had some past involvement), the Anglican Church because of its dominant position in the English culture in which I grew up, and the Catholic Church because of its wider dominance in West European culture of the past and present. It would involve false neutrality to assume that I can write about Christianity with indifference as to the differences between the non-conformist Protestant churches and the highly ethnicised churches of Greece and Russia, let alone of Syria or Armenia. In practising the Middle Way, we need to recognise our starting point and take that into account.

However, that does not imply religious relativism within Christianity any more than it does outside it. If the traditions of some churches can be more readily interpreted in an integrative way, then (taking into account how easy or difficult it would be for any one individual to work with those traditions), they are more likely to be preferable. For example, someone born within a Catholic context may find it easier to work within that context because of the power of that tradition for them, despite the obvious predominance of dogmatic beliefs in modern Catholicism. On the other hand, moving to a more liberal church may in other respects make it much easier for them to find an integrative path within Christianity. The ease with which one can access the raw material has to be weighed up against its malleability.

If the differences between churches are merely a matter of dogma, then this undoubtedly counts against them, as does a greater adherence to dogma in the present. However, any assessment of different churches in this respect has to be very approximate, because a given church may have integrative advantages in some respects that it lacks in others. A dogma that first strikes you as overwhelming (e.g. papal infallibility) may be softened by other integrative advantages (e.g. a stronger tradition of personal practice). So, what follows is an attempt to survey the 'forks in the path' - i.e. the key issues that have divided Christians and the possible arguments for following one fork rather than another. However, the limitations of any such survey as a guide to types of Christianity do need to be noted from the beginning. At worst, I hope, it may offer a starting point for further reflection in relation to your own experience of each church.

The Chalcedonian fork

The first fork in the path is that created by the Council of Chalcedon in 451 CE. This meeting of early church leaders followed up the Council of Nicaea of 325 CE and Council of Constantinople of 381 CE, each of which sought to resolve disputes about doctrine in the church, and each of which led to an increasingly explicit definition of the supposed metaphysical nature of Christ. Whilst the meetings of 325 and 381 produced the Nicene Creed that is still used in churches to this day, the 451 Council made the definition of the nature of Christ in the Nicene Creed still more explicit, stating that Jesus Christ is "At once complete in Godhead and complete in manhood.... recognised in two natures, without confusion, without change, without division, without separation...."[117].

These councils and their resolutions had been intended to remove conflicts in the church, and were instigated and supported by the emperors of the time who wanted a stable and unified church. The definition of Christ that they arrived at (as both completely divine and completely human) also has considerable advantages, precisely because of its defiance of Aristotelian logic, which may force people to engage with their experience of the ambiguities between ideals of perfection and human imperfection. However, the basic method adopted here – that of adopting a set of absolute beliefs that all must adhere to if they were to be accepted as Christians – was repressive and thus gave rise to more conflict.

It is hardly surprising, then, that it led to the first major split in the Church, in which monophysite, miaphysite and Nestorian churches[118] split off from the established 'Chalcedonian' church of the late Roman Empire. Monophysite churches, believing that Christ has only one (divine) nature, now include the Syrian Church and the Coptic Churches of Egypt and Ethiopia. The Armenian Church is miaphysite, meaning it believes that Christ has one nature but that it is both human and divine. Nestorian Churches, which believed that Christ has two natures but that they are not united, survive to this day but are much threatened in Iraq. The tendency of Christian fragility and fissiparousness was already set with the adherence to absolute 'belief' as the defining feature of Christianity.

However much we may deplore the overall assumptions that led to the split, however, they give no reason for preferring one side over the other. Both sides appear to share the assumption that entirely abstract metaphysical definitions of Christ are important in themselves, when they are very clearly merely tools of power. A monophysite interpretation makes no difference to the potential Middle Way function of Christ, because that function depends on the avoidance of metaphysical interpretation. Absolutising beliefs interfere with that Middle Way function because they interfere with our ability to engage with new conditions and values, and it makes no difference which particular absolutising beliefs we adopt. It is only when the Chalcedonian Definition allows us to understand and engage with the ambiguity between the divine and the human that it becomes potentially useful, but there is no reason why a monophysite definition should not play the same role, just as a non-Christian religious approach on the whole may do.

Whether you relate primarily to a Chalcedonian on non-Chalcedonian form of Christianity, then, is very likely to be simply a matter of your background, as it is for the vast majority of Christians. The Coptic, Syrian, Assyrian and Armenian Churches are highly ethnicised (as are also the Greek and Russian Orthodox Churches), and are thus not much more likely to attract converts from outside their traditional ethnic groups than are ethnic religions like Judaism or Hinduism.

What can be said, though, is that the introduction of creeds from this point in the history of Christianity brings in a highly destructive, toxic element. Creeds are very explicitly statements of absolute belief, and it is very hard to see how they could be reinterpreted to integrative effect. If you really 'believe' in the creed, you must reject alternative possibilities and believe that you have the final story: an approach that is completely opposed to the provisional spirit to be found in Jesus' teachings. This is simply an element that needs to be removed from Christianity if it is to become at all integrative rather than productive of endless conflict and repression. If you are in a Christian service when the creed is recited, I can only recommend silence.

The Orthodox-Roman fork

Fast forward to 1054 CE. At this point the Chalcedonian Church falls into two halves: the Greek-speaking East and the Latin-speaking West. Whilst all are still theoretically united by their adherence to the early councils, the Western part is ruled by a Pope who claims authority over the whole church. The Eastern Church, whilst recognising the Pope's administrative authority, takes that authority to be subject to the church councils and not extending to the modification of doctrine. In 1054 a dispute develops in which the Pope's authority is tested and rejected by the Eastern Church. Again this is a question of the metaphysical definitions of the creed: the Pope wished to insert a *filioque* ("... and the son") clause stating that the Holy Spirit proceeds from the Son as well as from the Father.

On this occasion, the use of metaphysical belief as a means of attempting to establish power is especially transparent. The *filioque* clause in itself made no difference to anything, except that it either showed the Pope's authority over the Eastern church or its absence. Once again, by insisting on a certain metaphysical doctrine, the power of one side was insisted upon and the result was a conflict and a split – this time between the Orthodox and Roman Catholic churches.

Once again, there is not a great deal to choose between the two sides. Whilst the Pope may have been the guilty party in directly creating the split through belief in his divinely-appointed power, both sides were equally absolute in their beliefs that the *filioque* clause either should or should not be part of the creed. Again, which side of the divide you find yourself is very likely to be a matter of background rather than abstract choice. Perhaps the main advantage of the Roman over the Orthodox side today is the universality that is enshrined in the very name 'catholic' (but is also shared by Protestants), and thus the avoidance of the degree of ethnicisation that is maintained in the Orthodox churches (Greek, Serbian, Russian, Bulgarian, Romanian etc.). In 5.c I discussed the universality of Jesus' teachings: a universality that the Pope's authority (whatever its other drawbacks) at least helped to establish in the Western church.

The Reformation fork

The split between Protestantism and Catholicism, initiated by Martin Luther nailing his theses onto a church door in Wittenberg in 1520, has become by far the most important one in Christianity because of the subsequent worldwide influence of West Europeans. As a result, it is Roman Catholic and Protestant Christianity, rather than any other type, that have not only fought bloody wars in Western Europe, but also competed for converts in the Americas, Africa, and even Asia and the Pacific. The separation of the Church of England from Rome by Henry VIII in 1536, though formally separate from the Lutheran Reformation, has become closely enmeshed in many of the same issues. Judging this particular 'fork' is a massive question, because of the huge reverberations of the Reformation in world history and the cultural complexity of Catholic versus

Protestant differences. I have chosen to attempt a manageable synthetic overview here, rather than the kind of detailed survey the subject really demands, which would require another book.

The most important division between Catholics and Protestants concerns the source of authority, with Protestants attempting to use the Bible as the only source of authority, while Catholics accept the authority of the Bible only as interpreted by the 'living magisterium' of the Church. In practice, this means that in the Catholic Church the authority of the Pope is paramount, as the Pope trumps every other authority in the church (especially since Papal infallibility was claimed in 1869), and the Catholic Church does not accept appeals to the Bible without that authority. The Protestant churches, on the other hand, stress the individual's autonomous interpretation of the Bible without the need for intercession between God and humans by a priestly hierarchy.

Both sides here are obviously making absolute appeals to authority of a kind that are not compatible with the Middle Way. Both recognise the limitations and drawbacks in the other's sources of authority, but in both cases the scepticism is selective, and there is a failure to extend the same critical awareness to sources appealed to in their own tradition. Catholics often recognise the drawbacks of attributing absolute authority to a text that has been interpreted in a way that is subject to individual delusion, and they are right that no text has an absolute representational meaning distinct from the context of its interpretation. Protestants are often guilty of naïve representationalism, and of a failure to recognise the multiple biases and embodied limitations to which their interpretation of 'God's word' is subject. On the other hand, the absolutisation of tradition, and particularly of the authority of one man authorised by that tradition to make absolute doctrinal pronouncements, is equally subject to delusion on the Catholic side. In both cases the problem is not the sources of authority themselves, but the absolutisation of those sources of authority exclusive of alternatives, and the belief in revelation attached to these sources. In either case, this appeal to authority merely distracts from the more basic human ignorance of 'God's will' to which both Catholics and Protestants are equally subject.

This disjunction in sources of authority has also led to a number of other differences of both doctrine and practice between the Catholic and Protestant traditions. Protestants are likely to disagree with Catholic approaches to monasticism, the role of priests as intermediaries, the celibacy of priests, the non-ordination of women, hierarchical church government, salvation by faith, devotion to saints, belief in purgatory, the doctrine of mortal sin leading to damnation, the practice of confession, the use of images, transubstantiation of the eucharist to become the body and blood of Christ, and the taking of the bread only by the laity in the eucharist.

On some of these issues it is the Catholic side that seems to have taken more of an absolutist stance, on others the Protestant. For example, Catholic intransigence on the power, celibacy and necessary maleness of priests has placed the Catholic Church increasingly out of step with modern conditions. The belief in mortal sin has become notorious for its tendency to produce unjustified, psychologically destructive guilt in the Catholic population. Absolute Catholic opposition to artificial contraception, masturbation, abortion and homosexuality is associated with a tradition of Christian opposition to the body that has become hugely undermining of confidence in Christianity, making it increasingly fragile, dogmatic and out-of-touch in the world's eyes. On the other hand, though, the Protestant destruction of a rich monastic tradition in Protestant countries, the Puritanical destruction of images, accompanied by an impoverishing rejection of the imagination, and the ways in which belief in salvation by faith can undermine a sense of moral responsibility and encourage hypocrisy – all indicate ways in which the Protestant tradition has also been extremely subject to absolutising tendencies.

If, from this brief survey, Catholic absolutism on the whole seems to outweigh Protestant, one should also consider the tradition of individual practice that has been preserved in the Catholic tradition, but very much neglected in the Protestant in favour of social activity and corporate worship. The mystical tradition in Christianity is overwhelmingly a Catholic one, and it is the Catholics that have preserved the monastic institutions where mystical practice is most likely to be developed. The Catholic use of images has also preserved a rich artistic tradition.

However, the positive advantages of the Protestant tradition are perhaps even greater than this. It is only in the Protestant tradition that faith has come to seem an individual responsibility, and it is largely through the Protestant cultivation of literacy, printing technology and individual judgement that the scientific tradition, with its crucial recognition of provisionality, was able to develop in the West. Without Protestantism, too, there would be no toleration of the kind that ultimately emerged after frustrating conflicts between Catholics and Protestants in the seventeenth century. The seeds of liberalism, with its recognition that society benefits from the discussion of a wide range of ideas, would never have been sown. As Weber argued, there is also considerable evidence that Protestantism was responsible (by 'secularising' aspects of monastic tradition), for some of the key cultural changes that made the development of capitalism possible (such as an expectation of deferred gratification, book-keeping, free labour, and corporate property)[119], and thus much of the economic development that makes the positive achievements of modern society possible.

Protestantism has grown and flourished in a climate over-dominated by narrow left-hemisphere representations, but at the same time made a major contribution to the development of Western institutions unprecedented in world history and largely supportive of the wider recognition of conditions. Because of its place in that wider Western culture, Protestantism has proved much more adaptive during the modern period of rapid change when the Catholic response was often one either of dogmatic rigidity or very reluctant and limited reform.

Your choice of route at this fork is perhaps the most difficult one in the whole journey: as with all the other forks, your personal background makes a huge difference. In the end, though, I find it easier to believe that Protestantism (in its more liberal forms – see below) can feasibly let go of its limitations and dogmas than that an unwieldy and largely reactionary Catholic Church will do so. At the time of writing, the accession of Pope Francis offers new hope in the Catholic Church after a succession of deeply conservative and divisive popes, but his contribution so far has largely been to emphasise what is best in Catholic tradition rather than to change the institutional biases that created its dogmatic basis.

The Establishment fork

Though I'm not going to attempt to survey every issue that has divided different denominations of Protestants, there are three key ones that it is worth considering: national establishment, adult baptism, and democratic church government. The first of these, the belief that a church should be 'established' by having the support of national government, is the implication of the foundation of the Church of England by Henry VIII. In Britain this 'establishment' has been rejected by the 'non-conformist' churches such as the Methodists, Presbyterians, Baptists etc., the underlying issue being that of the separation of church and state. Similar issues are raised in nearly every country where the nation is dominated by one religious group with 'establishment' status: for example the Greek Orthodox Church in Greece, the Lutheran Church in Scandinavian countries, or the Catholic Church in Ireland.

The establishment of a national church may often seem more like an accidental political reality than something that can be argued for. If Henry VIII had not created the Church of England out of motives of virtually unalloyed political expediency, would anyone argue for it now? But given that it is here, and part of English tradition, Anglicans suggest that the advantage of a national church is one of inclusivity. Everybody gets embraced by the Church of England as the default church, which also maintains a mission to support the disadvantaged and uphold the spiritual welfare of the whole of society, beyond the Anglican communion. From the standpoint of the Middle Way this has attractions, as Anglicanism is obliged to be a 'broad church', listening to a range of voices, precisely because of its political foundation. Though there are absolutists of both an evangelical and an Anglo-Catholic kind within Anglicanism, they are contained precisely because the church is *not* defined in terms of doctrine alone. In some ways, then, the Church of England seems to have been a vehicle by which the English have discovered the Middle Way through experience.

However, the establishment of the national church unavoidably creates unfair political advantages for those who support it. Although these have been much moderated since the nineteenth century, the Queen is still head of the Church of England, Anglican bishops still sit in the House of Lords, Anglican schools are still by far the most common type of 'faith' school in the UK, and Anglican cathedrals and parish churches still have huge cultural capital in every area. The establishment of Anglicanism continues through a combination of appeal to tradition and status quo bias: the political system has adapted around it, and it would be impossible to gain agreement on any alternative, so change would just involve too much upheaval and political risk.

As long as this situation continues, however, there are risks. With every passing year, Anglican congregations continue to fall and the established Anglican institutions become less and less representative even of a substantial minority, let alone a majority, with only 1.4% of the UK population being regular attenders at Anglican services[120]. There is a danger of even greater alienation than already exists between most of the population and the church. We also rely on Anglican bishops maintaining helpful values, but there is already an anxious move towards evangelicalism in the Church of England to try to counter declining attendances[121]. The greater the gap between tradition and social attitudes, the greater the danger of polarisation. On the one hand, the established religion may adopt more alienated and power-based approaches to Christianity out of insecurity, and on the other, secularists may eventually succeed in making such sweeping changes that all the meaningful symbols and social support created by the Church of England may be damaged or even destroyed.

Rather than simply disestablishing the Church of England, I would suggest a gradual move towards the political use of the Middle Way. If, as I have argued in the previous chapter, the Middle Way offers a common element by which religions can be assessed, there are huge advantages in using the Middle Way (or something equivalent to it) as the accepted basis of the state's relationship to religion, capturing the best of what the Church of England has achieved but avoiding polarisation. For example, Anglican state rituals and state-supported Anglican education could be incrementally moved to being based on the more universal values of the Middle Way, simply by explaining Christian concepts in its terms and allowing people to interpret what was occurring either in Christian terms or in more universal Middle Way terms. The role of the head of state could be moved gradually towards a figurehead whose values more represent the Middle Way, by initially using it to interpret Christian symbols and making it clear how other religions could also be interpreted in terms of the Middle Way. Prince Charles' expressed desire to be 'Defender of the Faiths' or 'Defender of Faith' rather than 'Defender of *the* Faith' could then be readily fulfilled[122].

Used in this way, an established church offers the possibility of integration between the religious and political realms as well as offering a model for religious integration. The accusations of injustice to other groups could at least gradually be addressed. But this is a political vision, and if the political reality actually moves in the opposite direction towards polarisation between an established church and other interests, Christians might be better advised not to involve themselves in an established institution. In countries other than Britain, too, (such as Russia, say) the relationship between an established church and the state may be more supportive of authoritarian conservatism than any more integrative political approach, and thus be clearly repressive from the beginning.

The Baptist fork

In contrast to the complex and quite evenly weighted arguments about earlier divisions in Christianity, the one concerning adult baptism as opposed to infant baptism seems relatively straightforward. It is adult baptism that is depicted in the New Testament when Jesus is baptised by John the Baptist[123], but infant baptism was adopted during the early history of the Church, and remains the dominant practice in most branches of Christianity. It is only the Baptists and other Protestant groups descended from the Baptists and Anabaptists that practise 'believer's baptism', or adult baptism (usually by full immersion) as a mark of initiation into the Christian community.

Given that the reasons for infant baptism seem to have been overwhelmingly concerned with absolute beliefs about salvation, the Baptists seem to have a strong case here. When baptism came to be seen as necessary for salvation, a mark of acceptance into the covenant of grace created by Jesus' atonement, the anxiety obviously arose that children who died unbaptised would not be saved, leading to infant baptism as a formalistic means of saving them regardless of the children's understanding of the situation. This is clearly an absolute belief, of no relevance to the experience of the child or of anyone else apart from the anxiety generated by the need to fulfil a group-based norm. Though a rite of passage may be needed to mark the acceptance of a new baby into society, this does not need to be linked to baptism. By bringing baptism back into the realm of adult responsibility, the Baptists were returning this Christian ritual from absolutism and formalism to meaningful experience, a position that is obviously preferable from a Middle Way standpoint.

That does not mean that the Baptists don't have absolutisations of their own, of course, both in relation to their other Christian beliefs and also even in relation to baptism. The experiential significance of baptism, as mentioned in 5.a above, rests on the symbolism of fluidity, and very much depends on the embodied experience of immersion as an expression of confidence in an integrative process. Baptism is thus an expression of faith, but it is often interpreted, instead, as an expression of absolute belief. For baptism to express a faith in integrated experience, and thus to be taken responsibility for by the baptismal candidate, it thus needs to be done at an age when a certain integrative stability has developed in the individual. However, the Baptist churches often conduct 'believer's baptism' with adolescents as young as fourteen: a procedure that seems irresponsibly premature.

The Congregationalist fork

The Congregationalist fork within Protestant Christianity is concerned with the matter of church government. Congregationalists, along with Baptists and many other 'free churches', believe that individual churches should be democratically controlled by their congregations, and ministers should be elected by the church meeting. This system of church government contrasts with the hierarchical episcopal system used by Orthodox, Catholic and Anglican churches, and the Presbyterian polity in which the church is governed by a hierarchy of committees of elders. Congregationalism was founded on the belief that each individual has a relationship with God and should be able to make their own judgements about the interpretation of the scriptures.

Arguments about the best form of church government need to follow more general ones about the best ways of organising human society in general, and the Middle Way can be applied to this as to any other area of debate. In the 'Middle Way Philosophy' series, I have argued that an integrative politics requires us to look critically at organisational arrangements that entrench polarised assumptions in many varied respects. Democracy has a particular role in at least broadly supporting the integration of people with their leaders, but its success in addressing conditions depends entirely on the integration of the individuals who vote, as well as of those who lead and of the bodies that enact their decisions[124]. Though leaders who are generally more integrated than their followers can have a helpful role in challenging their deluded assumptions, this will not work if the leaders are not more integrated in the relevant ways, or if the followers are alienated from the leadership.

More democratic church government, then, is probably one of the best ways to try to avoid the appointment of religious leaders who are not more integrated than their congregations, or who are insufficiently in sympathy with them to lead them effectively. All forms of democracy are a blunt instrument, and can also be abused by unintegrated congregations and superficial populist leaders, but the best way of avoiding such abuse is probably by avoiding the absolutisation of Christianity in general and thus equipping ordinary Christians better to make adequate judgements about their leaders. An Episcopal Church hierarchy, on the other hand, can entrench its own interests and become very resistant to change when it is needed, as can be amply illustrated in the modern Catholic Church. There seem to be few reasons here for not taking the Congregationalist fork.

The liberal/ fundamentalist fork

Finally, there is a major division amongst Christians today between liberal and fundamentalist wings, with conservatives as a third option who only differ from fundamentalists in that their absolutisation is of a tradition and its leadership rather than of a text. The division between liberals and fundamentalists can cut across Protestant denominations, as it does for example amongst Baptists.

In seeking a Middle Way in Christianity, it is necessary to clearly avoid absolutisation of all kinds, which obviously makes it much more difficult, if not impossible, for a Middle Way Christian to work in the context of a fundamentalist church, as fundamentalism is almost definable in terms of absolutisation. It is not the fundamentalist's valuing of a text as a source of inspiration that makes him an absolutist, but the representationalist assumption that the text can contain revelatory truths from God in the form of words. However, the label 'fundamentalist' can obscure complexities of motivation in each individual or group to which it is applied. A fundamentalist of necessity needs to have many practical and experiential beliefs alongside their absolutist ones, and may, for example, maintain a caring community or support charities, at the same time as deducing justifications for the unjustified use of power from metaphysical beliefs. It is not inconceivable that a Christian seeking to avoid absolutising assumptions could still work in a community of fundamentalists with the purpose of developing their more helpful beliefs and activities.

The liberal Christian community, too, is complex. Though not as thoroughly entrenched in a web of absolutisations as the fundamentalists, they may still have a good many of them, because the dominant liberal model tends to be one of choosing absolutisations that happen to roughly fit modern conditions rather than questioning absolutisation altogether. Liberals generally maintain the absolutisation involved in belief in God itself, together with the belief that God offers revelation, but interpret their revelations more flexibly than do fundamentalists.

Liberal Christians face an ongoing challenge of reconciling the very idea of revelation with the need for adequate practical beliefs that may not easily fit any available Biblical source. For example, the ordination of women is easy to justify in terms of our experience that women can plainly offer spiritual leadership of a kind at least as good as that of men, but is much harder to reconcile with the Bible without a fair amount of circuitous, tendentious, and probably ad hoc interpretation. Should Paul's obvious opposition to female leadership be read as "temporary" or "cultural", and if so, why are not other teachings of Paul interpreted in a similar way? The potential value of Middle Way Christianity is that it could offer a great deal more consistency to liberal Christian teachings, by treating the Bible not as revelation, but as a source of inspiration whose importance is primarily cultural. In this respect, some more consistently liberal groups that have emerged from the Christian tradition, such as the Unitarians and the Quakers, lead the way, and tend to be more open to Middle Way interpretations of Christianity than any other churches.

e. Science and Christianity

The relationships between Christianity and science have been marred by polarisation, or at least the perception of mutual opposition. However, an all-too-common attempt to overcome that polarisation involves essentialising science, Christianity or both in a way that defines them into compatibility. These nearly always maintain some form of absolutising belief, but one adjusted so that science and religion have divided responsibility, or 'non-overlapping magisteria' as Stephen Jay Gould put it[125], for different areas of ultimate explanation. Thus, for example, we had eighteenth century deism, in which God sets up the universe with certain intrinsic natural laws but then sits back and allows the universe to run itself like clockwork. Here, though, we maintain absolute beliefs about a God that created the universe (even if he did not do other things attributed to him) and add absolute beliefs about the 'realities' discovered by science to boot. It would be a fruitless diversion to go into all the more recent theological variations on this attempt to reconcile science and religion within an absolutising framework. They all massively miss the point, not just of religion, but also of science.

The basic problem arises from the assumption that either religion or science gives us 'knowledge' that should be described in propositions about supposedly true facts – whether these are scientific, moral, or abstract generalisation. Basic sceptical argument, of a kind available to us both in Greek and Indian philosophy since ancient times, shows it to be impossible for us to ever be certain of ascertaining any such 'facts'[126], given that we are embodied creatures with limited senses and a capacity to understand the world only in terms of models we have already constructed. Since the rediscovery of scepticism in the sixteenth century, the implications of such scepticism have been systematically misunderstood in the West as a threat to provisional and justified forms of belief: but they are nothing of the kind. Scepticism has thus been wrongly perceived as a threat to both religion and science, and thus to be fought or refuted by both, when on the contrary it offers the basis of their reconciliation[127].

Science is most helpfully interpreted not as a source of 'truths' about the universe, but rather as a method for undermining delusions and developing ever more adequate provisional theories, in which the idea of truth should offer only symbolic inspiration. As philosophers and historians of science such as Lakatos and Kuhn have identified[128], scientific progress depends on a series of paradigms, which consist in basic sets of assumptions that create a basis for a programme of research. There are never absolute grounds for either accepting or rejecting a particular paradigm, but only a weight of evidence, as any attempt to disprove a paradigm is always dependent on certain interpretations that are open to doubt. The abandonment of older paradigms, such as those of Aristotelian science, are thus a matter of confidence. Scientists gradually drop an old paradigm and move to another because the older one has become unfruitful.

Modern science is overwhelmingly a socially-organised discipline pursued in teams, following rigorous procedures that attempt to avoid bias and thus justify or falsify empirical theories. It is largely social procedures, rather than individual thinking, that ensures the rigour of the method employed, with the peer-reviewed journal article being the most crucial social determinant of scientific acceptability. Scientific method ensures a degree of social integration in a particular sphere of enquiry. Though this approach has been remarkably successful in providing us with ever more adequate scientific theory and with technological applications, it can obviously only be applied to a limited range of general judgements: where a topic can feasibly be investigated, where there are tests and observations that can be made, and where the resources and the people are available to be applied to it. On every topic that does not lend itself to such investigation, as in every personal judgement, it is the responsibility of individuals to improve the adequacy of their judgements without such social support.

So, science is a method for maximising the adequacy of collective human judgements on a specific range of socially investigable issues. In broader terms, though, the quality of human judgements depends on their degree of integration, whether that integration is exercised at individual level or on a social level. Science only represents a specialised way of improving those judgements in some cases, dependent primarily on the social integration temporarily created by adherence to scientific protocols. For example, if one scientist fails to see an obvious alternative explanation for an apparently confirmatory observation, due to confirmation bias (being attached to her theory), a supervisor or colleague reviewing her paper is quite likely to do so, and thus the limiting delusions of one person are addressed in this specific instance.

If we interpret science in this integrative fashion, rather than as a discovery of 'natural laws' of a kind for which it will always have insufficient evidence, it is entirely compatible with a religion which is also interpreted as an integrative method rather than as a set of absolute beliefs. Religion and science do not need to make incompatibly different kinds of claim, only to be relatively focused on different types of method. The difference between them will not be a question of lying on different sides of an absolute boundary, but rather consist in a relative difference of focus that does not exclude overlap. Whilst religion is primarily concerned with individual practice, and the individual relationship to motivating symbols, science is primarily concerned with socially-organised investigation of general claims. They are complementary in the sense that an individual scientist can develop greater personal integration through their own practice which they can then apply to being a better scientist, whilst scientific investigation of the conditions affecting integrative practice can also helpfully inform that practice.

It is Christianity interpreted as an absolute belief that has frequently been in collision with science, not Christianity as an integrative faith. The instances of Christian conflict with science are well known: for example the church's treatment of Galileo, or the continuing conflict between Darwinian evolution and Creationism in the US. On both of these examples, however, the absolutisation of some form of traditional or scriptural authority on one side has been exacerbated by the absolutisation of non-absolute scientific results on the other. In these situations the main model for scientific naturalism seems to be Christian naturalism and vice-versa, the prime source of conflict being the constant recourse to claims about truth or falsehood to the exclusion of questions of method and process. Rather than simply persecuting Galileo, the Church encouraged Galileo in investigating and arguing the heliocentric theory, until he began to make absolute assertions about his discoveries which then provoked a clerical counter-reaction[129]. Young Earth Creationism is promoted precisely by secularist attempts to repress it and entirely exclude it from scientific discussion in schools, rather than incorporating it into a discussion of scientific *method* that would clearly show its much lower level of justification when compared to Darwinian theory. If it was really considered more important to teach scientific method effectively in schools rather than scientific 'truths', then the discussion of an example that shows defects in following that method should be welcomed.

Christian *faith* can also be positively linked to the development of science. After all, the central function of Christ as a Middle Way between finite limitations and infinite demands is one that addresses the scientific situation as much as any other. The scientific ethos is distinguished primarily by *confidence* in engaging incrementally with an infinite universe that we can never possibly know completely due to our finite and embodied situation. Rather than seeing knowledge about the universe only in absolute terms and concluding either that we are perpetually ignorant or that we already know the truth, scientific method involves an incremental and empirical engagement with the evidence to support provisional beliefs. In parallel, the Christian ethos, interpreted most helpfully, is distinguished by the confidence it offers in our integrated selves: that despite never reaching divine perfection and being indefinitely subject to sin, we can accept those limitations and still remain inspired by the possibility of integration.

It is thus no coincidence that science developed in its most influential and lasting forms in a Christian culture, which particularly arose in the later Renaissance of northern Europe, influenced by the Reformation. Just as the Reformation enabled the questioning of established religious doctrines and liberated individual religious thought, it also enabled the questioning of established Aristotelian scientific doctrines. The Reformation was also associated with the use of printing, which also helped to spread new scientific ideas. The founding of universities has also been crucial for the development of modern scientific culture, but universities began as secularised monasteries with a largely theological purpose. The scientific revolution that began in the seventeenth century was thus not driven by Christianity in general so much as by specific new developments in Christianity, but it also developed elements found throughout all Christianity.

The concept of the 'book of nature' was central to many seventeenth and eighteenth century scientists, many of whom remained devout Christians. Although the idea that God had created the world and that he could be discovered in observation of that world contained dogmatic elements of a rationalistic kind, it was also mixed with a new openness to observation of the world around us that parallels the openness to the God within found in the medieval mystics. The idea of the natural world created by God served as an inspiring symbol for a positive drive to investigate many different specific aspects of that world, just as God can operate as an inspiring symbol of the larger perspective of assumptions within ourselves.

Just as there was no conflict between religion and science for figures like Isaac Newton, there need be no such conflict today as long as both Christianity *and* science are interpreted as faith rather than belief, and as long as guiding concepts are always interpreted as archetypes rather than bases of absolute belief.

'Nature' and the idea of natural laws are archetypes for scientists whether they count themselves as 'religious' or not: but the idea of Nature is no more or no less necessarily dogmatic than that of God.

f. Meeting atheism

The polarised 'debate' between theism (usually Christian theism) and atheism is a disgrace of which both sides should be ashamed. Both sides should know better, since those who identify with theistic belief presumably have some experience of religious inspiration and religious faith, whilst those who identify with atheism usually have some experience of thoughtful enquiry of a philosophical or scientific kind. Both sides have good critical points to make which they *systematically over-interpret and fail to apply to their own position*, so as to score points and 'win', and as a result they create an entrenched war-zone out of what ought otherwise to be the most refined and helpful areas of human enquiry. Christians who claim to have experience of God or of God's love have no business reinforcing the assumptions of this debate by putting into it in its usual terms, but instead have a responsibility to integrate the conflict by questioning the framing of the ideas within which it is usually framed. Of course, atheists have a similar responsibility from their side.

The situation is made considerably worse by the ways in which terminology has been gradually adapted to reinforce the dualistic opposition and undermine any possibility of positions being seriously considered that could defuse the conflict. Foremost amongst these is the systematic attempt to either dismiss or appropriate agnosticism by defining it into either your own camp (appropriating it to your set of assumptions) or dismissing it as part of the enemy camp. Thus Anthony Kenny invented the term 'negative atheism', and George H. Smith uses 'implicit atheism' to describe the mere absence of belief in God found in agnostics of all kinds, whilst theists also often lump agnostics together with atheists. However, the absence of belief is crucially different from a negative belief denying the existence of God, because the absence of such an absolute belief can be integrated, whilst a negative absolute belief offers a barrier to integration. Similarly, those theists and atheists who unite in unholy alliance to dismiss agnosticism as indecisive (as already discussed in 7.a) are completely failing to recognise the value of agnosticism as an integrable position that respects experience where their opposed positions do not. Philosophers and theologians on the whole seem to have taken almost no interest in the psychological effects of the beliefs they are discussing.

As a taste of the kind of intellectual entrenchment we are up against here, let me quote George H. Smith from his substantial book 'The case against God':

> *Properly considered, agnosticism is not a third alternative to theism and atheism because it is concerned with a different aspect of religious belief. Theism and atheism refer to the presence or absence of belief in a god; agnosticism refers to the impossibility of knowledge with regard to a god or supernatural being. The term 'agnostic' does not, in itself, indicate whether or not one believes in a god.*[130]

Smith here completely separates 'knowing' from 'believing', despite the fact that where absolute beliefs are concerned they are identical. One can hold a belief about something one recognises as uncertain, whilst being aware of alternatives: for example, I can believe that my chair will not collapse when I sit on it. However, without alternatives one's beliefs are taken as practical certainties and thus are indistinguishable from knowledge. So, an agnostic is not only someone who recognises the impossibility of knowing God, but also someone who does not believe in God (but also does not deny God's existence). Smith goes on to claim that theistic agnostics are people who believe in God but recognise that knowledge of him is impossible – which makes no sense when one becomes aware of the practical nature and function of absolute belief. Instead, I would suggest, a Christian or other theistic agnostic is someone who has *faith* in God but does not *believe* in God, which means that he or she has a positive relationship to the meaning of God as an integrative archetype but avoids absolute beliefs about God. Smith's perspective can represent a whole host of ways in which narrow assumptions on the part of both atheists and theists have effectively ruled out solutions to the conflict through the very way they define their terms.

So, one initial move I suggest to make integrative discussion about atheism possible is to clarify the vocabulary. I suggest that 'atheism' should be taken to mean the denial of God's existence. As with any belief, one could hold that implicitly as well as explicitly, but when analysed, the belief labelled 'atheism' should involve the denial of an absolute. Agnosticism, in contrast to this, is a lack of absolute beliefs about God – and by extension about any other metaphysical claim. That avoidance of absolute beliefs is best founded on a practical recognition of the unhelpfulness of absolute beliefs, but that recognition itself is something that can only be gradually developed with integration. Agnosticism is thus an ongoing project based on one's practical and psychological state as well as one's 'beliefs', a recognition of the irrelevance of absolute claims that is rooted in experience, and in this sense it differs from theism and atheism, which consist only in the assumption of absolute positions so as to accord with a group and are thus fragile positions that can be rapidly converted into their opposites.

However fragile and metaphysical atheism may be as a position, however, atheism does employ some arguments that agnostic Christians can learn from. These point out weaknesses in Christian *belief* of a kind that those with genuine Christian *faith* should have no trouble in accepting. However, these are arguments against theism rather than for atheism. Exactly the same can be said about theist arguments against atheism, which are also often critically strong but give no support for theism as such. I will look below at atheist arguments based on the lack of evidence for God, and the problem of evil, which both fall into this category. However, there are also arguments based on particular views of meaning and rationality which are also a threat to faith in God, and I shall argue that these are mistaken in a more basic way.

Lack of evidence for God

The most common, and basic, argument for atheism is that which appeals to a lack of evidence for God's existence. Thus Richard Dawkins, for example, insists that God's existence is a matter for empirical investigation, and then argues that although it can't be ruled out completely, God's existence is highly improbable[131]. The only justification for this might be that Christians have, at times, appealed to supposed empirical evidence for the existence of God – such as order in Creation, irreducible complexity, an ultimate cause, the presence of morality or beauty, or religious experience. The failure of these kinds of arguments is well documented in the philosophy of religion, and I do not wish to go over them here. However, the very fact that Christians have had recourse to them illustrates an inconsistency between their traditional belief in God as a metaphysical absolute and their belief in God as a phenomenon at work in the universe. Such arguments are doomed simply because no finite observation can provide adequate proof of an infinite claim, so atheists are correct to criticise them.

However, the idea that God's existence could ever be 'improbable' reveals a failure to understand the significance of God for Christians and others. God is either the subject of an absolute metaphysical claim, in which case its attraction as a shortcut to power is precisely that it cannot be threatened by any criticism appealing to experience – its unfalsifiability – or else God is an archetype. Since an archetype is a term for a psychic function, it is a way of talking about the way that the structures of our brains relate to experience, not a claimed object of experience to be rendered probable or improbable. Archetypes can only offer a practically helpful or unhelpful way to discuss psychic functions, as judged in individual experience with the use of any other concept. The 'existence' of an archetype is not a relevant way to discuss it, any more than the 'existence' of, say, emotion, or metaphor, or symbol. One can either choose to reflect on one's experience in the terms offered by these concepts, or one can, if one wishes, refuse to do so, perhaps motivated by whether they divide or unify our understanding of phenomena in ways that prove helpful.

It is in that sense that one can argue that everyone has a God within, and thus that to talk about the 'non-existence' of God is like denying a whole dimension of one's experience. People can choose not to refer to that dimension of their experience using that term, but that will not stop the dimension being part of their experience. For those who live in a Christian or other theistic culture, too, not linking this dimension of one's experience with God as a cultural symbol may create a sense of deracination or even alienation in relation to that culture. My impression is that many Christians who experience God as part of their experience do feel this, and are puzzled by the atheist rejection of God, which may seem like tearing off a part of themselves. As long as they maintain the traditional absolutist ways of talking about God, however, they are likely to be unsuccessful in helping atheists to understand the problem.

There is thus no reason why Christians should not accept atheist criticisms that involve pointing out a lack of evidence for positive claims about God's existence. However, they can then offer a starting point for suggesting more adequate ways of thinking about God than in terms of his 'existence'.

The problem of evil

The problem of evil, as a supposed argument for atheism, states that if one accepts that God is defined as omnipotent, omniscient and benevolent, and that evil (in the sense of any conditions causing suffering) exists in the world, God cannot exist. For a benevolent God would want to prevent evil, an omniscient God would know about it, and an omnipotent God could prevent it. This argument does indeed identify a major problem with *believing* in God. It is indeed inconsistent to believe in a God with these attributes – ones that are pretty unavoidable if you conceive God to be perfect – and to recognise evil in the world. This evil is a matter of experience, so cannot be simply defined out of existence.

However, the problem of evil does not undermine *faith* in a God who is not a supernatural ruler of the universe, but rather an experience of integration. If we no longer seek to defend the 'existence' of a ruler of the universe, we do not have to worry about why he 'permits' evil. Evil and suffering are conditions that we encounter in experience, but are not things we need to 'explain'. The problem of evil in relation to an archetypal God simply becomes the question of how suffering can contribute to integration. We no longer need to provide a total explanation of *all* suffering, but only of that suffering that comes into contact with God in our experience.

The second century thinker Irenaeus had an inkling of this in the theodicy he offered to try to reconcile his faith in God to his experience of suffering, and this approach has also more recently been revived by John Hick in his 'soul-making' theodicy[132]. Here, the value of suffering in precipitating open feedback loops that challenge our previous assumptions is appreciated. Without suffering, or at least frustration, we would not be able to adapt to new conditions, nor integrate beyond our limited assumptions at any given point. However, this Irenaean argument works much better to support faith in God than belief in God.

The Irenaean argument that the value of suffering for us justifies *belief* in God founders on the problem of excessive suffering. We experience far more suffering than is needed to set us on integrative paths, and much of the suffering people experience probably has no such beneficial effect. For example, someone who dies of cancer in great pain might well have been able to integrate that pain much better if it was less severe, but in practice, due to the severity of the pain, was overwhelmed by stress and thus unable to maintain a wider awareness at the time of death. We might also sometimes be propelled to helpful effort by the suffering of others, but very often the extremity of such suffering (say, when we see TV pictures of a famine) overwhelms us and we feel powerless. The 'moral evil' of, say, a paedophile destroying a child's sense of trust and security for the rest of their lives is also especially hard to reconcile with the idea that *all* suffering is helpful to us. The Irenaean argument, like many other traditional religious arguments, has taken a helpful insight about the possible value of suffering in some cases and unhelpfully absolutised it.

However, if we think of God, not as responsible for all conditions, but rather as the principle of integration, the Irenaean theodicy can help us to maintain faith in such a God, as well as saving us from the theologically twisted position of defending evil. Here it is helpful to make a clearer distinction between 'suffering' and 'evil' than the traditional debate tends to do. Suffering is the result of conditions, but evil as we experience it is an absolutising response to conditions. Both can indeed be helpful to us, but not as general conditions, only as we encounter them in the process of integration.

Suffering, as already mentioned in 6.c, can help us by challenging an existing set of assumptions and thus stimulating us to consider alternative views that might be preferable. Evil, however, consists in unintegrated beliefs and desires that are taken to be the whole story. Without unintegrated beliefs and desires in the first place, no integration can occur, and the 'rational' process of calculating how to reach a narrow goal more efficiently can still contribute to our overall integration by providing the preliminary materials that can be integrated. Both evil in our experience and suffering as far as it stimulates or challenges us, then, are part of the necessary conditions for the integration of the whole psyche, and thus are synthesised in God.

We can maintain faith in such a God in the terms of our experience by reflecting positively on the potential value of suffering or evil whenever it threatens to cast us into despair: a much more profound faith than the 'belief' that a supernatural God somehow approves of all the evil and suffering in the universe. That we can make progress with this process of integration of evil despite its degree of influence over us is dependent on the Middle Way, with our confidence in it symbolised by Christ.

The meaning of God

The argument that God is meaningless is one that was put forward by the logical positivist school of philosophy in the early twentieth century, and was encapsulated in a notorious radio discussion between Frederick Copleston and A.J. Ayer. For Ayer, the only basis of meaning is verification: that is, a claim is only 'strictly' meaningful when one could at least in principle state in what circumstances it could be verified[133]. This led him to claim that not only claims about God, but also ethical claims, aesthetic claims, and pseudoscientific claims, were similarly meaningless.

Though fortunately logical positivism in its early twentieth century form has now been widely discredited, I still find it incredible that a philosophy that threatened such an impoverishment of intellectual life could be taken as seriously as it was at the time, and also remain dismayed at the extent to which key assumptions of the logical positivist programme remain uncontested in analytic philosophy – the school that is still overwhelmingly dominant and defines the nature of philosophy in UK and US universities. In particular, analytic philosophy maintains the unquestioned assumption of representationalism – the belief that the meaning of a statement depends on its truth-conditions – which, even if it is still sometimes formally contested in philosophy of language, overwhelmingly remains the unreflective starting point in epistemology, metaphysics, ethics, and every other application of analytic philosophy. Along with this go absolutised distinctions between reason and emotion, and relatedly of fact and value (again assumed by the logical positivists). These again are merely assumed by specialist analytic philosophers who continue to apply them in other areas, and who are effectively never allowed by the academic system of speciality to reconsider the mutual influence of different sets of assumptions working together. One effect of this continuing philosophical influence is the failure to appreciate that the *meaning* of God can be entirely distinct from any considerations of the truth of claims about God (already discussed in 2a above), and thus an ongoing block on serious intellectual recognition of the distinction between Christian belief and Christian faith.

The argument that God is meaningless is thus *the* central mistaken atheist argument, because it is built on a misapprehension of the way in which human beings experience meaning, together with the dogmatic assumption of an entirely abstract conception of meaning. It is this assumption about meaning, shared by logical positivists and traditional theists alike, that provides the basic intellectual conditions for the obsession with God's 'existence' to even make sense, since it is only by assuming that this 'existence' has a meaning distinct from experience that it can be considered, with its meaning assumed to depend hypothetically on the possibility of that existence.

Unlike the atheist arguments about evidence and evil, the argument that God is meaningless does not just contain a helpful point that has been absolutised. Rather, it reinforces representationalist assumption, which is itself one of the basic conditions of absolutisation. As long as it remains unquestioned, the whole approach offered in this book is likely to continue being misunderstood and dismissed out of hand.

If God's meaningfulness is, instead, recognised as prior to and distinct from beliefs about his existence, the logical positivist approach is revealed as circular dogma that attempts to define God out of consideration by assuming a constricted definition of meaning. For some reason, the fact that he could have a discussion about a concept that he thought was 'strictly meaningless' does not even strike Ayer as ironic. But of course, God is not meaningless even to Ayer, because he maintains and is using the concept in a way that relates in some way to his experience. We do not even have to go into what aspect of his experience it relates to (by introducing embodied meaning or the theory of archetypes) to recognise that point. When 'meaning' itself is appropriated as a tool of power, we seem to have reached the furthest possible point of abstracted self-deception.

The 'rationality' of God

Finally we must come to a point that is perhaps almost equally self-deceptive: the idea that belief in God is 'irrational'. I make no apologies for using scare quotes around the word 'rational', as (along with 'logical') it seems to me one of the most abused and manipulated words in the lexicon: one that pretends precision and justification when it often offers neither. Let us start by briefly considering what 'rational' might mean.

'Reason' is most basically deductive logic: that is, the drawing of a conclusion from the premises or assumptions with which one begins. Philosophical tradition also talks about inductive reasoning which begins with the uncertain and finite premises of observation and draws general conclusions from them. In either case, though, 'reason' can tell us nothing more than was already assumed in the premises, and offers no guarantee of the 'truth' of those premises. At best, extended reasoning can check a series of beliefs for their consistency with one another. A 'rational' belief is thus a consistent belief, but this may also mean a consistently deluded belief. It is for this reason that I have elsewhere[134] proposed a distinction between 'reason' and 'justification'. Whilst the evidence or principles we appeal to may provide a 'reason' that imparts consistency to our beliefs, to *justify* those beliefs we also need a recognition that they may be wrong (which in turn requires us to have access to alternatives).

Reasoning about God, then, obviously follows this pattern. When theologians try to 'prove' the 'existence' of God, they start off with certain premises that are judged 'true' *a priori* and apply them, perhaps also using evidence from observation, to draw a conclusion that they believe affirms the existence of God. The justification of those founding *a priori* principles is a long vexed question of philosophy, which again it would not be fruitful to go into here, but the criticisms made of them are usually simply applications of sceptical argument. Given that these claims are subject to sceptical doubt[135], like every other claim, there is no shortcut to certainty through this route. The 'rationality' (i.e. the justification) of theistic attempts to prove God's existence has thus rightly been criticised by atheists, but given that sceptical arguments only justify agnosticism, this is very far from proving belief in God to be 'irrational'. Religious believers start from a variety of absolute assumptions and use them quite consistently to reach absolute conclusions: an eminently 'rational' process. Young-earth creationism, for example, is entirely 'rational': if you accept the starting assumptions.

The atheist argument that belief in God is 'irrational' may go further by claiming that it is contrary to evidence that we should 'rationally' accept. This ignores the fact that all such 'evidence' relating to God is entirely a matter of interpretation, whether one is referring to design, religious experience or anything else, and that 'reason' has no implications for which assumptions we accept beyond consistency. If you have interpreted all your experience in terms of a world designed and ordered by God, as traditional religious believers have, it is secularist assumptions that are 'inconsistent' rather than religious ones. There is thus nothing 'irrational' about such a position.

Atheist arguments for the 'irrationality' of belief in God thus seem to be more indicative of the need to find an equally authoritative alternative to God than with any precise justification. 'Reason' is a term almost as vague and easily manipulated as 'God' or 'nature' have traditionally been, but one that people can get away with using only because it is vaguely associated with precise justification. In many cases, it may be a shortcut to pointing out the dogmatic features of metaphysical belief as they are recognised in the case of God: that is, to pointing out a lack of justification in the terms of experience. But if so, this critical perspective is rarely, if ever, extended to other metaphysical beliefs that are equally dogmatic, and is also never differentiated from the meaningfulness of God as an archetype. The concept of 'rationality' is probably much better simply dropped from our vocabulary, except perhaps in its strict logical sense of consistency in relation to assumed premises.

Overall, then, it seems that some common atheist arguments are actually over-interpreted arguments for agnosticism. Others, however, go beyond such potentially useful scepticism and offer an entrenchment of unhelpful assumptions. However, the objection to these is not limited to their use in arguments for atheism. Theists, too, may appeal to 'rationality' or claim that atheism is 'meaningless' on equally spurious grounds, and if taken seriously these approaches also threaten the possibility of justified ethics and aesthetics. Justifiable Christian objections to atheism, then, can hardly be separated from their objections to absolute belief in general.

g. Responding to feminism

As a final element of the interpretation of Christian agnosticism, it's important to recognise the extent of feminist challenges to the Christian tradition in recent decades. Pursuing Christianity as an absolute belief has the unfortunate side effect of tying it unhelpfully to the patriarchal cultures of the past, together with the absolute beliefs that were assumed in those cultures about the roles and powers of men and women. On the other side there can also sometimes be found over-compensating absolutisations in feminism. Christianity based on faith and recognising the need for critical awareness on these issues is best placed to navigate them.

There are perhaps three key issues on which feminism challenges Christian tradition:

1. The assumed sex of God
2. The suitability of women for church leadership
3. The tendency to reject the body and sexuality, with accompanying misogyny in many strands of Christian tradition

1. The assumed sex of God

The traditional Christian practice, following the Bible, has been to uniformly refer to God as male. At the same time, most theologians would acknowledge that God is in theory beyond sex, because sex is a feature of imperfection that is transcended by a perfect and infinite being. In practice, then, as in many other aspects of the human depiction of God, the abstracted idea of an absolute is appropriated to serve partial interests in experience. Those partial interests are ones that feminism has been alerting the world to: the predominance of patriarchal assumptions that have often been institutionalised into normality, but which continue to maintain a general expectation of male predominance. What better way to maintain male predominance in general than to depict the ruler of the universe as male?

However, if we are to see God in the most helpful way possible, it is important to avoid that appropriation. God represents something beyond *present* experience but nevertheless within the wider scope of *potential* experience, as I have argued above (especially in section 3). We cannot assume that we know anything about what God is like or what he/she wishes, which obviously includes his/her sex. Though the use of the male pronoun for God can be defended simply as a matter of avoiding clumsy constructions such as 'he/she', or the potential misunderstanding that can arise if one alternates pronouns, there's also little doubt that the continuous use of the male pronoun over a period of time gradually contributes to the unconscious identification of God with maleness.

Though God can't be assumed to be *generally* of one sex or another, nevertheless, an archetypal God encountered in embodied experience may be *symbolised* in terms of one sex or another. This raises the question of the relationship between the archetypes, particularly the anima/animus and God archetypes, as discussed above in 2c. The anima/animus represents the attractive other, which is thus likely to be the opposite sex, and it is possible that God, being the archetype of integration, may in individual cases take more of that form depending on what the individual most needs to integrate. Thus, for example, a man who had identified himself too narrowly with masculine qualities such as aggression, might most need to relate to a feminine form of God, expressive of more accepting qualities in himself. God might, for the moment, need to be most imagined as Goddess, but we also can't assume that form of God to be complete or final, as it consists only in compensation for the integrative limitations of a changing individual.

That both men and women have predominantly thought of God as male may well reflect the rigidity of their identification with God as something separate from them, and project the power they would unconsciously like to either have themselves or be protected by. For women (or men) who need to identify more closely with assertive masculine qualities, though, that way of symbolising God may continue to be helpful, as long as they explicitly recognise the respects in which God is themselves, so as to avoid projection. For others, quite the opposite may be needed. This relationship between the way one visualises the archetype of integration and the compensating integrative process one needs to go through oneself is already used in Tibetan Buddhism in the selection of visualisation practices, meditating on a symbolic figure that is geared towards individual psychological needs. For example, a man tending towards aggression who needs to cultivate their gentler qualities might visualise the feminine figure of Green Tara, the embodiment of compassion. The same process could be reproduced in a Catholic context through the choice of saints for special individual devotion or prayer.

The recognition of God's archetypal relationship to embodied human beings can thus free us from fruitless argument over whether God *is* in any sense male or female, but at the same time allow God to be represented as *either* male or female in an entirely contingent fashion.

2. The suitability of women for church leadership

The claim that women are not suited to ordination or church leadership seems to depend entirely on the absolutisation of tradition and scriptural authority (such as 1 Timothy 2:12). Such sources of information need to be set against the overwhelming weight of evidence that women can perform any leadership or teaching role at least as well as men can. Any Middle Way resolution of this issue needs to give appropriate weight to such experience, treating scriptures as potential sources of inspiration but not of divine revelation, so it is hard to see how any Christian not entirely dogmatic in their judgements can object on principle to the ordination of women.

However, this issue also raises the wider question of the function of ordination itself. The earliest function of ordination was that of priesthood, in which only the ordained could act as an intermediary between humans and God by performing the eucharist and other sacraments – as is still the case in the Orthodox and Catholic churches. This belief about the function of ordination seals the externalisation of God. Although the sacraments may be helpful in connecting with divine inspiration (as discussed in the next section), and others may help with this, this belief about the role of priests absolutises that role. In Protestantism, due to the concept of 'priesthood of all believers', there is no such role for the priest as intermediary, but ordination nevertheless confers a leadership role based on the discontinuity of a particular ceremony conferring a sudden step up in social status.

Whilst people need leadership which can offer an example of integration, the problem with formally conferring the discontinuous status of ordination on a leader is that their integration is likely to be lop-sided or asymmetrical. Where they may be capable of offering leadership or example in some respects, ordination tends to confer it in a range of respects. Thus in the modern churches, clergy may often need to be managers as well as pastoral leaders, teachers, and ritual officiants. They may not be good at all these things, but their status leads people to assume that they will be. Such discontinuous status may also create a discontinuous and unwarranted increase in trust from the laity – trust that has been abused in the many clerical abuse scandals that have come to light in recent years.

The barrier to the ordination of women has been very much due to this discontinuity, which requires appeals to authority to be maintained. If there was not such a discontinuity attached to church leadership, it would have been much easier for women to simply demonstrate their leadership skills and gradually be trusted in leadership positions: but instead the church became caught up in the positive feedback loop of not giving women authority because they were judged unsuited to it, then maintaining the judgement of their unsuitability because women had not been allowed into positions of authority. Fortunately, that loop is now being undermined by the number of Protestant churches that have allowed the ordination of women, but it would be undermined even more by the breaking up of ordination itself into a more continuous system in which people took up specific leadership responsibilities only in relation to the potential they showed for fulfilling them.

3. The tendency to reject the body and sexuality

However, by far the most basic and far-reaching issue that divides Christian tradition and its feminist critics is that of the body. From relatively early in Christian tradition, Platonic elements entered it that valued the soul over the body, the will over the flesh. This has taken a moralistic and ascetic form in the monastic tradition (where it can still be graphically illustrated by the practice of self-flagellation), but even in Protestantism this continued in the form of puritanism and the idea of faith in God as involving a voluntarist act of will over our recalcitrant desires. This can be associated with a strong left-hemisphere dominance in much Christian thought and practice (see 2.d above), with the left hemisphere being the seat of belief and will, and its dominance being to the detriment of the right hemisphere, with its wider awareness of the body.

From early in the history of Christianity, too, this has resulted in misogyny. One type of misogyny involves women being blamed for creating sexual desire in men. This appears to be a straightforward projection of men's own conflict over their sexual desires, and a failure to take responsibility for those desires and their effects. Another type of misogyny involves the appeal to the Eden myth to blame women for evil in the world and thus rationalise their inferior position by implying that women have less control over their desires than men. This latter form is clearly expressed in 1 Timothy:

> *Their [women's] role is to learn, listening quietly and with due submission. I do not permit women to teach or dictate to the men; they should keep quiet. For Adam was created first, and Eve afterwards; moreover it was not Adam who was deceived; it was the woman who, yielding to deception, fell into sin.* (1 Tim 2:11-14)

As discussed above in 4c, the Eden story can provide no justification for such interpretations. Not only is Adam depicted as falling to the same temptation, and not only would women in general not be responsible for the action of one of their number, but the whole story of the temptation and fall itself can be taken to symbolically depict the independent judgement of the left hemisphere that is initially necessary for integration to become possible. Yet this story has been constantly invoked to support patriarchal assumptions on the rare occasions when these were challenged.

Compounding Christian misogyny has been its continuation of the Jewish taboo against menstrual blood[136], which for a long time justified a ban on menstruating women attending the eucharist, and required a purification ritual to be undergone by women returning to church after childbirth.[137] There has also been an idealisation of virginity, beginning with that of Mary and continuing with a line of female saints whose most admired characteristic was often their repression of all sexuality. Modern Catholic prohibitions on masturbation and artificial contraception may also be connected to this anti-sexual tradition.

To find an integrative interpretation of Christianity requires considerable disentangling of this unhelpful tradition. Most basically, it seems to me, attitudes to the body and human desire are to blame, and it is these that have led to confused attitudes to both women and sexuality, together with perpetuations of the patriarchy that already existed before Christianity. Some, like Uta Ranke-Heinemann[138], have protested that this rejection of the body is not properly Christian, but the result of the influence of Gnosticism, Stoicism, and other classical influences on Christianity. However, it seems to me that liberal and feminist Christians would do much better to avoid essentialising responses that evoke 'true Christianity' of some kind. Christianity has been interpreted in this way, which we can identify as unhelpful, and part of the reason it has continued for so long is a failure to acknowledge our responsibility for the interpretation of tradition. Christianity as a whole is neither essentially misogynistic nor essentially not misogynistic: rather, we have the opportunity to interpret it in a way that recognises the misogyny of the past and takes responsibility for avoiding it in future.

As long as human desire itself is disassociated from human will, the result is likely to be conflict and alienation. Moral desire is still desire, alongside all other desires, and desire itself consists only of energy that in some way or another seeks to address conditions, though the beliefs that inform our understanding of those conditions can be more or less adequate, so it is a mistake to think of one desire as rightly overpowering another rather than of desires as integrating in relation to more adequate beliefs[139]. Christ can represent an integrative model precisely because his humanity requires a recognition and acceptance of all of our desires, rather than just the comparison of human weakness with absolute rules supported by the ascetic appeal to will. If the human body and its sexuality can be seen as part of the solution, contributing its energy to increasingly integrated, increasingly adequate judgements, there is no longer any need or temptation to see men and women as differing very much in their position in relation to God. They may have slightly different conditions to address, but the same need to integrate their sexuality and physical needs with the rest of their lives.

Embodied meaning also implies that the very meanings of the words used by both men and women to refer even to the holiest concepts are based on the body and built up through metaphors that depend on links to bodily sensation through the right hemisphere. That implies, for example, that those who engage in the discussion of sexuality from a prohibitory standpoint will almost inevitably do so with a degree of prurience, since the discussion of sexuality, however abstracted, is separated from sexual behaviour by social conventions rather than by any intrinsic disembodiment in the linguistically referential parts of the brain. It can be said with justice that those who are most obsessed by sex are often the celibate, especially when they speak or write disapprovingly about it. If celibacy is to have any beneficial effects it must be combined with practices that seek to integrate rather than merely repress sexual energy, and celibates must be free to abandon it if it does not work for them.

Needless to say, then, the avoidance of misogyny in Christianity can only be achieved alongside acceptance of embodiment by both sexes. Whatever the sources of the sexually repressive, Platonic, and misogynistic tendencies in Christianity, they can be counteracted by drawing from the inspiration of Christ as the principle that integrates human and divine rather than imposing an interpreted divine model.

8

Christian practice

a. Worship

Christianity, like any other religion, does not consist merely in scriptures or doctrines, but in a tradition that shapes people's behaviour in a variety of ways. It is especially the case if we are trying to give up the absolutisation implicit in saying that Christianity is merely a set of beliefs, that we need to chart its potential interpretation beyond those beliefs into a more habitual and embodied sphere. What does it mean to live a Christian life, if this is not interpreted in terms of absolute beliefs? One can say that Christianity is a faith, but that faith needs to derive a basis of confidence from practice. That practice, in turn, cannot consist of a blindly-followed set of habits or rituals. Practices need to strike a point of considered balance in the Christian's response to the world, so as to be open to new understandings and activities that are the basis of integration. So Christian practice needs to not only maintain Christian inspiration, but also sufficient challenge to prevent Christianity becoming a dogma.

Of common Christian practices that may need to be evaluated, some have already been sufficiently mentioned: the creed and baptism in 7.d, and ordination in 7.g. In a book with limited space, I do not plan to duplicate those discussions, where I argued that the creed simply needs to be discarded, baptism understood as an expression of faith rather than belief, and ordination interpreted much more flexibly and continuously. Of the classic seven sacraments of Catholic tradition, that leaves especially the eucharist and confession as worthy of further discussion below, together with a general discussion of rites of passage that will cover marriage, confirmation and death. In addition to the sacraments, however, in this section I want to more generally discuss the role of worship and the crucial modern relationship between Christianity and psychology. Christian ethics and political action are another aspect of Christian practice, but these will be left for my final section.

'Going to church' to participate in communal worship is perhaps most widely seen as the basic Christian act, followed closely by private prayer, which is also a form of worship. How can we understand the value of this worship, and what form should it best take, in an agnostic, Middle Way Christianity?

Though worship may often be assumed to be a method of inculcating belief, it is actually central to faith. Though traditionally the words used in creeds, and some of those used in sermons, hymns and prayers, may involve statements of absolute belief, worship is primarily a way in which people open up their experience to God. That implies that they are experiencing the meaning of God and Christ, and connecting religious symbol with personal experience: an activity of the integration of meaning[140]. Symbols can become more meaningful for being used and explored in a variety of ways, there is a re-connection with inspiration, and a temporary turn from the obsessive, chattering left hemisphere to the openness of the right. Where worship is communal, it can also mean sharing that integrative process with others and thus helping to unite the Christian community. The derivation of the term 'worship' is after all from 'worthship': it is a way of recalling and engaging with what we find of most worth.

Whilst this experiential process can often be valuable for all who participate wholeheartedly in it, the imposition of the idea of worshipping God as a supernatural entity into it, on the contrary, creates conflict and alienation. Since God as an absolute power is beyond our experience, this is hardly surprising. Worship of God as an absolute tends to involve the mindless reiteration of a mere abstract concept of God as perfection, rather than an engagement with our own living experience of God. Such a

God also does not need worshipping: rather it is us who need to reconnect with our archetypal experience.

My overwhelming experience of church services as a child was one of boredom, dreariness and alienation – leaving a negative impression so deep that I struggle to engage more positive emotions with Christian worship even today. I think this was because it was primarily about power: the power of a social institution imposed upon participants by appeal to the authority of a supernatural entity. I was there only because I was socially obliged to be there, or because it was the cost of social acceptance of some sort. None of my own energies or values were effectively engaged, because I was never consulted about what I wanted to happen, or about what kinds of ritual would best reflect and inspire my own integration process. Like God himself, the act of worship was thus always experienced as other, as an alienating imposition which of course was always accompanied by doubt about whether I was singing hymns to a grand delusion. Although these responses were very much the product of my own conditions, I find it hard to believe that they are not to some extent widely shared. Regular church attendance in the UK is continuing to fall and is now down to about 5%[141], whilst even in the supposedly religious US it may be as low as 22%[142].

Whilst some Christians have recognised that there is a problem in public responses to Christian worship, the most common responses to this have been evangelical. This generally involves even more reliance on absolute assumptions about God than previously, with attempts to make worship superficially more engaging, for example by using 'modern' hymns accompanied by guitars rather than organs. Charismatic pastors can spice up services with rhetoric, and Pentecostalists also succeed in drawing crowds through induced group hysteria. Group hysteria is not integrative, but merely binds people temporarily into a group under the sway of shared absolute beliefs, so should not be confused with the kind of genuine religious experience discussed above in 2b. This is thus not an adequate response to the decline in Christian worship.

My suggestions for the reform of Christian worship would instead involve a much more candid acknowledgement by all worship leaders that the object of worship does not have to 'exist', and is instead found in the direct experience of each worshipper. Given that the God being celebrated is also likely to be experienced differently in the varying integration processes of each person, the creation of worship should also be much more consultative and participative and less the mere imposition of tradition. There is no particular reason why a service has to be based around hymns, prayers, sermons and the eucharist unless the congregation finds these things valuable, and there are a great many other things they could do to ritually celebrate a shared appreciation of what God and Christ really mean in each person's experience: for example, video, creation of or listening to music, dance, creation and appreciation of visual art, poetry, a wide variety of symbolic actions to ritualise values, dressing up, drama, crafts, readings from a wide variety of texts, meditation, visualisation, structured reflection, spontaneous contributions from the congregation. Many of these activities are used occasionally in church services, and there are recent initiatives such as 'messy church'[143] that do try to engage people in Christian worship in some of these alternative ways, but these are often linked to an extension of the evangelical paradigm, which compromises the means but not the model of belief to go with it.

To get beyond mere beliefs and superficial concepts, and help people to engage with their wider and deeper experience, the use of periods of silence is crucial. A good deal of modern Christianity is just way too noisy and superficial. It is only in silence that people are likely to move into right hemisphere awareness rather than goal-focused left hemisphere activity, and thus engage with any kind of experience of God beyond the mere sharing of concepts and beliefs. It is also only in periods of silence that people are likely to be able to connect with their own emotions and bring those into the worship process, rather than merely overriding however they may be feeling through participation in communal worship. There is a long tradition of silent prayer and meditation in Christianity that can be further supported by drawing on techniques from other traditions (such as Buddhism). Even if people are not used to prolonged periods of public silence, they can become accustomed to it by interspersing periods of a few minutes' silence between other kinds of worship.

The distinction between silent prayer and meditation is sometimes emphasised by Protestants who are suspicious of meditation, but my own impression is that there is very little genuine experiential distinction. Silent prayer is sometimes described as 'waiting on God', and involves an openness to wider experience that is very similar to that cultivated in the less structured forms of Buddhist meditation, such as the Zen *Shikantaza* or 'just sitting'. The more one engages directly with experience, the less labels like 'God' matter, because we are dealing with the same kinds of brain processes. The more structured forms of meditation – which can vary from a very non-conceptual focus on the breathing, a coloured disc or set of sounds to a structured reflection or visualisation – offer techniques that can help one focus better in prayer, avoid obsessive and interfering trains of thought, and contact ongoing sources of inspiration. All such activities are integrative, not repressive, and it is a complete misunderstanding of them to think in terms of 'emptying the mind' or other such terms that convey the repression rather than integration of thoughts. Both prayer and meditation are about filling the mind rather than emptying it, filling it with directly experienced openness: with energy, positivity, love and awareness rather than the trivial fluff that more frequently obsesses us.

If public worship is to avoid the two extremes of superficiality and mass hysteria, it needs to be closely linked to individual practice of prayer and meditation. Where people in the congregation do not have experience of private prayer, they can be encouraged and supported in it by public worship that provides a way in. Those who come to a service in search of inspiration and restoration as well as communal sharing, though, will only be refreshed if they are able to connect to experience as well as rouse their emotions and relate to symbols. The less religion relies on absolute beliefs as a shortcut, the more imperative it will be to get worship right and to use it as a tool of integration.

b. Middle Way practices and psychology

Since Christian practice only differs from wider Middle Way practice in terms of the cultural tradition in which it is expressed, it is probably helpful here to also review some wider Middle Way practices that I have written about in more detail elsewhere, but to relate them to the teachings of Jesus as discussed in 5c. These practices particularly draw on the Western psychological tradition, and also to a lesser extent on aspects of philosophical practice.

There is a widespread perception of conflict between Christianity and psychology, but this is nearly always based on an unnecessarily rigid view of the presuppositions of each which concentrates on absolute belief rather than the evidence from experience that supports the practice of each. For example, Christianity is assumed to require belief in the soul, freewill and an intrinsically sinful human nature, and this to be at odds with supposed psychological assumptions of materialism, determinism and the value of self esteem[144]. The standpoint of the Middle Way, however, involves clear agnosticism on all these metaphysical points *on either side*, liberating Christians to follow the spirit of Christ in valuing human experience as a guide to more adequate provisional beliefs, and thus allowing them to make use of the many fruitful discoveries made by psychology and neuroscience in recent years to inform Christian practice.

The whole debate about metaphysical assumptions appears nonsensical once one has the courage to rise above it by simply recognising that both moral and factual claims based on experience do not have to be absolutised. Thus, for example, we can recognise an experience of choice and responsibility which is central both to the practice of Christianity and of psychotherapy, without absolutising this into an assumption of either freewill or determinism. We can use evidence about brain function (which is enormously informative today) without adopting reductionist or materialist assumptions, because we don't have to assume that the information we get from observing the brain is the only or the final story. Rather, information about the brain can help us to understand and clarify our interpretation of the inner experience of having a mind[145].

If Christians will only set aside the metaphysics and investigate the riches of psychology with an open mind, they will find a huge amount there of practical value. If they want to actually get to grips with sin and delusion (rather than relying deterministically on the grace of God to sort it out for them), it will be especially important to understand the interrelated sources of rigid belief, overwhelming craving and fear and the variety of cognitive biases that can interfere with our judgements. Nor is having some sort of psychology in any way optional, and traditional forms of Christianity often just assume a cruder and less adequate form of psychology because that is associated with the Biblical context, rather than combining the insights that can be found in Jesus and other Christian sources with a more adequate psychology. To practice the seven principles of Jesus' Middle Way teachings as explained in 5c above (synthesis, integration, universality, scepticism, provisionality, love and balance), and to actually make progress as well as recognise our limitations, it will be most important to draw on a psychological perspective. I will make some suggestions here of practices, largely psychologically and some philosophically orientated, that can help with all seven of these aspects of Jesus' teachings.

1. Synthesis

Synthesis demands that our approaches to every aspect of experience are inter-related. Thus religion is not just for Sundays, ethics cannot be separated from factual judgements, and religious considerations cannot be separated from moral ones. The practice of synthesis is often described today as 'thinking outside the box' – i.e. being able to override boundaries between areas of experience to creatively bring one to bear on the others. Our tendency to 'think within the box' involves a number of biases identified in psychology, which can be practically addressed though probably not entirely overcome.

Confirmation bias is a central concern of science that should also be a central concern of Christians in their moral and religious judgements. Confirmation bias is the tendency to only consider information that confirms the beliefs you already have, and is well documented as a universal human tendency[146]. It is thus obviously also a tendency that Christians often exhibit: for example by associating mainly with other Christians, by reading Christian theology rather than considering the insights that might be offered by secular sources or other religions, or by dismissing alternative viewpoints when they do encounter them, rather than listening to them and learning from them. *Domain dependence* is a related cognitive bias that works against synthesis, in which people are unable to apply ideas or insights that they understood in one context across in another[147]. This is particularly common when people are obliged to engage with psychology to make them more efficient in a work context, but do not apply it to their personal lives.

To cultivate synthesis is at one and the same time to work with these biases, recognising how much they limit our judgement. We can cultivate synthesis through a variety of measures. Meditation (or prayer) will work to help cultivate the overall awareness needed to become aware of alternatives to our current view. Deliberately exposing yourself to alternative viewpoints in your reading, internet browsing and social media use is another helpful practice: here Jesus' embrace of tax-collectors and sinners can be a direct inspiration. On the whole it is probably more effective to engage with 'near' alternative viewpoints than 'far' ones, to take into account our embodied limitations. For example, if you are a political liberal, engage first with moderate conservatives, rather than neo-Nazis whom you will probably just end up in conflict with.

Much can be learnt from scientific approaches in our personal judgement. For example, when confronted with a new claim, a scientist might well want to ask how widely that claim has been or could be tested in practice, and in what circumstances that claim would be abandoned. Before abandoning a theory of some kind, it's also crucial to compare it to the available alternatives rather than considering the theory in isolation. These are not only features of scientific method, and should not be identified with 'materialism' or other confining metaphysical assumptions: rather these are general ways of working with any human judgement so as to work towards a more adequate view. Even to avoid the seven deadly sins of traditional Christianity one needs these kinds of practices. For example, to avoid excessive pride, one needs to look beyond the assumption that one's own achievements or possessions are of overriding value. There's nothing wrong with positively 'taking pride' in what one has done, in the sense of valuing it, but if we ask how wide a field of experience the belief that one's own achievements are valuable has been measured within, in what circumstances one might find greater achievements, and what might be alternative candidates for praise, one has greater resources for reflection that would undermine an excessive reliance on such pride. The same could be said about the values that underlie greed, sloth, gluttony, envy, wrath and lust, all of which involve the absolutisation of values that have not been compared beyond a certain limited context. Synthesis is an important aspect of the solution to these sins.

2. Integration

Integration brings together desires and associated beliefs that have previously been in conflict. In 5c I have already discussed some of the ways that Jesus both taught and practised integration, with the practices of prayer and of forgiveness being obviously important in any Christian context. Integration is a psychological term, originally used by Jung, but also by modern psychotherapists such as Daniel Siegel[148] and Paul Gilbert[149]. Light can also be cast on the nature of integration by research on the asymmetry of the brain hemispheres. Integration occurs when desires that were previously in conflict are reconciled, because the beliefs associated with those desires have been reconsidered and reframed in a way that addresses the conditions better and makes the conflict unnecessary.

Elsewhere I have analysed the practice of integration into three interdependent types: desire, meaning and belief, each of these being the subject of a volume of the *Middle Way Philosophy* series[150]. Integration of desire refers to the unification of previously opposed energies, integration of meaning to the recognition of new symbols as both cognitively and emotionally meaningful (which enables alternative beliefs to be considered), and integration of belief to the actual reframing process whereby conflicting assumptions are reconsidered. In these books I have also given a more detailed account of the practices that can support each of these forms of integration than can be offered here. Here I will only offer a summary suggesting a range of practices that will to some extent overlap with ones discussed elsewhere in this book.

The integration of desire can be most immediately cultivated through meditation and mindfulness (in which I would include many forms of prayer). It is the openness to new experience from the right hemisphere that is crucial here, but this in turn can only be made possible by the relaxation of anxieties and cravings: chemical stimuli from the amygdala and striatum at the back of the brain that keep our conscious activity focused on narrow ideas of what we want to gain or avoid. Bodily awareness is probably the best way to calm down the insistent and obsessive thoughts that these anxieties and cravings tend to produce, and just going through this relaxation regularly can have an integrative effect on our experience and judgement. Meditation does not need to become an end in itself, is not about stopping all thought, and involves a temporary internal focus so that we can be more effective in our external judgements.

This individual practice, however, also has its correlate at a social level. Where conflicting desires take the form of opposition between different individuals who each identify with those desires, the same basic approach can be used: namely, temporarily relaxing the obsessive flow of responses in order to help people consider alternative points of view. Forms of mediation, such as Marshall Rosenberg's Non-violent Communication[151], may often begin by getting opposing people to recognise each other's viewpoint and needs, in the process broadening the desires of each so that they might start to want to benefit the others and meet their needs as well as fulfilling their own. Nothing is gained in these sorts of situations by the idealistic renunciation of one's own desires: rather one's desires (which, as an embodied being, one is never likely to lose) need to be put in a bigger context with those of others. It seems that Christianity has often promoted an unhelpful psychology of self-denial that is merely a reaction away from the demands of the self, rather than a much more helpful Middle Way that includes it.

The integration of meaning gives us access to new significant symbols (such as words, grammatical structures, cognitive models, significant objects, visual images and music) that we have not previously engaged with or recognised as meaningful, and thus have been unable to actively consider as the basis of new belief. The barriers to recognising, engaging with and understanding new symbols may be predominantly emotional or predominantly cognitive, but always involve a mixture. Christians need to be engaging with the integration of meaning because in order to love your enemies, it is essential to understand your enemies.

The integration of meaning can be practised in a range of ways which may focus on engaging with new meaning in oneself or in others. For example, *focusing* is a practice developed by Eugene Gendlin[152] that involves working with a facilitator to open up and clarify our semi-conscious thoughts and feelings, thus making meaningful what was previously denied. Learning new languages and engaging in mediation processes can also help to make meaningful both what others are saying and what we have not been listening to sufficiently. However, it is the arts that are probably the prime established practice for the integration of meaning, whether we are creating new art or appreciating what others have done. In both cases new possibilities are opened up and made meaningful for us, whether as part of a creative process that articulates our own feelings, or as a broadening awareness of becoming aware of new possible symbols used by others. Christianity has a rich tradition of work in the arts, especially poetry, visual art and music, which can especially help us to make the archetypal God, Christ and other archetypes more immediate and meaningful.

Indeed, worship, as discussed in the previous chapter, is probably best seen as a medium for integrating meaning, and in that sense as an artistic and practical event. Just as in art we may encounter a striking new visual representation that adds to our understanding of God, in worship we make such symbols of God more meaningful by focusing special attention on them.

The integration of belief is the reconciliation of opposing beliefs by reconsidering and reframing assumptions, and often we can only reach a stage where we are capable of this by prior practice of the integration of desire and of meaning. Since beliefs are rendered incompatible by absoluteness[153], the process of integration of belief is most basically one of sorting absolute elements of a belief from provisional ones, so that the absolute ones can be avoided and the provisional ones brought into creative dialectic with their apparent opposites. When one's beliefs are provisional, it is always possible to make comparisons with alternatives, and to compare their degree of justification through experience of some kind (not necessarily full scientific verification), this being just as much the case with claims about value as with factual claims. If we accept a more integrated claim that takes into account more conditions as better justified, provisional beliefs can always be integrated by being tested and proving more or less adequate compared to the alternatives available.

To get to grips with this process in the complexity of our experience we need both to cultivate awareness of absolute beliefs that might sabotage the integration process, and engage our provisional beliefs with each other. Though both of these processes can be supported by integration of desire and integration of meaning processes, they more basically involve critical thinking, by which I mean a process of reflection on our assumptions and their justification rather than merely an analysis of reasoning.

Both cognitive psychology and philosophical education offer help with this process. Cognitive psychology offers a great deal of research on a whole range of cognitive biases, which are distortive tendencies in the human constitution: for example, they can distort our judgements by absolutising a particular time, a view of oneself or of an object, a particular value or particular boundaries. One of these, confirmation bias, has already been mentioned, whilst I have surveyed a long list of others elsewhere[154]. Philosophical education has also applied the skills of philosophy beyond their traditional field in the form of critical thinking or thinking skills, one major focus of which is the avoidance of fallacies, which also often identify absolutisations. If they really want to get to grips with sin through its causes in human judgement, Christians should be engaging with both critical thinking and bias awareness.

In practice, though, we have a situation where most people overwhelmingly associate (nay, define) Christianity with its absolutisations. Instead of working in harmony with psychologists, therapists, and educators to challenge absolutisations and thus help people get closer to God's profound challenges, Christians are in many cases working directly to *maintain* bias and prejudice. For example, the Texas Republican Party's 2012 platform opposed the teaching of critical thinking that "have the purpose of challenging the student's fixed beliefs". On the same educational platform support is offered for "school subjects with emphasis on the Judeo-Christian principles on which America was founded"[155]. In this case, as in others, this is due to their identification with authoritarian politics as well as an absolutised account of divine revelation, and that's an issue I'll be returning to in 9.f.

However, for the moment it only needs to be noted that this kind of identification does not help people to become more integrated in any respect, or to address conditions better. The needs of Christians are not magically different from those of anyone else in this respect because they 'believe' something different. As Jesus said, "If your right eye causes your downfall, tear it out and fling it away" (Mt 5:29). I suspect that the eye by itself is never the source of our downfall without the assumptions that accompany its use, but for 'right eye' here, substitute any belief that seems just as indispensable. Without the ability to consider that you might be wrong, talk of love, peace and harmony are empty verbiage.

3. Universality

Universality, as discussed in 5c above, is the applicability of the Middle Way to any situation of any person. Wherever there is a judgement to be made, we could make that judgement in a way that focuses on experience and avoids absolutes, or we could veer into assuming absolutes. That judgement can be made regardless of the decisions you have made before (however much of a sinner you are), and regardless of how easy or difficult your situation is. To put this into more accustomed Christian language, one could say that Christ is always present for us, and that the attempt to take a divine perspective always involves moving beyond the limitations of each human perspective.

To recognise that universality in practice requires integration, because we need to be able to accept alternative desires, meanings and beliefs as starting points for the Middle Way or places where Christ dwells, without cutting them off as 'other'. All the practices mentioned above for integration should thus also help us to recognise this universality. The recognition of universality also involves the process of synthesis, which produces cognitive and emotional connections between one sphere and another.

4. Scepticism

Scepticism is the practice of consistent critical awareness. Most of us do not have too much of a problem being critical about something that adversely affects our interests, but the challenge of sceptical practice is to be aware of the limitations of *all* beliefs, whether these are positive or negative, and whether they are associated with your group or another group. Consistent scepticism is intellectual and ethical liberation. It is the basis of the recognition both that we will never get everything absolutely right, and that provisional and uncertain views are acceptable without any need to strain for absolute ones of a kind that we are incapable of. Scepticism in Christian tradition has often been experienced as holiness: the experiential ability to move beyond 'worldly' assumptions so that they no longer have power over us.

To practice scepticism it is helpful to be aware of basic sceptical arguments. I have discussed these elsewhere[156], but they include awareness of the effects of our embodiment, the limitations of our senses, the cultural limitations of our interpretation, the uncertainty created by past error and the possibility of total or partial delusion in our present experience, the danger of infinite regression in all justifications, and the impossibility of the language we use to state our beliefs even gaining its meaning from a relationship with reality.

In a culture rife with the misunderstanding of scepticism as a negative, and with the merely *selective* use of it in the Church and in Christian theology, it is challenging to try to use scepticism in a balanced fashion. Nevertheless, it is doing so that gets us to the heart of the insights of Jesus as they can be most usefully applied in human experience. It is crucial to be able to practise scepticism in relation to beliefs associated with Christianity as well as those that we might perceive as opposed to it, as was explored above (7f) in relation to atheism. Awareness of cognitive biases and fallacies is also a crucial way of developing sceptical awareness in relation to one's own assumptions.

A sceptical practice of Christianity will require, whenever we come across a claimed belief, to ask ourselves "Why should I believe that?". If you can justify your belief in the terms of experience, then adopt it provisionally, but be prepared to let go of it if you encounter a better alternative based on more integrated experience. If the belief is absolute and lies beyond anything we can experience, then it is likely to interfere unhelpfully with your practice of provisional belief. Do not react against it (as this will likely lead you into the opposite absolute), but gently set it aside. In that way, what you do believe, whether ethically, spiritually or factually, will be adequately rooted in your experience.

Do not underestimate the ubiquity and prevalence of absolute beliefs that need to be set aside in this way. It is not only beliefs about God that can take this form, but also ones about things, facts, people, ourselves, moral and aesthetic values, responsibility, times (past, present or future), meanings, and boundaries[157]. All of these need a balanced sceptical treatment, for which study of the absolute beliefs, cognitive biases and fallacies associated with each of these areas can be very helpful.

5. Provisionality

However, scepticism by itself is of no positive value without provisionality. Scepticism helps us to recognise ways that any beliefs we identify with may be wrong. Provisionality, however, combines this critical awareness with awareness of alternatives. As long as we are able to consider alternatives to a given belief, it remains provisional, even if in practice we maintain a lot of faith or confidence in it. The availability of alternatives, even when we don't believe in those alternatives, depends on the imagination. Alongside the strong and well-worn channels in our brain, representing the beliefs we rely on, we also need weaker links: resources offering alternatives that we may need to adapt to new circumstances in future.

One of the key ways in which provisionality has been recognised in Christian tradition is through *repentance*. In order to move to better ways of thinking and living, we need to recognise the limitations of the old ones: that they have been narrow and sinful. To repent of our sins, though, we need to be aware of an alternative. That's why repentance often accompanies conversion in Christian tradition, for example in the life story of St Augustine of Hippo[158]. The New Testament word for repentance, *metanoia,* means a change of heart or mind that is most basically dependent on flexibility. Conversion where there is a lack of such flexibility can be sudden and fragile, as in the story of Saul's conversion in Acts 9, but even here the move from a narrower to a more integrated state is marked by the recognition of new possibilities: "Immediately it was as if scales had fallen from his eyes" (Acts 9:18).

That's why it's so helpful not to just rely on one tradition of discourse, even though we can also acknowledge the ways we may be rooted in it. Christians who practise provisionality will find it helpful to engage with other ways of thinking, whether these take the form of other religions or of alternative ('secular') Western traditions. That doesn't mean attempting to swap one's identity for something alien, but rather using the alternative perspective as a stimulus to help develop the understanding initially offered by the Christian tradition in one's own experience.

Other ways of cultivating provisionality particularly can involve engaging with those we have an initial negative response to, and setting up contexts where we are obliged to do this, such as mediation practices or encounter groups. It can also be aided by learning other languages – both in the sense of the speech of other nations and in the sense of different groups with their own ways of using language. Every kind of practice of integration as noted above can also help to create the conditions in which greater provisionality becomes possible.

6. Love

Christianity is often distinguished from other religions for its degree of emphasis on love. The love concerned is *agape*: that is universal and unconditional love rather than sexual or other attached forms. However, the Christian understanding of love has often suffered from over-analysis which separated *agape* so much from ordinary human forms of love that it became a strained abstraction. Thus, for example, monks and nuns have often been strongly discouraged from forming 'particular friendships'. However, psychology confirms that universal and unconditional love (if it is even possible in anything like a pure form) needs to develop from more basis experiences of infantile attachment, self-esteem and social bonding[159]. Past Christian idealisation of love has often been damaging because of dogmatic assumptions and a failure of synthesis in relation to it. We can only attain divine love by growing up, nurtured by the roots offered by human love.

To develop love from the roots up there are a variety of practices, that have developed particularly in the Buddhist and psychological traditions. I have always found it extremely odd that the Christian tradition talks most about love, but does very little to actively cultivate it, and other traditions, such as Buddhism, which is more likely to talk about the interdependence of wisdom and compassion, have a far stronger tradition of practical exercises to actually develop love. In Buddhism, the cultivation of loving-kindness practice involves getting into contact with positive feelings of goodwill via the body, then extending gradually to oneself, a good friend, a neutral person, an enemy and then the whole world[160]. Though I've personally never found this an easy practice, even struggling with such a practice seems preferable to singing a hymn or intoning a prayer about love and leaving it at that in the vain hope that love itself will magically follow.

Paul Gilbert, the modern developer of compassion-focused forms of mindfulness, also offers a wide range of integrative practices designed to help us develop compassion: for example, structured reflections to work with anger and anxiety, cultivate courage, and develop more awareness around our tendency to unreflectingly blame ourselves or others[161]. Considering the stress on love in Christianity, it is surprising that these or similar practices like them are not used in every church. Is it not the *responsibility* of Christians to cultivate love, and thus to try to engage with the psychological conditions that help it develop?

7. Balance

To find and maintain a balance between divine and human seems, if anything, the most central defining Christian practice of all. What is a Christian if not someone who follows Christ, and what is Christ if not the balancer, the mediator, the transformer, the bridge-builder that we find within ourselves? Every time our awareness recurs to the ideal, and we engage that ideal with the limited and human rather than abandoning it in despair as being beyond us – every time we do this we are going through a process of balancing and adjustment between positive and negative extremes – the Middle Way.

Such balancing is not so much a practice that one could do in isolation, as a way of doing all the other practices that have been mentioned. Every practice offers its challenges and standards, set by ourselves or others. If praying, we want to connect with God. If meditating, we want to maintain our mindfulness. If creating art, we want to find a creative flow. But these things do not always happen. We can give up in frustration and despair, or alternatively we can recall that the failures *are always part of the process*. It's only by accepting the crucifixion, symbolically speaking, that we can reach the resurrection. We tack back and forth between the goal and the failure, and somewhere in between we find a working point. It's a working point that will vary in every situation with every purpose, but there will always be a working point of some kind. Perhaps, then, by finding it, we will be able to succeed to a greater extent – but never perfectly.

That's the uncomfortable balance, the 'stretched hanging' as Jung described it, between the divine and the human in every moment. It's right at the coalface of experience, and is worth far more than all the pious idealisations of the absolutising tradition.

c. The eucharist

The eucharist is the most important of all Christian sacraments in both Catholic and Protestant churches. That's because it is part of the day-to-day routine of the church, not merely the ceremony accompanying an exceptional event. I have never yet 'taken communion' myself, but nevertheless the eucharist helped shape my childhood. On a regular basis, before the remains of lunch were cleared up and before he set out for his afternoon visits to the housebound and hospitalised, my father would cut a block of bread off the loaf, remove the crust, and cut the remainder into little cubes, whilst I watched in fascination. These little cubes of bread would go into his communion box along with a little bottle of made-up blackcurrant cordial. I later realised that such casual treatment of the bread and 'wine' would probably scandalise a Catholic or high Anglican, by whom the communion is constantly treated as a holy object – in theory the actual body and blood of Christ. But for my father as a Baptist, their significance was clearly 'only' symbolic.

I trust that this symbolic significance does not need arguing for by this point, and that no Christian who really 'believes in' transubstantiation (or even its weaker Lutheran version, consubstantiation) will have read thus far. Powerful symbolism simply does not need metaphysics: indeed, it is undermined by it. For the full power of the eucharist, a Christian has to *imagine* the bread and wine as the body and blood of Christ: how could the belief that it 'really is' that body and blood operate as anything other than a cognitive distraction to an imaginative process? The disputes that arose about the issue at the time of the Reformation only go to show quite how much of a cognitive distraction it can be.

The eucharist is potentially a very powerful ritual, because of its degree of embodiment. It does not just consist of saying (or singing) fine words, but of actually eating and drinking something. What's more, the ritual space in which the eucharist occurs ensures that the eating and drinking will be done with great awareness and reflectiveness. The corporeality evokes that of Jesus' own body and its suffering. Indeed, there could be no more powerful reminder that *we are* Christ – that we symbolically take in parts of his body to our own. However, if the awareness of bodily suffering is not to become an end in itself, the accompanying awareness is crucial. We recall bodily suffering *so that* we can be free of automatic positive feedback loops: so that we can think again in provisionality about whatever cycles we may be caught up in.

Our understanding of the eucharist obviously depends on what we think the atonement is about. If atonement is seen as a magical shortcut to the end of sin, the eucharist can simply be seen as a ritual spell we cast to activate this shortcut. The actions, no matter how embodied, will merely reinforce belief in certain ideas that remain entirely abstracted from our actual engagement with what we experience as sin. If, on the other hand, atonement is primarily the at-one-ment of Christ in us, the symbolised body and blood of Christ can be directly connected to our own pain and its potential fruits in provisionality.

It is obvious that in a very large part of the Christian world the eucharist is so formalised that it is primarily a social ritual, which merely provides an absolute basis of group membership for those who participate in it. The rituals that surround it have become so rigid, even in the 'free' Protestant churches (let alone in the Catholic and Orthodox churches) that the ritual probably has precisely the opposite effect from that of encouraging provisionality. The rigid bounds of the ritual space also mean that few carry positive effects from the ritual to the rest of their experience.

I think there is much that the clergy could do to help frame the eucharist in a way that helps it to become a ritual that celebrates provisionality rather than dogma. One is to impart as much practical mindfulness to the occasion as possible. The use of meditation beforehand, for example, could help put people in a mood that is itself more provisional before the ritual begins. Another is to stress the Biblical symbolism that determines the wider meaning of the bread and wine, as discussed in relation to Jesus' miracles in 5.d above. The bread reminds us that only integrated hunger can be satisfied, the wine that fluidity can become the basis of rich transformation. Bread and wine in the gospels are symbols of the integration that can follow when suffering is wisely responded to, rather than only of suffering as an end in itself.

A Middle Way in relation to the eucharist, as with any tradition, will work with it as part of the Christian legacy, of great significance within the terms of that legacy. However, at the same time it will not be unalterable, and its significance will need to be the generation of faith rather than the reinforcement of belief. There are several formalistic requirements surrounding the eucharist that seem to be very much the result of absolute belief rather than faith, and that in my view interfere with the helpfulness of the ritual. These include limitations on who conducts it and who participates in it, as well as attitudes to the bread and wine themselves.

The requirement in the Orthodox, Catholic and Anglican churches for an ordained priest to conduct the eucharist is closely tied to the belief that it is some kind of magic rite that can tap into Jesus' atonement seen as an external cosmic event. The church as the agent of God on earth (represented by its priest) is seen as having the power to reconcile God and humanity through the sacraments, rather than the purpose of the sacrament being to have a beneficial effect on the individual who participates in it. As discussed in 7g above, such discontinuous significance being put on ordination also creates an unhelpful idealisation of clergy who are likely to be at best asymmetrically integrated in some respects. There is thus no good justification for the conduct of the eucharist being reserved for priests. Though it needs to be a solemn ritual, anyone willing and able to conduct it with the right degree of seriousness and confidence, and commanding sufficient trust in the congregation, should be able to conduct it.

Similar issues of unhelpful discontinuity apply to the question of who should participate in the eucharist: typically it is only baptised (and, in denominations that practice infant baptism, also confirmed) Christians who do so. However, this limitation is entirely dependent on the idea of accepting Jesus' atonement as an external, supernatural act. If the key issue is simply whether people find the eucharist sufficiently meaningful and beneficial, and participate in it with sufficient seriousness, there is no need to bar the unbaptised from the eucharist: provided, of course, they wish to participate. Breaking down that barrier could contribute to reducing Christian exclusivity, and recognising the degree of commonality they have with many non-Christians.

With regard to the bread and wine themselves, the literalism invested in transubstantiation by Catholics and High Anglicans means that it must be preserved as sacred. Any unused bread and wine must either be ceremonially kept or finished off by the priest (a requirement that sometimes contributes to alcoholism amongst Catholic priests). Of course, this involves an indefensible absolutisation of a symbolic process. If we are to avoid projecting symbolic archetypes, it is actually important that we distinguish the symbol in our minds from an external object that we might otherwise project it onto. Throwing away the bread and wine, or consuming it in an ordinary way, would actually involve a psychologically healthy reminder of that distinction.

Though by most non-Christian standards, the eucharist is a most peculiar ritual, there is no reason why it should not become a powerful and inspiring reminder of our commitment to challenge ourselves and to re-examine our assumptions. However, instead of this it is much more strongly associated with deeply entrenched dogma. We do not need to perform the eucharist to save our souls, but for those who wish to perform it, it may well be a useful method of stretching our souls.

d. Confession

The practice of confession is one of the seven sacraments in Roman Catholicism, and has a central place in regular Catholic practice, due to the requirement for Catholics to attend confession and gain absolution before attending mass. Confession has been rejected in the Protestant tradition because of the belief in salvation by faith, which took away the motivation for confessing and absolving sin as a way of re-accepting Christ's atonement and thus gaining 'salvation by works'. This is a great shame, because confession, if not freighted with absolutism, can be a very useful practice. The very idea of confession just did not figure in my Protestant upbringing, and I have had to experience its potential value in a Buddhist context[162]. Protestants are missing a possibly important tool of moral practice, because of an irrelevant debate about absolutisations concerning salvation.

Let us first review what the basic process of confession is, or might be if shorn of the unnecessary superstructure it has acquired in Catholicism. An individual Christian recognises that they have committed an action (or perhaps even maintained an intention) of which they are ashamed and that they recognise as morally negative (the basis on which they might fairly judge it to be morally negative is one that I will discuss in the final chapter of this book). They may recognise their action as morally negative because they have previously committed themselves to maintaining a certain moral standard, or because they recognise others as upholding a moral standard to which they aspire and that they have fallen short of. In recognition of their fault, they confess it to another person who shares (and preferably exemplifies) the moral ideals they are seeking to follow. By doing this, they are able to reinforce their commitment to improving their moral practice by having it socially reflected, so the action may well help the person to avoid committing the same negative action again, thus developing greater integration as they remove a source of conflict within themselves, and bringing them closer to the archetype of God within themselves.

This picture of how confession might be effective contrasts with all the unhelpful elements that have been incorporated into the Catholic practice of confession. Firstly, there are rigid and absolutised moral rules that are often at some remove from people's moral experience: notoriously including the prohibition of masturbation and of the use of artificial contraception. To begin with, these distort and undermine confession, as well as ethical practice in general, by associating morality itself with stupid and out-of-touch rules rather than with the development of moral experience. If people are asked to confess breaches of rules they do not perceive as genuine moral rules, but only as impositions of authority, they will rapidly become either alienated from the whole process or unhelpfully guilty.

Secondly, in Catholicism the process has become associated with a formalised penance and absolution, in which the priest represents the supposed power to forgive sins that is authorised by Christ's atonement. This involves a fundamental misunderstanding of the process of atonement as a supernatural process, rather than an integrative process gone through by an individual themselves. A penitential act may be helpful to us when we are trying to integrate the conflicts created by guilt and shame and try to develop a more helpful state of mind in which we can start again with a new commitment to moral practice. However, formalising that penitential act so rigidly reduces and trivialises it. When we have completed the formal act we may not be genuinely penitent, or we may still have much further to go over a period of time to integrate our guilt and shame. The Catholic church has failed to adapt its practices to anything like an adequate psychological understanding of the process of repentance, and thus made them increasingly irrelevant at best, or alienating at worst.

If confession is to be more helpful to Christians, it needs to be separated from absolute assumptions. Our moral commitment is not made to a supernatural authority, but rather to a more integrated self. To help us become more integrated, we can give ourselves rules, structures and institutions that may make demands on us, and remind us of our commitments. But the purpose of these is instrumental, not absolute. It is thus ourselves as individuals who need to be responsible for deciding when we have committed a sin that we want to confess. The church may offer us guidelines, but they can hardly be more than that, and their provisionality needs to be constantly born in mind without loss of moral urgency or moral purpose.

The question of whom we choose to confess to also needs to be much more flexibly understood. The church does not have a magical ability to forgive sins, but leaders in the church may (contingently) be the people we trust to receive our confessions and respond to them appropriately in confidence. On the other hand, for many people, a friend, spouse, counsellor or psychotherapist may be a better recipient for confession. It is the relationship of trust that matters far more than the formal role.

It's crucial that the confessor, whoever he or she may be, is able to hear and accept the confession, because the sharing of it is the crucial part of the psychological effectiveness of confession. By recognising that someone else knows about your fault, the conflict it creates is eased and it is seen in a slightly bigger perspective. It's also crucial that the confessor's response to the disclosure is balanced: neither disproportionately horrified, nor denying that a fault has occurred. The confessor simply needs to make it clear that the confession has been fully understood, perhaps by reflecting it back and perhaps by asking questions to get further details. It may also be helpful to put the offence in a broader perspective without belittling it, for example by giving information about how common the offence is (if the offender is inclined to exaggerate its uniqueness) or what effects it is likely to have (if the offender is inclined either to exaggerate or dismiss those effects). But the confessor should not exhort or advise from a morally absolute position beyond the actual moral commitments the person has arrived at for themselves.

Much the same points can be made about penance. Formalistic penances such as saying ten Hail Marys have become a kind of joke that makes a laughing-stock of Catholicism the world over, and are probably best dispensed with entirely. It is the person who makes the confession who should decide, in discussion with the confessor, what the penance should be, if any, depending on what would have the most integrative effect for the person concerned. In many cases it may involve apologising and making amends to the victim of the offence, if there is one.

Approached in such a way, that respects the experienced variations between individuals both in moral commitment and justified guilt, confession could become a sacrament of great moral value and worth: one that I would also urge Protestants to embrace. Confession is still an acknowledgement of fault before God, and need lose none of its power in that respect, but might actually become morally efficacious instead of an institutionalised moral failure.

e. Rites of passage

There are many semi-estranged cultural Christians for whom rites of passage are the only remaining link with their religion. They attend the occasional christening, wedding or funeral service, and for many, a religious sentiment adheres to these ceremonies even when it has been forgotten or alienated elsewhere. Why should this be the case?

The obvious answer is that it is at these key moments of life – and death – that we are at our most open to the power of religious meaning. When experience has shifted substantially, when we can no longer rely so much on the old assumptions because the conditions have changed, then we have to look beyond the established patterns of everyday meaning and belief represented in our prosaic left brains. Like dinosaurs after the meteorite hits, we are either laid low or we adapt. To adapt we need to look to the wider sphere, the unexpected as we might experience it in the more open right hemisphere – to God.

Of course, rites of passage also have a social function of mobilising support and reassurance from the community at a time of transition, whether the occasion is happy or sad. But that is a function that could be fulfilled by any kind of social ceremony, without it necessarily needing a religious edge. We see this in the variety of rites of passage that are often celebrated by families or work colleagues by holding a party or going out for a meal: significant birthdays, significant anniversaries, retirements, leaving a job, moving house, or special achievements. The adjustment is rarely so profound here that we feel such a need to reconsider our entire view of ourselves. However, having a baby, marriage (at least in a traditional framework) and death or bereavement do have this effect. It is then that we are more likely to turn to God, and use the occasion to integrate profoundly new and different experiences with old ones, in addition to seeking social support.

It is thus clear that rites of passage in Christianity, as elsewhere, have an important integrative function, and that this function can often be better fulfilled by contact with meaningful archetypes that remind us of a wider perspective. Unfortunately, as in the rest of Christian tradition, though, Christianity as an absolute belief has often interfered in this process by imposing dogmatic beliefs on the whole context in which the rite of passage takes place. I think a strong case can be made that these absolute beliefs have a very negative effect on rites of passage, and should be banished from them.

Baptism and confirmation

In the case of christening (infant baptism), except in those churches that practise adult baptism, I have already discussed some of these absolutisations in 7d above. As it is primarily due to the belief in salvation after death being dependent on the discontinuous acceptance of Jesus' magical atonement through baptism that infant baptism has ever been practised, a ceremony that might be a hugely integrative experience for an adult, symbolising a commitment to integration, has often become one of which the chief participant (the child) understands nothing. The very idea of adopting a religion of which you understand nothing is a travesty of the experiential power of that religion.

It could be argued that christening also has a value for the parents, for the godparents, and for others who symbolically welcome the new baby to the community. This is obviously correct, in the sense that having a baby is a huge upheaval and a point at which a rite of passage could be invaluable – for the adults involved. In recognition of this, the Baptists and other denominations that practise adult baptism tend to substitute a dedication ceremony for christening, in which the focus is on the parents pledging the child to a Christian upbringing in the church. However, absolutisation still rules here in the terms of what the parents are pledging themselves to, whether the ceremony is a baptism for the baby or not. If they are committing themselves to bringing up the child in Christian *beliefs*, they are most likely pledging themselves to alienation and conflict, as well as ignoring the child's autonomy in deciding its own beliefs. On the other hand, if they pledge themselves to helping the child encounter the living archetypal God in experience, they are engaging in a spiritual act of huge value both to themselves and the child, and the commitment may later help sustain them when the going gets difficult. Much the same may be said of the role of godparents in assisting with such spiritual support.

The same kind of absolutisation over the role of baptism, leading to infant baptism in most churches, simultaneously created the rite of confirmation. Confirmation occurs, for most cultural Christians, at the time when a coming of age ceremony is needed to mark the difficult passage from childhood to adulthood. Traditional coming of age ceremonies involve initiation through the overcoming of difficulty, creating a sense of confidence in newly won strength (especially for young men), and simultaneously allow experiential bonding with the tribe through the sharing of this initiation and ritual acceptance of the new adult member. Confirmation, however, uses an absolutising shortcut for both these things. Instead of working through difficulties, the new Christian has to merely passively accept beliefs, with deep and critical questioning of those beliefs by comparison with alternatives discouraged. The ritual acceptance by the adult group, then, is superficial because it depends only on that shared metaphysical undertaking, and is likely to be fragile.

The whole term 'confirmation' itself indicates the major error here in the way most Christianity responds to adolescence today. Adolescents need to establish their own intrinsic motivations for their values, in the spirit of Jesus and his questioning, rather than following rules and accepting prefabricated belief systems, otherwise their maturity is blocked. Rather than 'confirming' something that is already assumed, then, they need to be creating and discovering values through their own integrative process. It is hardly surprising, then, if most adolescents, when offered alternatives in an open society, find no meaning in Christianity. Those who are left are most likely to either be very extrinsically motivated and dutiful, or desperately seeking a refuge from extreme insecurity. If only people with this kind of psychological profile become Christians, the effect is likely to be a positive feedback loop of greater and greater superficiality and literalism becoming dominant in the churches, and the churches in the developed world getting more and more out of touch with a world in which people (even if often economically forced into extrinsic motivation in their work) increasingly seek intrinsic motivation in those areas they can more readily control.

My suggestion for the reform of the whole sorry situation surrounding christening and confirmation, then, is a clear abandonment of the absolute beliefs about salvation that stand in the way of adult baptism, and a return to adult baptism in all churches with a dedication ceremony for infants. However, the dedication for infants needs to involve a dedication to an integrative path rather than a set of beliefs, and baptism also needs to be understood as a commitment of faith rather than one of belief. As a ritual of transition into adulthood, baptism also needs to be accompanied by an initiation process involving full confrontation with both intellectual and possibly also physical difficulties (depending on the situation of the person being baptised). It could happen at any point in adulthood when the person is mature and integrated enough to take such a step, and should not happen prematurely in early adolescence through motivations that are largely extrinsic.

Marriage

In the case of marriage, there can be much more debate about whether a discontinuous upheaval in people's lives is any longer necessary, and thus whether marriage needs to be a rite of passage with great emphasis put on it, or whether it is mainly a social event in which a couple are supported in their commitment to each other. Absolutising moral teachings from the church have done their best to keep marriage as discontinuous as possible. By emphasising virginity and disapproving of sex or cohabitation before marriage, the church for the most part still tries to ensure that a virgin bride and groom enter their first physical intimacy only after the wedding ceremony, and thereafter they are suddenly thrust into married life all at one go. Fortunately, modern couples in Western countries overwhelmingly ignore these rules, even if they have a church wedding. They do so, for the most part, on a sound basis of experience: you are much better committing yourself to a person you already know, and have already lived with and had a sexual relationship with on a trial basis. Not only then does marriage have to be much less of a trauma, but it stands a much greater long-term chance of success.

Even if we remove the discontinuous stress that traditionally attends marriage, though, the development of a committed relationship can still be a crucial integrative step for both partners. In marriage one is constantly challenged by the intimate otherness of one's partner to come to terms with the corresponding aspects of oneself. As long as both partners are engaged in a continuing process of integration, and are not attempting to dominate one another, they are better equipped to overcome the conflicts that new conditions may throw up. Then one can indeed claim that the traditional Christian model of a threefold marriage – between two human partners and God – has a relationship to experience. The image of the other in each is a field of integration in which they are stretched, an external demand like that of God, in relation to which they can only maintain a degree of imperfect practice.

If one can maintain the role of God in the marriage in this way, then it seems to be worthwhile to maintain marriage as a Christian rite of passage (though not necessarily with all the trappings that have become associated with it – white dresses, bridesmaids, photographers, special cars etc. really are optional). For a couple that does not have an understanding of God that in some way relates to their experience of integration, however, a Christian marriage is a travesty in which people repeat words they don't mean when they pledge themselves to God as well as each other. The integrity of the ceremony often seems to have been greatly undermined, with again Christian 'belief' being the chief culprit by distracting people from the integrative experiences that could be most meaningfully associated with the ceremony. Christian marriage is trivialised when people either believe that God's supernatural intervention will magically help their marriage, or on the other hand go through the motions and merely talk about God for the sake of social expectations.

Death

Of all the rites of passage, funerals are perhaps the one of which everyone seems to feel the most visceral need. Births and marriages, after all, are usually long expected and prepared for, and can usually be experienced as part of a process of transition: but death involves a sudden and sometimes completely unexpected change in which a person abruptly disappears from our lives. Not only do we need social support to be demonstrated at such a time, but we also need access to new inner resources to reconfigure our lives. But positively, bereavement is an opportunity for integration. The space left by the lost person, and our own identifications with that person, now needs to be filled by parts of ourselves that may previously have been hidden or undeveloped. For example, a widowed man may need to start doing the housework or cultivating the relationships he previously left to his wife, and in the process discover a neglected 'feminine' part of his own experience.

As I write on this topic, the loss of my father, to whom this book is dedicated, is still fresh in my mind from only a year ago. This book is itself a product of such an integrating process for me, as his death prompted me to try to engage more deeply with the relatively neglected Christian in me. My experience of the funeral was pivotal to this. Previous Christian funerals, including that of my mother, had been pretty much alienating experiences, in which I fretted at the absolutisations that were being imposed on me, when all I wanted to do was engage with my experience of the person I had lost and integrate it in solidarity with others. The insistence of the Christian community that I had to do that by 'believing' in absolute claims that had nothing to do with my experience of the person was a massive barrier to that process of integration, and resulted in the funeral being a focus of feelings of conflict rather than a context for adjustment. However, at my father's funeral, that changed only because I made a personal resolution to participate as actively and positively as I could. Since I had no control over the overall format of the service, of course some of those conflicts were still there, but they became far less important and faded into the background when I was able to give stronger outward expression to my own integration process.

I think everyone should have that opportunity to experience a funeral of the close friend or relative as a meaningful and helpful occasion, not as another battle in an entrenched cultural war between belief and unbelief, whether waged outwardly or inwardly. This should not just be a matter of declaring a truce sufficient to allow 'non-believers' the opportunity to participate in some minor role that would not cause too much offence to believers. Rather, the causes of the conflict need to be addressed at their root by the interpretation of Christianity in terms of experiential faith, and the clear articulation of it in those terms in funerals rather than in terms of conflictual belief.

In the case of funerals, those absolute beliefs involve not only ones about the existence of God as a supernatural entity, but also about the afterlife, and implicitly about the soul as a vehicle by which the dead person can reach that afterlife. The belief that the dead person still exists in some way is popularly supposed to be a 'consolation', but I would suggest that this 'consolation' is an outward projection of an integrative process. People may start to integrate the beliefs and values associated with their bereaved situation in relation to their previous situation, but attribute this integration to an outward supernatural mechanism that is easier to conceptualise: but it is basically what cognitive psychology calls an attribute substitution[163]. Confronted with the question of what has enabled them to adjust, people substitute an apparently simpler set of concepts about the afterlife for a more complex, difficult set of explanations involving psychological processes. Such simplified substitutions remain popular because there is no possible way of challenging them in the terms of experience; as nobody, by definition, has ever experienced life after death (as opposed to *near* death experience) and returned to tell the tale.

The question of whether afterlife actually occurs or not is a massive distraction from this far more important practical question of how we adjust to death when still alive. If atheists go so far as to deny the existence of the afterlife, or discuss it in the irrelevant terms of probability, then they are also entering into such a distraction. Rigorous agnosticism, I would suggest, is the approach to the afterlife best justified by a helpful interpretation of Christian teaching as faith rather than belief. We simply do not know, nor will we ever know, nor can any possible 'evidence' tell us anything about such a matter. Helpful funerals assist people in coming to terms with the fact that they do not know, using the meaningful archetypes that will enable people to put their loss in a bigger perspective. Unhelpful ones prevent people from doing this by feeding them with fragile dogmas.

The implicit conflict surrounding afterlife beliefs is often evident in the way they are treated: with embarrassment, vagueness, and evasion. Central to classic Christian doctrine on the afterlife is the belief that souls go to heaven or hell (or purgatory in Catholicism), yet strangely enough funeral leaders seem to refrain from any suggestion that the deceased may have gone to hell, however obviously they may deserve it. Vaguer ideas, such as that the deceased may still be with us in spirit, seem to be more popular, because they avoid the idea of judgement. But, of course, even these vague ideas about spiritual continuation after death fly in the face of any evidence available to us. A person looking down on us after death would have to see without eyes and experience without a brain. The whole idea of them being able to do this is a left brain abstraction of an embodied process and goes far beyond 'experience' as we know it. We have absolutely no need to turn our requirement to integrate the *meaning* of the dead person into such literalistic beliefs about their *existence*.

Nor do we need to maintain afterlife beliefs to maintain a connection with Jesus and his most helpful teachings. Jesus discusses *judgement* a good deal in the gospels, as in the passage of the sheep and the goats discussed in 5f above, but does not link such judgement to the afterlife. As I argued there, such judgement can be most helpfully interpreted as *our* judgement. There is certainly no reference in the gospels to continued existence after death in which a disembodied person continues to dwell with us, of the kind vaguely adumbrated in so many Christian funeral addresses to avoid talking about judgement. The whole concept of the surviving soul is a Platonic import largely foreign to the Judaic tradition in which Jesus moved. The standard Christian 'beliefs' referred to in the funeral context bear very little relationship to any version of Jesus' message, let alone one that attempts to interpret helpfully on pragmatic grounds, and a funeral that tries to stay closer to Jesus' message thus most of all needs to maintain his provisionality and scepticism and apply these to death.

I can greatly respect clergy who make the best of the circumstances in Christian funerals, by acknowledging that death is a mystery and putting all the emphasis on our adjustment to that mystery. Linked to this could be the archetypal use of God and Christ to give a wider context to our adjustment. However, not all clergy have this practical emphasis, and those that do still have to contend with liturgy that often promotes a traditional supernatural interpretation, as well as sometimes a popular expectation of 'consolation'. Only institutional reform based on changes in theological approach can really change this, not so as to take the Christianity out of funerals and make them 'humanist', but rather to make it entirely clear that Christianity is a religion conducted by, maintained and participated in by humans, whose first requirement is for meaning and an integrative process rather than abstraction and alienation.

9

Christian ethics and politics

a. The contradictions of revelatory ethics

In this section I will argue that the Middle Way and Christian agnosticism potentially offer a far more justifiable, relevant and adequate ethics than what has passed for 'Christian ethics' in most of the two thousand years since Christ. 'Christian ethics' as normally understood is probably most realistically viewed as a vast institutionalised failure, in which 'oughts' are clung onto for the perverse reason that they *don't* work to change anyone's behaviour. Although there are many different versions of 'Christian ethics', what they nearly all have in common is the belief in a God who offers revelatory moral instructions. The disputes tend to lie only in the question of what form those instructions take.

For example, throughout Christian history, Christian ethics have extolled the virtues of peace, whilst professed Christians have engaged in continual war. Modern Catholic ethics continues to forbid the use of artificial contraception, but in the overwhelmingly Catholic countries of Spain and Italy the fertility rates have now dropped to 1.34 per woman (Spain) and 1.46 per woman (Italy)[164] precisely because the vast majority of Catholic couples completely ignore this rule. In any other sphere of life, a theory that so massively failed to match the outcomes would have been reconsidered long ago, but because ethics is routinely based on absolutisation, the gap is accepted.

Ethics does not have to be based on absolutisation – whether that is the positive absolutisation of traditional Christian ethics, or the negative absolutisation that denies the universality of ethics through relativism. There is an alternative based on experience and the Middle Way, in Christianity as in any other context, in which ethics do offer a normative challenge and stretch us, without being dogmatically unrealistic.

Any ethics needs to offer us guidance on how to judge each action, and thus how to live our lives. Each judgement is made in a specific situation – a situation that is freighted with the circumstances, our mental state and assumptions – but nevertheless we need to be able to respond to that specific situation. An ethics that is to be of any help to us needs be applicable in that situation as well as many others, to tell us relevantly how to move forward. It also needs to give a justifiable indication of how we *ought* to act, not tell us what we would have done anyway, nor merely give us ideals that are of no relevance to our current situation. Christian ethics as most generally understood – as revelatory ethics – do none of this. Its general rules that supposedly represent the moral will of God are unjustifiable because based on nothing more than dogma, irrelevant because abstracted from experience, irreligious because they lead us away from rather than towards God, and impossible to follow because they consist of general ideals rather than advice that is adequate to the circumstances.

Revelatory ethics are unjustifiable because in identifying a source of ethical knowledge in Christian tradition, they necessarily ignore the fact that such claimed ethical knowledge has to be interpreted by embodied human beings. If the source of revelation consists of a verbal command, whether from the Bible, Papal edict or any other source of authority, that command will have been both selected from possible alternatives and interpreted against other possible interpretations. The verbal formula itself is incapable of offering absolute justification, because its meaning depends, not on a relationship between the proposition and its potential truth or falsity, but on the accretion of synaptic links built up by each individual who interprets it through their embodied experience. Those individuals, interpreting the verbal formula, also have a responsibility for their interpretation that is undermined by any attempt to impose one interpretation through power. Even if the revelation is believed to be non-propositional, in the form of the person of Jesus for instance, there is still the same issue of selectivity and interpretation if that example is to be used to support any moral belief: what version of Jesus do we seek to imitate, in what way and how closely? In judging these things, we already have a responsibility for our ethics that takes it a long way from sole reliance on the justificatory source of moral authority.

Revelatory ethics are irrelevant because we do not make judgements through a simple process of deduction from a moral instruction. Ethical judgements involve a complex amalgamation of judgements about what we take to be true in a given situation, what motives arise for us in that situation, how others are likely to respond to our judgement, what options we find meaningful, and sometimes what options we think are good. The vast majority of judgements for most people are not consciously considered in a moral light in which different alternatives are possible, but rather decided according to social norms. We are all subject to a whole range of biases identified in cognitive psychology, in which social norms work directly or indirectly to determine our judgements in a positive or negative way: for example, few people will stand against *social proof* by using the evidence of their immediate experience to contradict what everyone else is saying (like the boy in the story of the Emperor's new clothes), and social proof can also work indirectly by making one view seem obvious that we then constantly select from our experience to reinforce (*confirmation bias*). Ethics of a kind that wants to avoid institutionalised failure must address these wider issues of how we actually make judgements, not just the idealised and thoroughly outdated model in which a general commandment is straightforwardly applied to a specific action in an apparent vacuum.

Revelatory ethics are also irreligious because their

assumptions about God work against the experiential archetype that is at the heart of integrative religious motivation. A God who is co-extensive with our own capacity for integration can be a profound source of moral challenge, but only because we *share* these motives as our own more integrated motives. Revelatory instructions, on the other hand, may often be imposed on us from without and have no necessary relationship to our own motives. God is love, but revelatory ethics are a form of power. A Christian who consults their own experience through prayer and contemplation, for example, may arise from this to find the church imposing a ruling on her that directly opposes the position she has just reached in her own experience, with this being not a challenge that forms the basis of further negotiation, but a matter of mere obedience, in which the possibility of the church being mistaken does not arise.

Revelatory ethics are impossible to follow because of their absolute nature, and in this respect depart from Jesus' rejection of Pharisaism. If God is said to provide a commandment to behave in one general way rather than another – whether it is not to commit adultery or to love one another – this takes no account of the individual's cultural or historical starting point, their motives, or their capacity to obey such a commandment in a practical context. There may be some for whom adultery is already a way of life, or others for whom just considering the possibility of loving their enemy rather than hating them (still very far from doing it) would be a massive moral step. But an absolute and discontinuous commandment, when unfulfilled, then reinforces the impression of the formalistic irrelevance of ethics rather than engaging with people's incremental capacity to actually practise ethics.

If Christians have still often ended up with a revelatory ethics, it is not because there has been no awareness of their potential limitations, nor that there has been no awareness of the possibility of ending up back with the Pharisees. St Paul's pivotal discussion of the contrasting roles of the law and the spirit in Romans 7 and 8 has had a big influence on Christian awareness of these matters, yet that discussion is also so ambiguous that it can be interpreted in terms of the magical shortcut of belief in the atonement as a moral panacea rather than as a challenge to take full human responsibility for ethical judgement. Paul recognises both an unavoidable experience of moral conflict, and the imperfection of all human moral responses, yet nevertheless takes these as indications that the law is admirable[165]. The following passage offers what might be read as a crucial anti-revelatory message for Christian ethics:

> *It follows that there is now no condemnation for those who are united with Christ Jesus. In Christ Jesus the life-giving law of the Spirit has set you free from sin and death. What the law could not do, because human weakness robbed it of all potency, God has done: by sending his own Son in the likeness of our sinful nature and to deal with sin, he has passed judgement against sin within that very nature, so that the commandment of the law may find fulfilment in us, whose conduct is no longer controlled by the old nature, but by the Spirit.* (Rom 8:1-4)

It is easy to see how this passage could be read, down the centuries, as offering a shortcut. All you have to do, it seems, is accept the Holy Spirit into your life, in order to find a release from guilt and sin. Not that you stop sinning, of course, but at least you cease to feel bad about it because you have the consolation of a special pass from God. The basis of salvation by faith as suggested by Augustine and Martin Luther among others, this passage as commonly interpreted is apparently a recipe for hypocrisy and institutionalised failure, despite Paul's recognition of the limitations of the law, because the resolution of the problem remains absolute and does not engage with the human experience of responsibility.

But this passage also bears a more helpful reading. Christ Jesus, in individual experience, can be read as an actual experienced process of engaging with the gap between moral ideals and human experience. The life-giving law of the Spirit that sets us free is the actual experience of integration that we may have in temporary glimpses, and that may inspire us towards incremental engagement with sin as we encounter it in narrowed experience based on limited and absolutised assumptions. The 'old nature' is a world interpreted in terms of these narrow assumptions, but we need to decisively move beyond it. To engage with sin in that way we have to put it into a bigger, integrative context, not simply oppose it with alternative narrow assumptions that happen to be reinforced by authority. Rather than simply opposing sin on its own terms we need to respond to it with love, so as to integrate it with the remainder of our experience. If this is what Paul meant – as opposed to a magic shortcut – his writings can be a helpful source of inspiration in the complex moral judgements of life. But in the end, as I have been arguing in relation to the Biblical sources throughout this book, it is not a historical or textual argument that needs to determine this so much as our confidence in taking responsibility for our interpretation.

b. Ethics in the Spirit

So, what does Christian ethics in the Spirit actually look like? In some ways, no different from the ethics practised by Christians throughout the ages, when they have been motivated by experience rather than by dogma. Experience is the starting point, but far from being a source of relativism because everyone's experience is unique, experience is a source of universality, because human experience is consistently subject to the same kinds of absolutising distractions. 'Christian ethics' thus does not differ from the ethics of any other tradition, religious or secular, insofar as it depends on that universal moral experience, but differs only in the language and cultural context in which it is recognised and applied[166]. Far from the traditional picture, in which Christian ethics are distinctive because they are derived from absolute claims that are not shared by other traditions, a Christian ethics based on experience sets out to avoid such absolute claims.

Ethics in the Spirit is also not distinguishable from other aspects of religious or integrative practice. Ethics isn't a separate box to be opened only when we confront a particular sort of dilemma, to be left shut all the rest of the time. When we worship, worship should be a morally positive action at that point, just as if we meditate or study or reflect. Ethics is also not separate from the assessment of facts or the judgement of aesthetic priorities. When we judge in the best way, taking into account *both* our own individual needs and the conditions of the world at large, we are judging ethically.

Nevertheless, 'ethics' does refer to an area of concern, which is the values we apply to our judgements. The fact that this area of concern is not isolated from all the others makes an issue 'moral' only as a matter of emphasis. In one broad sense, all issues are moral, but in a narrower sense, 'moral' more specifically refers to issues that are *more* matters of value, where assumptions are *more* likely to differ depending on one's culture, religion or philosophical approach.

It is also important *not* to assume that if we don't hermetically separate ethics from factual issues, ethics are thereby reducible to factual issues. Ethics do not become 'naturalistic' because the boundaries with scientific beliefs become blurry. We could just as well say that scientific beliefs become 'moralistic'[167].

We 'ought' to follow such an ethics, not because of the command of a supernatural being, but because by following it we address conditions better: in other words, rather than being the 'command' of God, it brings us closer to God on the basis of our own responsibility. We are not simply selves isolated from

God, expecting to magically connect to him by doing certain things or even by having certain motives: rather, by acting as more integrated beings, we gradually cease to be restricted by narrow assumptions about either ourselves or the world. We stretch our selves into something closer to the integrated God that we have glimpsed, and in the process address more of the moral requirements in the world.

To focus on ethical experience does not mean just adopting the first intuition that comes up in our experience. Rather it means making the most of the breadth offered by our experience over a period of time, trying to reach an integrated interpretation of that experience. Even if you believe God has spoken to you at one point, do not simply rush out and do what you believe he has told you to do, because God can speak in many ways, and apparently say different things at different times. Your interpretation of God is your responsibility, so whenever you can (unless circumstances demand otherwise), take opportunities to wait and reflect, especially when a judgement has important consequences. God may offer alternatives that are quite the opposite of what you first thought: but only slow reflection, as opposed to fast thinking based on entrenched assumptions, will help you find them and weigh them up.

There are three traditional ways of thinking about moral judgement, corresponding to theories of normative ethics, which I will consider in the next three sections. These three ways involve putting the emphasis on principles (deontology), on consequences (consequentialism) and on virtues (virtue ethics). All three of these approaches have been used by Christians to try to articulate Christian ethics, though on balance there has often been a preponderance of deontology. I shall argue that all three of these approaches are needed for an integrative ethic, and indeed that the tendency to absolutise any one of them by assuming it is the whole moral story is the basis of the mistakes that have been made in Christian ethics through history.

c. Principial forms of ethics

Christian ethics are most commonly associated with principial types of ethics: that is, with the belief that the right way to act can be expressed in a principle or rule of some kind. The Ten Commandments from Exodus 20 are examples of rigid rules that are taken to be morally binding because they are associated with divine revelation, whilst a wider and vaguer rule such as 'love your neighbour as yourself' is probably better described as a principle. Christian principial ethics are most commonly Biblical, and may be cherry-picked from any part of the Bible, but are by no means limited to Biblical revelation, as the Catholic rules against masturbation and artificial contraception (based on natural law reinforced by papal authority) illustrate.

Three kinds of problems dog principial ethics, of a kind that may already be guessed from the foregoing pages:

1. The revelatory justification of the principles
2. The loss of justification when principles are interpreted
3. The idealisation of principles

If the principles gain their normative ethical power from their revelatory origin, this obviously involves an appeal to an absolute God who must have supplied those principles. This, to begin with, is a misunderstanding of the relationship between God and ethics. We feel morally responsible because of an experience of an ethical demand that comes from our own wider experience, and it is a mistake to project that moral requirement onto an external agency.

Even if there were to be such things as right principles, the fact that they have to be interpreted by embodied beings means that the rightness they might have abstractly had in theory is immediately lost. The meaning of the principles being formed by metaphorical relationships to embodied experiences connected to synaptic links, there is no way that they can maintain the already impossible abstract rightness they are said to have possessed as they become the varied property of an individual. Let's take the rule 'Do not commit adultery' interpreted by an embodied being. For one embodied human being, the meaning of 'adultery' is a remote hypothetical, an inconceivable form of disruption to a happy and committed partnership; whilst for another, it is an immediate temptation breathing from another person in front of her, singing in her blood, and perhaps offering a few moment's respite from a dysfunctional, even abusive relationship. 'Adultery' and its prohibition does not have the same meaning for these two people, and its rightness or wrongness cannot possibly be equivalent.

Even if we were to set these two problems aside, revealed principles very often simply command things we cannot do. However much Jesus may command us, it is psychologically impossible for most of us to give all our goods away to the poor, or even to give up some degree of coveting what others have. We can work with these things, but divine commandments generally do not tell us to work with our possessiveness and covetousness and reduce our mental dependence on our goods: they tell us to give them up. Whilst principles consist in idealisations as what we might do, they are, as I have already argued above, institutionalised failures.

But all these problems do not necessarily tell us that principles are morally useless, nor that they have no connection with God. Let us set aside the traditional picture, and instead think anew about how moral principles may reflect the God we really experience.

There is a traditional term for God's inner moral demand, which is conscience. This has been interpreted in a variety of ways: though it is popularly supposed to be the voice of God, Christian thinkers such as Aquinas and Butler have seen the conscience rather as a human response to God: a faculty that we use to sort through conflicting priorities and that involves both reason and emotion. What is helpful about much of this theological tradition on the conscience is that it confirms that a Christian should follow the voice of conscience despite its imperfection. What is unhelpful about it is the separation between the voice of God and the human judgement. The voice of God, at one and the same time, may be experienced as a distinct voice, projected ahead of all others, and as the integration of all other voices. We cannot trust an isolated voice of God, which may correspond more to Freud's account of the 'conscience' – that is, as an internalisation of external authority – rather than an integrated perspective. On the other hand, the human faculty that brings together the different voices in a dialectical process of engagement offers the best shot at justification we can manage as embodied creatures.

When we adopt moral principles, at their best they can operate as reminders of a more integrated state and the resolutions we reached in that state, despite their limitations as verbal formulae. For example, after drinking too much alcohol and recognising the various drawbacks of doing so, I might adopt a principle never to drink in future, or only to drink a maximum of one glass of wine. This principle then offers me a reminder, even in the midst of a convivial evening with friends, of the reasons for abstention. This adoption of a principle for oneself is sometimes described as a precept, or (perhaps more rigidly) as a vow, but the advantages of such an approach over an externally revealed principle are obvious: we take responsibility for them, they flow from our own experience, and are a good deal more meaningful to us because of that relationship with our own experience.

The other disadvantages of revelatory principles can also be overcome by this approach. A principle that I have taken on for myself as a matter of conscience means whatever it means to me, and the difference in interpretation with others then becomes less significant. Of course, if I adopt a principle such as abstention from alcohol and others interpret it differently, discussion and negotiation may then follow, but this at least will avoid the association of ethics with absolutised power. The danger of it being a mere idealisation is also reduced, because I have adopted that principle on my own responsibility, and thus should be able to judge how realistic it is at the time I adopt it. However, I can still adopt an idealistic principle on the basis of an insufficiently integrated judgement, and for that reason will need to take care in the principles I adopt.

The principles we adopt in this way can come from any source. I could get my principles from a passage of scripture, from a friend's suggestion, or directly from my own awareness of mistakes I do not wish to repeat. However, if we are to take responsibility for the principles we seek to live by, they cannot be simply adopted unreflectively from any source, including scripture or the church. Conscience, then, needs to be seen not as an aid to following an ethics laid down elsewhere, but as our best guide to what is ethical. For example, if I have not undertaken to follow a principle in which committing adultery is wrong, it is not wrong for me to commit adultery.

Of course, this raises issues for social ethics. If someone else does something that we consider wrong, on what grounds can we hold them responsible, if they have not broken a principle to which they *ought* to have adhered, independently of their own experience? Here we need to make a clear distinction between *holding* people responsible and them *being* responsible. You cannot make a person be responsible, but holding them responsible is often a necessary social, political and legal function. Much confusion has arisen in Christian ethics from the projection of this social, political and legal responsibility onto individual experience, but the criteria of individual judgement in ethics cannot be wholly determined by social expectations. We can adopt social expectations into our world view, and expect ourselves to conform to the principles recognised in social ethics that we have scrutinised and found helpful and acceptable, thus integrating social pressures with other values in our own experience: but this cannot indicate any necessary requirement for us to accept social ethics. It is rather surprising that Christians should ever think otherwise if they take Jesus (who constantly questioned the social ethics of his context) as in any way their model.

No, the principles of social ethics need to be socially determined, just as political principles and law need to be politically and legally determined, all of these necessarily agreed at a social level in order to provide a basis of shared action (there will be more about this in 9.f below). The wrongness of actions such as murder or theft in the vast majority of cases is of course not only a matter for the law, but we feel them to be wrong only to the extent that we recognise the values that would forbid them. Those values might arise from compassion for others, from a desire for rational consistency in a society where people respect each other, or from reflection on the effects of such actions. If we do not feel those values, we need to cultivate them before that wrongness becomes part of our moral experience.

Idealised principles applying to the whole of society must, of course, remain meaningful. They may even have a crucial archetypal meaning, and thus act as a source of inspiration, for those who use them. Christians who read the Bible and encounter Jesus' command to love your neighbour as yourself are hardly likely not to pay attention to it, and may indeed find it highly significant as an indication of Jesus' response to the world around him. Yet, the fact that Jesus may have held such a moral instruction to be of great importance does not imply that Christians should believe that this instruction defines their ethics. All they need to do is reflect that any attempt to follow this instruction requires a process of interpretation and application, and that this process alone makes the instruction *theirs* rather than Jesus'. An idealised ethic can easily be seen as part of a heroic archetype, from which the image of a hero derives its identity: but this archetype needs to be integrated, not projected outwards.

The principles that Christians adopt should thus be seen not as absolutes, but as helpful tools for integration. A moral resolve made in a more integrated state can be applied in a less integrated one. But even such a principle, even if adhered to with strict personal discipline in which others support us, can never be absolute simply because it remains a verbal formula subject to ambiguity and interpretation. Unlike social and political norms, they can never be the basis of accusations against others or of 'holding people responsible'. As long as they remain within the sphere of experience, moral principles can be the basis of moral stretch, and inject rigour into our moral practice. As long as it remains better to judge in one way rather than another, too, we can recognise our personal responsibility for the principles we follow without becoming relativists.

d. Consequentialist forms of ethics

Mainstream Christian ethics, with only a few notable exceptions, has overwhelmingly rejected consequential forms of moral judgement that decide the morality of an action according to its consequences. For example, we should not steal a loaf of bread to feed a starving child, nor abort a severely disabled foetus in order to save it from a life of intense suffering. St Paul apparently rejects the idea that we should "do evil that good may come of it" (Rom 3:8) and thus that the end justifies the means. One reason that can be given for this approach is that God's commands are said to prescribe both means and ends. As imperfect and fallible beings we are also very likely to misjudge the consequences of our actions because of lack of full understanding of the surrounding conditions, or indeed manipulate consequential reasoning by using it to justify our own narrow goals. Contrary to our expectations, the severely disabled foetus may still be able to lie a fulfilled life that is an inspiration to others, and explaining our desperation to the baker rather than stealing from him may enable poverty to be addressed rather than conflict created. Given our ignorance, our obsessiveness, and the tendency of our well-intentioned acts to produce unintended consequences, it can be argued, we should rely on higher authorities to guide us in our means as well as our ends.

However, it is that very imperfection and ignorance that also makes us unable to know the nature of God's commands, or even whether or not God 'exists' or issues any commands. The traditional theistic rejection of consequential reasoning involves selective scepticism, as the very reason we make mistakes in consequential reasoning is the very same reason we make mistakes in our beliefs about supposed moral truths given by revelation. We have no alternative but to rely on our own judgement, and indeed to do otherwise is an abnegation of responsibility. What we consider to be a consequential shortcut as opposed to a principled stand may also seem to arbitrarily depend on how we define the rules. Why is surgery acceptable when lying is not, given that surgery involves clear harm to someone's body that good may come of it? In both cases the consequential justification depends on our fallible judgements about the results.

Nevertheless, human over-confidence that the ends justify the means is at the base of many disasters: for example, the Three Gorges Dam with its environmental and social side-effects, and the 2003 US invasion of Iraq with its poorly-planned aftermath. Unforeseen side-effects can also happen in personal lives: for example, we move house in order to fulfil career ambitions, but the new conditions involve perhaps a long commute or new financial outlay that more than undermines whatever we feel we've gained from the move. If we can't compensate for the effects of our ignorance by finding a perfect source of moral advice, the best we can do instead is to make decisions that try to take into account our limitations.

We thus cannot rule out the need for consequential reasoning, but nor can we absolutise it. Some crucial goals can only be fulfilled by sacrifice – including, controversially, that of Jesus himself. No gardener would ever pull up a weed, nor would a parent cause temporary pain to a child by frustrating their ill-considered wishes, without consequentialist reasoning. As argued in 6c above, it is necessary to go through a process of frustration in order to recognise new conditions and go beyond previous assumptions, and that process of frustration may in many cases need to involve suffering in order to drive us to reflection. We will need consequentialist reasoning in order to help others learn, as well as to make essential adjustments to our society, environment or bodies. Those Christians who in theory stick to deontological or principial views of ethics seem not to acknowledge that by necessity they must engage in consequentialist thinking themselves on a regular basis.

The morality offered by God comes from our own glimpses of an integrated state, but those glimpses offer varied forms of moral challenge rather than a consistent system of absolute ethics. There is no reason to assume that those moral challenges should always take the same kind of form. At some points, we are stretched towards greater integration in our judgements in we can resist the temptation to absolutise a principle and instead think about the implications of following that principles. At other times, however, a principle may well be needed to break a tendency to absolutise particular consequences as trumping all other considerations.

For example, the Catholic teaching theoretically requires people not to use a condom when engaging in sex, even when this creates a risk of spreading HIV, clearly seems to involve an over-narrow focus on principle at the expense of consequence that is reminiscent of the Pharisees. On the other hand, the decisions made by businesses, often supported by governments, to engage in activities that result in long-term environmental destruction, such as the development of tar sands oil extraction in Alberta, justified by the profits, employment and economic activity this will produce in the short term, are focusing narrowly on a certain sphere of consequence whilst breaking wider principles of sustainability. In each of these cases, it is by taking the alternative form of moral thinking more seriously that people can challenge their more restricted assumptions, and thus more directly interpose the integrated perspective represented by God in experience.

There can be no absolute formula as to when we are justified in using consequentialist moral reasoning as opposed to principial reasoning, but there is nevertheless a clear basis of judgement within each individual's experience. If your judgement is based on the consideration of a narrow range of options, it is less well justified. On the other hand, the recognition of approaches that would otherwise have been repressed or ignored is likely to offer new challenges to our moral thinking and may result in unexpected solutions. The more genuinely we can consider alternatives outside the range we would previously have considered, the more fully we can justify our stance. That's why many Christians who have over-relied on the absolute interpretation of revelatory moral rules would be more likely to develop a genuinely godly ethics by abandoning their narrow adherence to those rules and considering the consequences of their actions according to the evidence available.

e. Virtue ethics

Virtue ethics offers a third form of moral assessment in addition to the principial and consequentialist. This focuses on the development of character over the whole period of one's life, with the great advantage that it then starts to engage with some of the embodied complexity of actual moral decision making, which are made by complex developing people rather than abstractly reasoning left brains. The development of character has an obvious compatibility with the development of integration over a lifetime, and has been theorised both by Aristotle and by the Christian tradition in ways that can be adapted to an integration model. Some of the most common difficulties in virtue ethics, such as how we know what virtue is, and of how we can avoid a relativism of virtues, can be easily resolved using an integration model. Given that the same problems dog Christian developments of virtue ethics as any other kind, the same answers can be applied. Overall, Christians should be able to draw on the idea that good is virtue as a third type of tool in their moral toolbox, another way of challenging their moral judgements that once again should not be absolutised by being assumed to offer the whole story.

Since virtue is best described as the ability to make good judgements, it is clear that integration provides the best account of virtue. That's because good judgement is interfered with by biases, fallacies and metaphysical beliefs all of which can be avoided by preventing our absolutising response to them. Integration prevents that absolutising response by putting the assumptions made into a bigger context. The more we are in the habit of making more integrated responses where we don't accept that absolutising response, the more virtuous we will be – and also the more godly, because we will be working towards the integrated state. Christian accounts of virtue are not generally cast in terms of integration, but can nevertheless readily be interpreted in those terms.

Perhaps the most influential Christian account of virtue is that of Thomas Aquinas[168], who sought to reconcile Aristotelian accounts of virtue with the revelations recognised by the church. This led him to formulate *natural law* as the moral basis that he claimed every human could access through experience and reason, and *natural virtues* that he claimed enable us to interpret and apply this natural law. This allowed him to formulate the respects in which pagans could be virtuous, but to also maintain the superiority of Christian teaching he saw natural law as supplemented by revelation and also by distinctive *theological virtues* that enabled this revelation to be interpreted and applied.

Though Aquinas' sources of information in both natural law and revelation are obviously absolutised and dogmatic, his understanding of the way in which virtue enables us to interpret belief is a much more useful one. Having adopted a particular moral principle – such as, say, avoidance of lying – it is our characteristic attitude to this, developed through study, training and reflection, together with our understanding of each situation, that enables us to make a judgement about when lying might be taking place and when and how to apply the principle. Aquinas takes the principles as given, but even if we have ourselves adopted the principles and committed ourselves to them, we still have this issue in interpreting them. It is our degree of integration that will help us in a situation like this, because if we either absolutise the principles by interpreting them rigidly, or if we let them drop because of the difficulties, we have given way to the polarising pressure created by conflict. The more integrated we are, the better we will be able to interpret these principles.

This point can be reinforced by an interpretation of both the natural and the theological virtues that Aquinas identifies[169]. The four natural virtues for Aquinas are justice, temperance, fortitude and prudence. Justice involves a rightness in judging when a principle has been broken, which could obviously be undermined by either positively absolutising the principle (too much severity) or negatively absolutising it (too much laxity). Temperance involves a similar balance in relation to pleasures that might distract us from our judgement: we can remain temperate because we remain in the wider awareness of the Middle Way rather than thinking that every new pleasure or pain that afflicts us is the whole story. Fortitude also demands equanimity in the face of hardship and difficulty, so that we are not put off positive intentions by an absolutised response to that difficulty. Prudence demands a wider awareness when we make a decision as to what bad effects may follow from it, so that we do not act hastily, dominated by automatic fast thinking.

The theological virtues, faith, hope and love (charity), are seen by Aquinas as going beyond these natural virtues, and as being required to interpret Christian revelation. All of these virtues have already been discussed in this book. Faith can be understood as a positive confidence in an integrated perspective (see 2b). Hope involves positive projections into the future which is another dimension of that confidence, particularly from a position when all seems lost that is actually on the creative cusp of new integration (see 6c). Love, as discussed above in relation to Jesus' teachings (5c), involves the ability to stretch our identifications beyond the narrow range they might have subsequently had. All of these Christian virtues, then, can also be seen as aspects of integration, and also as needed from interpreting all Christian moral teachings.

However, Aquinas' distinction between natural and theological virtues is clearly the product of his time and of his project, which was to bodge together unquestionable Christian revelation with wider Aristotelian moral insight. If we are to adopt a critical universalism like that discussed in 7c, whereby other traditions (including the pagan ones) may also provide helpful paths, but all paths need to be assessed in terms of the Middle Way, then it is clear that there are no clear grounds for Aquinas' view that Christian revelation provides a necessarily superior element in our understanding of human virtue. The value of our understanding of human virtue lies, in the end, in its application, and if the key element in all cases is integration, then it is the way in which the 'natural virtues' and 'theological virtues' are interpreted to support that integration that matters, rather than which concepts we appeal to. A Christian who appeals to love, may still in the end be less integrated, and thus less loving, than a pagan who appeals only to temperance. Nevertheless, Aquinas's account of the theological virtues does provide a culturally distinctive model that may be an inspiration for many, Christian or not.

In more recent times, the discussion of Christian virtue ethics has been decisively picked up by Stanley Hauerwas[170]. Hauerwas stresses the value of distinctively Christian virtues within a Christian community following a Christian tradition, and whilst he maintains a belief in revelation, he also recognises that Christian revelation only makes sense as such within the distinctive cultural developments of a Christian community built on Christian symbols and stories. The interpretation of scripture, as well as the celebration of Christian stories through ritual, provides the necessary context in which a communal embodied meaning for revelation can emerge, and he opposes the cherry-picking of scripture for decontextualised propositional moral claims.

Hauerwas' approach is helpful in one key respect, which is its move away from abstracted understanding of moral meaning of the kind that tends to create absolutisations. Though he continues to treat revelation as central to Christian faith, what he means by revelation is non-propositional and contextually dependent. Nevertheless, he refuses to yield to any form of universalism, and instead follows Alastair MacIntyre[171] in seeing traditions as both adaptable in the face of new experience and incompatibly competing with each other. Christianity, then, still seems to offer virtues that can be found nowhere else, even though those virtues can't be reduced to decontextualised verbal formulae.

In this Hauerwas seems to be following the negative absolutisation of the postmodernist movement, which tends to conclude, from the fact of there being rival forms of absolute claim, that there is no justifiable way of judging one as being better than another beyond the assumptions adopted by each tradition. But we do not have to conclude, from the contextual dependence of each moral judgement and its meaning, that there can be no moral priority between these judgements, or that such moral priority cannot be assessed beyond the terms of a given tradition. Traditions are not absolute or discrete entities, but interact in ways that create new inter-traditional forms of discourse in which the virtues of each can be re-interpreted in ways comprehensible to the others. The constant emphasis on linguistic and cultural specificity in postmodern thinking can also lead us to neglect what we really do have in common: a human physical structure, including a brain structure in relation to which we can understand the universal implications of phenomena such as absolutisation, bias and archetype.

Christian virtues, then, cannot be hermetically sealed from those of other traditions or wider society in ways that make them completely impossible to interpret beyond a Christian community. Rather we can say that Christian tradition offers some culturally specific ways of interpreting universal human virtue. Generally speaking, human beings are more virtuous when they are more integrated, because they have fewer barriers that prevent them from engaging with conditions; but nevertheless, the development of those virtues is inter-dependent on those of a community which is also itself subject to assessment according to its degree of integration. Where the Christian community is in conflict because of dogmatic responses to conditions and reactions against that dogmatism, the cultural traditions on which Christians can draw are much less advantageous than they are when the community itself is integrated.

The development of virtue is thus a third type of moral approach that can be used to challenge Christian moral judgement in any particular situation. Rather than resting on one kind of moral principle and absolutising it, Christians need to be willing to stretch towards God by sometimes using moral principle, sometimes consequences, and sometimes the development of virtue as the prime stimulus to their moral judgement. Which of these takes precedence depends entirely on the situation, as well as on the past moral limitations of the person concerned.

What is meant by a stretch towards virtue also depends on what kinds of virtue a given person already has, but can be generally understood as the prioritisation of practice as discussed in section 8, particularly 8b above. A focus on personal practice might mean, for example, a structured communal retreat, a solitary retreat for meditation, reflection and study, an educational course or a shift to a new long-term situation that makes such practices more feasible. However, for those who are more experienced it might also well mean contributing to the integration of the community at large by teaching or supporting others, or by taking on other responsibilities in a community. These kinds of priorities will always have to be balanced with considerations of the consequences of doing or not doing them, and of the principles that one might be following or breaking. So, for example, it is hard (though not impossible) for parents with young children to go on a meditation retreat. Whatever they do to help themselves develop or contribute to a wider community will also have to be weighed in terms of its effects on their children; but at the same time this duty should not be absolutised, because children also benefit from having more integrated parents.

The need to see virtue in relation, not only to the integration of individuals, but that of a wider community, provides us with an opening to the final section, which passes on from the ethics of individual judgement to questions of social and political organisation. Just as Christianity offers culturally specific ways of supporting the individual's development of virtue, it also offers a distinctive approach to the socio-political.

f. Christian political values

The Christian challenge to power can be traced long back before Jesus in the Old Testament. The law of the Israelites itself, though it maintained political authority, reconstituted the role of that authority as enforcing laws that were coherently just, rather than the authority itself also constituting the law. When justice failed in the Israelite kingdoms, prophets such as Amos railed against that injustice, and attributed misfortune to God's punishment of the unjust betrayers of his covenant. Against this background, Jesus' advocacy of the poor is a revival of that tradition; but one that goes further, because it challenges a wider range of the interests of the powerful. Rather than merely appealing to a law that had not been kept, Jesus challenged the legalistic use of the law and appealed to a spirit of justice behind it. Rather than appealing to justice alone, too, Jesus combines justice with love.

In the psychological analysis of Jonathan Haidt[172], justice (or fairness) is one of six basic socio-political values found in all human minds, alongside care, freedom, loyalty, authority, and sanctity. Whilst conservatives are likely to give expression to all of these values, progressive liberals and socialists are likely to give sole emphasis to justice and care, and have little patience with the greater emphasis on values of loyalty, authority and sanctity found on the right. A strong case can be made for the importance of all of these values in a functioning society, and we all have bonds of loyalty with friends and family, a recognition of the need for authority in practical enterprises such as work-places, and a sense of the sanctity of our bodies and environments that would react against many forms of intrusion or contamination. Yet any of these values can be absolutised. For example, we could absolutise authority and create totalitarianism, or we could absolutise justice and end up with a dysfunctional form of communism in which other key human motivations are undermined.[173]

Given this need for a basic balance of political values in society, how can we understand the significance of Jesus' advocacy of justice and care? Not, I would suggest, as an absolutisation of these values. For all his rebukes to the rich and powerful, some of Jesus' most significant sayings involve a balancing process in which different values are combined.

> *Do not suppose I have come to abolish the law and the prophets; I did not come to abolish, but to complete.* (Mt 5:17)
>
> *Pay to Caesar what belongs to Caesar, and to God what belongs to God.* (Mt 22:21)

At the same time, all of these institutions are given an air of provisionality by the comparison with the kingdom in which Jesus thinks they are to be properly integrated. In the kingdom (see 5.f above), the conflicts between rich and poor, the conflicts between pure and sinful, the conflicts between men and women are all resolved: for there is exaltation for the humble, acceptance for the repentant sinner, and no more marriage, for men and women are "like angels in heaven" (Mt 22:30).

Jesus's challenge to power, like that of the prophets before him, is thus remedial in nature. He operated in a society in which loyalty, authority and sanctity had become over-dominant and absolutised. Many other traditional societies show the same bias towards these values, but we should not assume for that reason that that bias is universal. It is always possible, whether in a smaller or a wider context, to infantilise by absolutising care or to stifle autonomy by imposing a particular model of equality. In many societies, however, it is still an appropriate emphasis to see inequality and lack of care for the disadvantaged as overriding problems. Apart from the suffering of the poor, injustice is a major source of conflict and of limited opportunities for individual human development.

In Jesus' time, the absolutisation of authority had become a tool of power: for the Romans, for the Jewish leaders, and for individuals who repressed alternative voices within themselves. It is easy to confuse the absolutisation of authority with authority itself, but the interpretation that Jesus was neither an anarchist nor a revolutionary can be supported not only by the famous 'pay to Caesar' quotation, but also by the wider role of scepticism, provisionality, balance and integration in Jesus' teachings (as discussed in 5c) and by the role he plays in Christianity as Christ the mediator. The rigidity of authority had a close relationship to the rigidity in people's hearts, so there is little doubt of the importance of social and political judgement in Christian teachings.

However, the potential weakening of that remedial challenge to power in Jesus' teachings is already evident in Paul, who brings in absolute divine sanction to political authority of a kind that goes much further than Jesus' equanimity about paying taxes:

> *Every person must submit to the authorities in power, for all authority comes from God, and the existing authorities are instituted by him. It follows that anyone who rebels against authority is resisting a divine institution, and those who resist have themselves to thank for the punishments they receive.* (Rom 13:1-2)

It is the unconditional nature of this submission that offers a dangerous new element quite inconsistent with a critical Christian faith as opposed to an absolutising Christian belief. The arrogance of assuming that God can be known to have providentially created all authorities, despite our knowledge of the sinfulness of the human beings that form those authorities, is quite contrary to Jesus' attitude of balanced scepticism against authorities. Whilst some[174] have attributed the authoritarian streak in the Christian tradition to the political establishment of the Christian church under Constantine and the ensuing corruption of Christian motives by power, the tendency towards authoritarianism evidently goes back much earlier than that.

This authoritarianism supported the divine right of kings, regardless of the quality or justice of their kingship, and the subsequent ease with which warmongers and dictators have been able to claim Christian support through the centuries. Yet at the same time alternative possibilities were incubated by the Christian tradition: the emphasis on an individual relationship with God in Reformation Protestantism paving the way for the Enlightenment with its social contract theories, democracy and human rights. The subtle and ambiguous position suggested by Jesus' challenges to authority continues to stimulate a wide range of political attitudes, but the only thing we can be clear about is that Christianity does not have one essential or absolute political value.

The Middle Way in politics is no different for Christians than for others, even if it can be inspired and culturally supported by Jesus' teachings or by other aspects of the Christian tradition. We cannot absolutise political authority, but nor can we reject its practically necessary role. We can find some conditions addressed in most if not all ideological approaches, but need to remain resolutely agnostic in the face of absolutised ideologies that repress alternatives. We can welcome liberal democracy as a clumsy and imperfect but nevertheless often helpful mechanism for preventing political absolutisation, limiting social conflict, and keeping a variety of policies under discussion. An absolutised Christian polity should be seen as a contradiction in terms.

The use of power by rulers or political institutions does not have to be an *unconditional* use of power. As discussed in relation to human dominion over the environment in 4b, there are ways of justifying the use of power in terms of the integration of that use. In the case of subjection to political authorities this implies that obedience to such authorities is *not* unconditional in the way Romans suggests, but rather dependent on the relative integration of the judgements of the political authority when compared to the subject. The question of how we can judge the integration of a judgement by a political authority compared to that of a possibly rebellious individual is one I have gone into elsewhere[175], and do not have space for here. However, the idea of a rebellion against the state justified by integration is far from foreign to Christian thinking, given that the experience of integration is that of God, and that many martyrs, starting with Jesus himself, have defied the state on grounds of conscience.

The test of whether a Christian has a godly political viewpoint, whether this is used to defy the state, take political office, or merely to determine her vote, needs to be entirely one of personal integration, as far as this can be estimated. A Christian in conflict with themselves through repression is not in a good position to make incrementally objective moral or political judgements, and the adherence to absolute Christian beliefs may well be the basis of such conflicts. For example, Catholic priests, monks or nuns who are in a state of unacknowledged conflict over their sexuality due to ill-advised celibacy are hardly in a good position to make judgements about the welfare of children, however much they may make an appearance of holiness in other respects. Similarly, Christians who manage to combine Christian beliefs with racism or homophobia are likely to be in so much unacknowledged conflict because of such beliefs (and the energy they have to put into maintaining them), that they can hardly be trusted to be making spiritually inspired political judgements. These are thus similarly not people who should be placed in positions of social or political responsibility. On the other hand, much wiser leadership is more likely to be offered by those with a record of making integrated judgements, whether or not they show the dominating behaviour that is likely to be sought in leaders.

Though political leadership may involve wielding power, it should not be based on a predilection for power, but rather on spiritual strength, ability to engage with other views, awareness of one's own needs and those of others, and confidence based on integration. In that respect Jesus' upending of worldly political priorities is best interpreted in terms of genuine faith rather than Christian belief:

Blessed are the poor in spirit; the kingdom of heaven is theirs.

Blessed are the sorrowful; they shall find consolation.

Blessed are the gentle; they shall have the earth for their possession.

Blessed are those who hunger and thirst to see right prevail; they shall be satisfied. (Mt 5:3-6)

10

Conclusion

At its best, Christianity heals. "Make me an instrument of your peace," prays St Francis, "Where there is hatred, let me sow love." If Christians are serious about this, it is imperative for them to address the conditions that prevent peace and love. These are conditions found primarily in the human brain, in the dominance of one part of the frontal left hemisphere that too often believes it knows the whole story. You can remain stuck in that story and continue to rationalise the beliefs of the past, or you can begin to examine alternatives. The kind of love of which Jesus spoke cannot occur without opening our minds to these alternatives, and for that reason it is crucial that Christianity stops undermining its own objectives.

In this book I have argued for a distinction between faith and belief, that Christian faith is a matter of experience, Christian belief a matter of absolutisation. Faith involves confidence, not in the perfect, but in the imperfect. Faith is embodied, and involves the recognition that meaning is dependent on our brains and bodies rather than ultimate states of truth or falsity. Faith depends on a connection to a source of meaning which is always earthed in our physical experience, however abstractly its expression has been built from metaphor.

Conflict occurs between our own desires as well as between ourselves and others, so love needs to be established within as well as beyond us. Faith has a mutually supportive relationship with integration, the process that overcomes conflict, allowing opposed desires to become united through the critical reframing of the beliefs that are associated with them. But the process of integration is constantly blocked by absolutisation. The practice of the Middle Way is thus constantly required as a practical navigation process between opposing absolutised forces, positive and negative.

I have argued that it is a massive misunderstanding of God to identify him with an outward projected form, rather than the glimpse of potential integration within our own experience. The belief in God as an outward supernatural entity turns him into a ready tool of power, exploiting our human need to be accepted by a group by making group membership conditional on an unquestionable absolute claim beyond experience. Even within the individual, the absolute God becomes repressive rather than integrative. If we interpret God in accordance with the Middle Way, he can instead become a source of inspiration and of authentic responsibility.

I have argued that the Bible and the Christian tradition need to be interpreted in accordance with a recognition of our responsibility, not as a shortcut to absolute authority. We need to abandon the belief in revelation and clearly avoid absolutisations in the Bible. Nevertheless, there is a great deal of material in the Bible that can be interpreted in an integrative way that can still then provide inspiration for Christian faith. This begins with seeing the Creation as symbolic of a creative process in ourselves, and the fall as a necessary and positive stage of integration.

In order to make a helpful reading of the gospels, it is not necessary to enter into contestable historical revisionism with its accompanying implicit appeal to historical authority. Instead, the teachings of Jesus as they are found in the traditional four gospels can inspire us towards synthesis, scepticism, provisionality, universality, integration, love and balance. We need to recognise Jesus as a flawed figure, but also one of striking integration. As the symbolic Christ he becomes a powerful archetype of the Middle Way, representing the integration of the human with the divine.

We can also draw on the mystical tradition in Christianity,

which centrally shows us the inspiring effects of past Christians concentrating on experience of God rather than belief about him. They have blazed a path of Christian agnosticism which is courageous rather than indecisive in putting the conditions of love before those of dogma. That agnostic path can also be fully compatible with other religions – provided they too are interpreted in accordance with the Middle Way. It can also be compatible with scientific method, with many of the arguments adopted by atheists, and with feminist arguments against patriarchal assumptions in Christian tradition. It does not have to ally itself necessarily with one form of Christianity over another, although it must be acknowledged that it would be much harder to pursue a Middle Way interpretation of Christianity in a theologically conservative or fundamentalist church. Instead, the Middle Way is a tool with which we can potentially interpret any tradition in a helpful fashion.

I have argued that the Christian Middle Way is practical, and that Christian practice needs to take much more account of the resources offered by psychology, engaging in a range of integrative practices. Amongst these, however, Christian worship and the sacraments can continue to form a prominent part provided they are interpreted in integrative and non-absolute ways.

In Christian moral and political practice, the Middle Way offers a balancing function whereby a variety of approaches can be prioritised at different times depending on the extent to which they realistically stretch our existing identifications. Principles, virtues and considerations of consequences thus all need to have their place in Christian ethics. Christian ethics can be made far more effective if it is separated from absolutised principles, not offering absolute requirements for all like those of social ethics or law, but nevertheless allowing one option to be better than another for an individual in a specific situation. The arbiter of which option is the best is God, but that God being the process of integration within us, he is found in human experience rather than in absolute moral or political revelations.

Whilst power does have to be used by governments, the justification for that power is also not absolute, but depends on the integration with which it is used. Since governments need to address a wide variety of conditions, they should not adopt a single absolute ideology, even in the service of such laudable concepts as justice or freedom. Instead, Jesus' approach to politics suggests a remedial balancing whenever one kind of ideological approach becomes over-dominant, in this respect following the pattern of Middle Way ethics.

Overall, then, I argue that Christianity when responsibly interpreted does not differ from the Middle Way, and that the distinctively Christian is a matter of culture and symbol. That does not imply relativism or determinism of birth or culture, for our journeys may take us in or out of Christian culture, and the strands of religious traditions are not mutually exclusive, but nevertheless, to be Christian is to adopt certain cultural expressions of the Middle Way.

By offering a Middle Way through Christ, the Christian tradition offers a symbolic strength that should not be underestimated. In Christian faith, the Middle Way is a person, thus bringing out all the distinctively personal aspects of the negotiation between ideals and realities, perfection and imperfection. The fact that the Middle Way is more explicit in their tradition should not lead Buddhists to assume that it is necessarily superior in the extent to which it supports the practice of the Middle Way. After all, science and democracy are offspring of Christianity in a way in which they are not offspring of Buddhism, and both of these, whatever their limitations, are powerful modern traditions for avoiding absolutisation that interferes with our engagement with conditions.

* * *

But let me conclude on a more informal note. Supposing you are a Christian, more or less liberal or lapsed or sceptical, who has read this book, and recognised the value of separating faith from belief. You may well ask "What now?"

I have been at pains to offer a broad argument applicable to a wide range of situations, which means that I cannot possibly offer any specific prescriptions. If you accept that argument, it will probably be the beginning, not the end, of your difficulties. Do you take this book as a call to institutional reform of Christian churches? As a prescription for an individual interpretation of Christianity, whatever church you find yourself in? Or as a call for an individualistic approach to Christianity beyond church institutions? In many ways it is, or can be, any or all of these, because they are interdependent.

In the longer term, Christianity will only become of more benefit to the world if it turns to faith, gives up the promotion of absolute belief, and reforms its institutions accordingly. Yes, that means institutional decisions to, for example, abolish the creed, train both clergy and lay people in non-absolute interpretations of scripture and liturgy, stop making exclusivist claims and start listening more carefully to critics. But these things take a long time, and may never happen at all. In the meantime, as an individual, you may have to decide whether to work with a church that is sufficiently integrative in its attitudes, constantly testing your ability to interpret it in helpful ways. Alternatively, you may feel that you would be better off outside the church altogether, or perhaps starting your own church.

Whichever of these courses you adopt, I have only one final warning to offer. The Middle Way is subtle and requires time to understand, absorb, and make part of one's practical approach. It is not even well-developed intellectually, and a great deal even of current academic discussion may well drag you away from it. If you have an intuitive sense of the importance of a Middle Way interpretation of Christianity, don't forget that this may need a certain amount of nurturing and protecting at first until it becomes better established. It is probably unwise to subject yourself to very testing circumstances where you end up defying a group, whether you are trying to lead it into reform or merely maintain your own integrity whilst participating in it, before your understanding of the Middle Way is well-developed. Ideas about the Middle Way will be readily dismissed on the one hand, or appropriated on the other, and you need to have a clear idea of when it is (or is not) important to stand your ground. Only a process of practice guards us from turning the Middle Way into another absolutisation, and you need to give that practice enough time to operate before putting it to too severe a test.

I have founded the Middle Way Society as a support group for the development and practice of the Middle Way, cutting across traditions. It is *not* a Buddhist group, whatever the name might suggest to you, but a group in which people from any context can learn more about the Middle Way in theory and practice, and contribute their own insights from their own experience. It is not a new religion, but aims to support the better interpretation and practice of all religions. Do come and find us on our website, *www.middlewaysociety.org*, and join in if we can help you on your path.

What of my own path, with which I began? The process of writing this book has led me to acknowledge, to a greater degree than before, how much I am culturally Christian. However, whether that will ever lead me to join any church remains an ongoing question that remains open. I am also deeply influenced by Buddhism, and in many respects prefer to straddle two traditions. Nor do I want anything to risk interfering with my capacity to communicate Middle Way Philosophy in a way that crosses traditions and brings them into fruitful synthetic contact with each other. But that is a response to the very specific conditions of my own life. Let me conclude with the words of Jung:

There is only one way and that is your way. You seek the path? I warn you away from my own. It can also be the wrong way for you. May each go his own way.[176]

Notes and References

Note on references in this book

This book attempts to balance accessibility with a reasonable academic standard of referencing. However, it is also a book based on interpretative argument rather than new scholarship about Christianity or its sources. There are thus many general assertions about Christianity in it that are assumed in the argument, but are not themselves new or controversial. Where such uncontroversial factual assumptions are concerned I have adopted the criterion that if it can be easily looked up in a basic textbook or on Wikipedia, it does not need referencing. References have thus been confined to major sources of information, sources of quotations, or sources of further justification on potentially controversial points.

Biblical references

All Biblical references use standard abbreviations for the books of the Bible, with quotations taken from the *Revised English Bible* unless otherwise indicated. Direct quotations from the Bible have been attributed in the text, whilst other biblical references are included in the notes below.

Endnotes

1 Jung (2009) p.331
2 See, inter alia, Lakoff (1987), Johnson (2007), Lakoff and Johnson (1980). I also discuss this in more detail in Ellis (2013b) section 1.
3 See Ellis (2013b) section 3 for more detailed discussion
4 See Ellis (2001) 4e for a critique of Wittgenstein's arguments
5 See Ellis (2015) section 3 for extensive evidence of these features of absolute belief, surveyed in relation to cognitive biases.
6 Taylor & Doria (1981)
7 Asch (1956)
8 Janis (1982)
9 Ross, Greene & House (1977)
10 Many of these are on display at www.theflatearthsociety.org
11 Hay (1990)
12 Bolte-Taylor (2008)
13 Deikman (1980)
14 Ramachandran & Blakeslee (1998)
15 These four archetypes are a functional simplification of the wider range of archetypes Jung discusses in a number of places, especially in Jung (1968). I discuss my functional adaptation in more detail in Ellis (2013b) section 4.
16 Jung (1969)
17 Also see Ellis (2015) 3.n
18 McGilchrist (2009)
19 Ibid. chapter 2
20 Harrington, Haaland & Knight (1998)
21 Ellis (2015) 3.n
22 Tweedy (2013)
23 Mt 6:1-18

24 Mt 7:1-5
25 Jn 7:53-8:11
26 Augustine (2009)
27 Sartre (1980)
28 Ex 19:17-25
29 Ex 34:26
30 Ex 20:3
31 Murata & Chittick (1994) p.29-32
32 Aquinas (1920) 1.1
33 Kierkegaard (1962)
34 Coleridge (1983)
35 Auerbach (1953)
36 McGilchrist (2009) ch.7
37 Brahmajala Sutta 2.3-2.6 (Walshe 1987 p.75-6)
38 2 Mac 7:28 "God did not create them from what already existed".
39 Plato (1977)
40 See Diamond (2005)
41 Singer (2004)
42 Pinker (2012) p.827 ff.
43 Hick (2010)
44 I'm grateful to Emilie Åberg for helping me see this point.
45 Gen 3:12-13
46 McGilchrist (2009) pp.20-29
47 Marx (1977) p.77 ff.
48 McGilchrist (2009) pp.138-140
49 Rom 5:12-21
50 Jung (2009) p.359-360
51 Ellis (2001) 3.f.ii
52 See Funk et al (1996) and a number of other works
53 Elford (2000)
54 Jn 12:1-8
55 Jn 4:8-15
56 Lk 10:29-37

57 E.g. Lk 16:19 ff
58 Lk 19:1-10
59 Lk 18:16
60 Jn 8:1-11
61 Elford (2000) p.107
62 Mt 21:12
63 Elford (2000) p.107
64 Mt 25:1-13
65 Verney (1985)
66 Ex 3:14
67 Verney (1985) pp.24-5
68 The REB's 'In very truth I say to you' has been altered back to 'Amen, amen I say to you' as it is rendered in some earlier translations: this is closer to the Greek and appears to be more a matter of emphasis than a truth claim.
69 Gen 28:12
70 Verney (1985) p.28
71 See previous footnote on 'Amen, amen…' In addition, here, I have altered the REB's 'born again' to 'born from above', which is closer to the Greek ανωθεν.
72 Verney (1985) pp.43-44
73 Lk 8:5-13
74 Wrede (1901)
75 Mk 1:25, 1:34, 3:12, 5:43, 7:36, 8:26
76 Mk 8:30
77 Mk 9:9
78 E.g. Jn 11:26-27
79 Zech 9:9
80 Hume (1999) ch.10
81 Lk 7:1-10
82 Mk 2:1-5
83 Lk 8:43-48
84 And also Ellis (2015) 3.n
85 McGilchrist (2009) p.392 ff

86 Verney (1985) pp.29-37
87 Bays (2009)
88 Schweitzer (1910)
89 Verney (1985) p.162
90 Jung (2009) p.295
91 Ibid. p.299
92 Edinger (1987) pp.72-3
93 Mt 26: 38 & 40-41; Edinger (1987) pp.73-4
94 Mt 26: 51-2
95 Edinger (1987) p.92-3
96 Hall (1974) p.81, quoted by Edinger (1987) p.98
97 Lk 23:39-43
98 Jung (1959) §79
99 Ellis (2012. 2013 a & b, 2015)
100 Mk 16:1-8; Mt 28:5-7
101 Lk 24:31,36 & 51
102 Lk 24:16; Jn 20:14; Jn 21:4
103 Jn 20:26
104 Lk 24:38-43; Jn 20:26-9
105 Jung (1958) §149
106 Jn 20:24-9
107 Acts 2:5-12
108 For more details see Ellis (2015) p.147 ff.
109 Pseudo-Dionysius (1924) Caput V
110 James (1902) pp.379-382
111 Angela of Foligno (1908)
112 McCullough (2012)
113 Ignatius of Loyola (1914)
114 Bernard of Clairvaux (1884) sections 8-10
115 Eckhart (1981)
116 Hildegard of Bingen (1990)
117 Chalcedonian Definition, quoted in Davies (1987)
118 Strictly speaking, the Nestorian Churches had already split off from the rest at the earlier Council of Ephesus in 431 CE.

119 Weber (1930). Also discussed in more detail in Ellis (2001) 3.f.x.
120 Church of England figures quoted in http://www.telegraph.co.uk/news/religion/12095251/Church-of-England-attendance-plunges-to-record-low.html
121 Ibid.
122 http://www.telegraph.co.uk/news/uknews/theroyalfamily/3454271/Prince-Charles-to-be-known-as-Defender-of-Faith.html
123 Mk1:9-10
124 See Ellis (2013a) section 6 & (2015) section 7.
125 Gould (1997)
126 See Ellis (2012) 1.a & b for more detailed discussion
127 See Ellis (2012) 1.c
128 Lakatos (1974), Kuhn (1996)
129 Johnston (1994)
130 Smith (1979) p.10
131 Dawkins (2006) ch.4
132 Hick (2010)
133 Ayer (1936)
134 Ellis (2012) section 5
135 Ibid 1a
136 Lev 15:19-24 & Lev 20:18
137 Ranke-Heinemann (1990) pp.21-7
138 Ibid.
139 See Ellis (2013) 1a for a more detailed discussion
140 See Ellis (2013b) for more detailed discussion of this concept
141 http://www.brin.ac.uk/figures
142 Hadaway & Marler (2005)
143 http://www.messychurch.org.uk/
144 Jones & Butman (1991)
145 See Ellis (2015) 4c & 4e for fuller discussion of the agnostic stance on freewill-determinism and mind-body questions
146 Wason (1960), Mynatt, Doherty & Tweney (1977)

147 Taleb (2012) pp.38-9
148 Siegel (2010)
149 Gilbert (2009)
150 Ellis (2013a, 2013b & 2015)
151 Rosenberg (2002)
152 Gendlin (2003)
153 See Ellis (2015) 3.a for a more detailed account
154 Ibid. section 3
155 https://www.washingtonpost.com/blogs/answer-sheet/post/texas-gop-rejects-critical-thinking-skills-really/2012/07/08/gJQAHNpFXW_blog.html
156 Ellis (2012) 1 a & b. Also (more briefly) Ellis (2014) pp.18-23 and (2011) ch.1
157 See Ellis (2015) section 3
158 Augustine (1907) books 6 & 7
159 Fraley (2010), Bowlby (1988)
160 Salzberg (1995)
161 Gilbert (2009)
162 Many of the ideas in the rest of this section have been inspired directly or indirectly by Sangharakshita's approach to confession in Buddhism. He writes about this in Sangharakshita (1995) ch.2.
163 Kahneman (2011) pp.97-104
164 2015 figures from http://indexmundi.com
165 Rom 7:16
166 I discuss the nature of this wider Middle Way ethics in Ellis (2012) section 7. That discussion can offer a more detailed version of what follows here, though one also not specifically geared to make connections with Christian culture as this is.
167 Johnson (2014) offers a set of detailed arguments that supports the inseparability of facts and values. Johnson describes himself as a 'naturalist', but his naturalism is so subtle it practically disappears.

168 Aquinas (1920) I-II.49 ff.

169 Op. Cit. II-II

170 Hauerwas (1984)

171 MacIntyre (1981) ch.15

172 Haidt (2012)

173 This argument is developed in more detail in Ellis (2015) 4.h

174 E.g. Kee (1982)

175 Ellis (2013a) section 6

176 Jung (2009) p.125

Bibliography

Angela of Foligno (1908) trans. Mary Steegmann, *The Book of Divine Consolation*. Chatto & Windus: https://archive.org/details/BookOfDivineConsolation

Aquinas, St. Thomas (1920) trans. Fathers of the English Dominican Province, *Summa Theologiae. http://www.newadvent.org/summa/*

Asch, Solomon (1956) *Studies of Independence and Conformity: 1. A minority of one against a unanimous majority*. Psychological monographs

Augustine, St., of Hippo (1907) trans. Pusey, *Confessions*. Dent.

Augustine, St., of Hippo (2009) trans. Holmes & Wallis, ed. Knight, *On Grace and Free Will. http://www.newadvent.org/fathers/1510.htm*

Ayer, A.J. (1936) *Language, Truth and Logic*. Penguin.

Bays Jan Chozen (2009) *Mindful Eating: A guide to rediscovering a healthy and joyful relationship with food*. Shambhala.

Bernard of Clairvaux (1884) trans. Marianne Caroline & Coventry Patmore, *The Love of God*. Burns & Oates. *https://archive.org/details/saintbernardlove00bernuoft*

Bolte-Taylor, Jill (2008) *My Stroke of Insight*. Hodder & Stoughton

Bowlby, John (1988) *A Secure Base: Clinical applications of attachment theory*. Routledge.

Davies, Rupert E. (1987) *Making Sense of the Creeds*. Epworth Press.

Dawkins, Richard (2006) *The God Delusion*. Black Swan.

Deikman, Arthur J. (1980) 'Deautomatisation and the Mystic Experience' and 'Bimodal Consciousness and the Mystic Experience', both from ed. Richard Woods, *Understanding Mysticism*. Athlone Press.

Diamond, Jared (2005) *Collapse: How societies choose to fail or survive*. Penguin.

Eckhart, Meister (1981) trans. Edmund Colledge & Bernard McGinn, *The Essential Sermons, Commentaries, Treatises and Defence*. Paulist Press

Edinger, Edward F. (1987) *The Christian Archetype: A Jungian Commentary on the Life of Christ*. Inner City Books.

Elford, R. John (2000) *The Ethics of Uncertainty: A new Christian approach to moral decision-making*. Oneworld.

Ellis, Robert M (2001) Ph.D. thesis, Lancaster University, published 2011) *A Theory of Moral Objectivity*. Lulu.

Ellis, Robert M. (2011) *Truth on the Edge: A brief Western philosophy of the Middle Way*

Ellis, Robert M (2012) *Middle Way Philosophy 1: The Path of Objectivity*. Lulu.

Ellis, Robert M (2013a) *Middle Way Philosophy 2: The Integration of Belief*. Lulu.

Ellis, Robert M (2013b) *Middle Way Philosophy 3: The Integration of Meaning*. Lulu.

Ellis, Robert M. (2014) *Migglism: A Beginner's Guide to Middle Way Philosophy*. Lulu

Ellis, Robert M (2015) *Middle Way Philosophy 4: The Integration of Belief*. Lulu.

Fraley, Chris (2010) 'A brief overview of adult attachment theory and research': *https://internal.psychology.illinois.edu/~rcfraley/attachment.htm*

Funk, Robert W. et al (1996) *The Five Gospels: What Did Jesus Really Say? The Search for the Authentic Words of Jesus*. Harper Collins.

Gendlin, Eugene T. (2003, rev ed.) *Focusing*. Rider.

Gilbert, Paul (2009) *The Compassionate Mind*. Constable.

Gould, Stephen Jay (1997) 'Non-overlapping magisteria': *Natural History* 106 pp.16-22. *http://www.stephenjaygould.org/library/gould_noma.html*

Hadaway, C.K. & Marler, P.L. (2005) 'How many Americans attend worship each week? An alternative approach to measurement': *Journal for the Scientific Study of Religion* 44:3, pp.307-322

Haidt, Jonathan (2012) *The Righteous Mind: Why good people are divided by politics and religion*. Penguin.

Hall, James (1974) *Dictionary of Subjects and Symbols in Art*. Harper & Row

Harrington, D., Haaland, K. & Knight, R. (1998) 'Cortical networks underlying mechanisms of time perception': *The Journal of Neuroscience* 18:3

Hauerwas, Stanley (1984) *The Peaceable Kingdom: A primer in Christian ethics*. University of Notre Dame Press.

Hay, D. (1990). *Religious Experience Today: Studying the facts*. Mowbray.

Hick, John (2010) *Evil and the God of Love*. Palgrave Macmillan.

Hildegard of Bingen (1990) trans. Columba Hart & Jane Bishop, *Scivias*. Paulist Press.

Hume, David (1999) ed. Beauchamp, *An Enquiry Concerning Human Understanding*. Oxford University Press.

Ignatius of Loyola (1914) trans. Elder Mullan, *Spiritual Exercises*. http://www.sacred-texts.com/chr/seil/

James, William (1902) *The Varieties of Religious Experience*. Longmans.

Janis, Irving L. (1982) *Groupthink: Psychological Studies of Policy Decisions and Fiascos*. Houghton Mifflin.

Johnson, Mark (2007) *The Meaning of the Body: Aesthetics of human understanding*. University of Chicago Press.

Johnston, George Sim (1994) *The Galileo Affair. Scepter Press.*

Jones, Stanton & Butman, Richard (1991) *Modern Psychotherapies: A comprehensive Christian appraisal*. Intervarsity Press.

Jung, C.G. (1958) *Psychology and Religion*. Routledge

Jung, C.G. (1959) trans. R.F.C. Hull, *Aion: Researches into the Phenomenology of the Self*. Routledge.

Jung, C.G. (1968: 2nd Ed) trans R.F.C. Hull, *The Archetypes and the Collective Unconscious*. Routledge

Jung, C.G. (1969: 2nd Ed) 'A psychological approach to the dogma of the trinity' from *Psychology and Religion: West and East.* Princeton University Press

Jung, C.G. (2009), ed. Sonu Shamdasani, *The Red Book (Reader's Edition).* Norton.

Kahneman, Daniel (2011) *Thinking, Fast and Slow*. Penguin.

Kee, Alistair (1982) *Constantine versus Christ*. SCM Press.

Kierkegaard, Søren (1962) trans Swenson & Hong, *Philosophical Fragments. Princeton University Press*

Kuhn, Thomas (1996: 3rd Ed) *The Structure of Scientific Revolutions*. University of Chicago Press.

Lakatos, Imre (1974) 'Falsification and the methodology of scientific research programmes' from *Criticism and the Growth of Knowledge* ed. Lakatos and Musgrave. Cambridge University Press.

Lakoff, George (1987) *Women, Fire and Dangerous Things: What categories reveal about the mind*. University of Chicago Press.

Lakoff, George & Johnson, Mark (1980) *Metaphors we live by*. University of Chicago Press.

MacIntyre, Alasdair (1981) *After Virtue.* Duckworth

Marx, Karl (1977) ed. David McLennan, 'Alienated Labour' from *Selected Writings*. Oxford University Press.

McCullough, Lissa (2012) 'Simone Weil's Phenomenology of the Body': *Comparative and Continental Philosophy* 4:2 pp.195-218

McGilchrist, Iain (2009) *The Master and his Emissary: The Divided Brain and the Making of the Western World.* Yale University Press.

Murata, Sachiko & Chittick, William (1994) *The Vision of Islam*. I.B. Tauris.

Mynatt, Clifford, Doherty, Michael & Tweney, Ryan (1977) 'Confirmation bias in a simulated research environment: and experimental study of scientific inference': *Quarterly Journal of Experimental Psychology* 29:1 pp.85-95.

Pinker, Steven (2012) *The Better Angels of Our Nature: A history of violence and humanity.* Penguin

Plato (1977) trans. H.D.P. Lee, *Timaeus* (from *Timaeus and Critias*). Penguin.

Pseudo-Dionysius (1924) trans. John Parker, *Mystic Theology. https://en.wikisource.org/wiki/Dionysius_the_Areopagite,_Works/Mystic_Theology*

Ramachandran, V.S, and Blakeslee, S. (1998) *Phantoms in the Brain: Probing the mysteries of the human mind.* William Morrow.

Ranke-Heinemann, Uta (1990) *Eunuchs for the Kingdom of Heaven: The Catholic Church and sexuality*. Penguin.

Rosenberg, Marshall (2002) *Nonviolent Communication: A language of compassion*. Puddledancer Press.

Ross, Lee, Green, David, & House, Pamela (1977) 'The false consensus effect: an egocentric bias in social perception and attribution processes': *Journal of Experimental Social Psychology* 13:3 pp.279-301

Salzberg, Sharon (1995) *Loving-kindness: The revolutionary art of happiness*. Shambhala.

Sangharakshita (1995) *Transforming Self and World*. Windhorse.

Sartre, Jean-Paul (1980) trans. Philip Mairet, *Existentialism and Humanism*. Methuen

Schweitzer, Albert (1910) trans. W. Montgomery, *The Quest for the Historical Jesus*. Black.

Siegel, Daniel (2010) *Mindsight*. Oneworld.

Singer, Peter (2004) 'Taking Humanism beyond Speciesism': *Free Inquiry*, 24, no. 6 (Oct/Nov 2004), pp. 19-21

Smith, George H. (1979) *Atheism: The case against God*. Prometheus Books.

Taleb, Nassim Nicholas (2012) *Antifragile: Things that gain from disorder*. Penguin.

Taylor, Donald and Doria, Janet (1981) 'Self-serving and group-serving bias in attribution': *The Journal of Social Psychology* 113:2, pp.201-11

Tweedy, Roderick (2013) *The God of the Left Hemisphere: Blake, Bolte Taylor and the Myth of Creation*. Karnac.

Verney, Stephen (1985) *Water into Wine: An Introduction to John's Gospel*. Verney Books.

Walshe, Maurice (1987) *The Long Discourses of the Buddha: A translation of the Digha Nikaya.* Wisdom Books.

Wason, P.C. (1960) 'On the failure to eliminate hypotheses in a conceptual task': *Quarterly Journal of Experimental Psychology:* 12:3, pp.129-140

Weber, Max (1930) trans. Talcott Parsons, *The Protestant Ethic and the Spirit of Capitalism.* Routledge.

Wrede, W. (1901) *Das Messiasgeheimnis in den Evangelien: zugleich ein Beitrag zum Verständnis des Markusevangeliums.* Vandenhoeck & Ruprecht.

CHRISTIAN ALTERNATIVE

Christian Alternative
THE NEW OPEN SPACES

Throughout the two thousand years of Christian tradition there have been, and still are, groups and individuals that exist in the margins and upon the edge of faith. But in Christianity's contrapuntal history it has often been these outcasts and pioneers that have forged contemporary orthodoxy out of former radicalism as belief evolves to engage with and encompass the ever-changing social and scientific realities. Real faith lies not in the comfortable certainties of the Orthodox, but somewhere in a half-glimpsed hinterland on the dirt track to Emmaus, where the Death of God meets the Resurrection, where the supernatural Christ meets the historical Jesus, and where the revolution liberates both the oppressed and the oppressors.

Welcome to Christian Alternative... a space at the edge where the light shines through.
If you have enjoyed this book, why not tell other readers by posting a review on your preferred book site. Recent bestsellers from Christian Alternative are:

Bread Not Stones
The Autobiography of An Eventful Life
Una Kroll
The spiritual autobiography of a truly remarkable woman and a history of the struggle for ordination in the Church of England.
Paperback: 978-1-78279-804-0 ebook: 978-1-78279-805-7

The Quaker Way

A Rediscovery

Rex Ambler

Although fairly well known, Quakerism is not well understood. The purpose of this book is to explain how Quakerism works as a spiritual practice.

Paperback: 978-1-78099-657-8 ebook: 978-1-78099-658-5

Blue Sky God

The Evolution of Science and Christianity

Don MacGregor

Quantum consciousness, morphic fields and blue-sky thinking about God and Jesus the Christ.

Paperback: 978-1-84694-937-1 ebook: 978-1-84694-938-8

Celtic Wheel of the Year

Tess Ward

An original and inspiring selection of prayers combining Christian and Celtic Pagan traditions, and interweaving their calendars into a single pattern of prayer for every morning and night of the year.

Paperback: 978-1-90504-795-6

Christian Atheist

Belonging without Believing

Brian Mountford

Christian Atheists don't believe in God but miss him: especially the transcendent beauty of his music, language, ethics, and community.

Paperback: 978-1-84694-439-0 ebook: 978-1-84694-929-6

Compassion Or Apocalypse?

A Comprehensible Guide to the Thoughts of René Girard

James Warren

How René Girard changes the way we think about God and the Bible, and its relevance for our apocalypse-threatened world.

Paperback: 978-1-78279-073-0 ebook: 978-1-78279-072-3

Diary Of A Gay Priest

The Tightrope Walker

Rev. Dr. Malcolm Johnson

Full of anecdotes and amusing stories, but the Church is still a dangerous place for a gay priest.

Paperback: 978-1-78279-002-0 ebook: 978-1-78099-999-9

Do You Need God?

Exploring Different Paths to Spirituality Even For Atheists

Rory J.Q. Barnes

An unbiased guide to the building blocks of spiritual belief.

Paperback: 978-1-78279-380-9 ebook: 978-1-78279-379-3

The Gay Gospels

Good News for Lesbian, Gay, Bisexual, and Transgendered People

Keith Sharpe

This book refutes the idea that the Bible is homophobic and makes visible the gay lives and validated homoerotic experience to be found in it.

Paperback: 978-1-84694-548-9 ebook: 978-1-78099-063-7

The Illusion of "Truth"
The Real Jesus Behind the Grand Myth
Thomas Nehrer
Nehrer, uniquely aware of Reality's integrated flow, elucidates Jesus' penetrating, often mystifying insights – exposing widespread religious, scholarly and skeptical fallacy.
Paperback: 978-1-78279-548-3 ebook: 978-1-78279-551-3

Do We Need God to be Good?
An Anthropologist Considers the Evidence
C.R. Hallpike
What anthropology shows us about the delusions of New Atheism and Humanism.
Paperback: 978-1-78535-217-1 ebook: 978-1-78535-218-8

Fingerprints of Fire, Footprints of Peace
A Spiritual Manifesto from a Jesus Perspective
Noel Moules
Christian spirituality with attitude. Fourteen provocative pictures, from Radical Mystic to Messianic Anarchist, that explore identity, destiny, values and activism.
Paperback: 978-1-84694-612-7 ebook: 978-1-78099-903-6

Readers of ebooks can buy or view any of these bestsellers by clicking on the live link in the title. Most titles are published in paperback and as an ebook. Paperbacks are available in traditional bookshops. Both print and ebook formats are available online.

Find more titles and sign up to our readers' newsletter at
http://www.johnhuntpublishing.com/christianity
Follow us on Facebook at
https://www.facebook.com/ChristianAlternative